THE NEW
COMPLETE
BOOK
OF PASTA

THE NEW COMPLETE BOOK OF PASTA

An Italian Cookbook

by

MARIA LUISA SCOTT

and

JACK DENTON SCOTT

With Photographs of Italy by
SAMUEL CHAMBERLAIN

and Drawings by Melvin Klapholz

CONSUMERS UNION • MOUNT VERNON, NEW YORK

For Maria Cifelli Limoncelli,
who taught us that the kitchen is
the true place of creation

Library of Congress Cataloging-in-Publication Data
Scott, Maria Luisa.
The new complete book of pasta.
Includes index.
1. Cookery (Macaroni) 2. Cookery, Italian. I. Scott,
Jack Denton, 1915–   . II. Title.
TX809.M17S35   1985   641.8'22   85-8979
ISBN: 0-89043-145-0

Consumers Union Edition
First printing, February 1987
Manufactured in the United States of America

Book design by James Udell

Grateful acknowledgment is made to the Samuel Chamberlain
Collection at the Essex Institute, Salem, Massachusetts,
for permission to use the photographs in this book.

The NEW Complete Book of Pasta is a Consumer Reports Book published by Consumers Union, the nonprofit organization that publishes *Consumer Reports,* the monthly magazine of test reports, product Ratings, and buying guidance. Established in 1936, Consumers Union is chartered under the Not-For-Profit Corporation Law of the State of New York.

The purposes of Consumers Union, as stated in its charter, are to provide consumers with information and counsel on consumer goods and services, to give information on all matters relating to the expenditure of the family income, and to initiate and to cooperate with individual and group efforts seeking to create and maintain decent living standards.

Consumers Union derives its income solely from the sale of *Consumer Reports* and other publications. In addition, expenses of occasional public service efforts may be met, in part, by nonrestrictive, noncommercial contributions, grants, and fees. Consumers Union accepts no advertising or product samples and is not beholden in any way to any commercial interest. Its Ratings and reports are solely for the use of the readers of its publications. Neither the Ratings nor the reports nor any Consumers Union publications, including this book, may be used in advertising or for any commercial purpose. Consumers Union will take all steps open to it to prevent such uses of its material, its name, or the name of *Consumer Reports.*

SAN FRUTTUOSO—*Liguria*

Books by Maria Luisa Scott and Jack Denton Scott

The Complete Book of Pasta
Feast of France
(with Antoine Gilly)
Informal Dinners for Easy Entertaining
Mastering Microwave Cooking
The Best of the Pacific Cookbook
Cook Like a Peasant, Eat Like a King
A World of Pasta
The Great Potato Cookbook
The Chicken and the Egg Cookbook
The Complete Convection Oven Cookbook
The Complete Book of Pies
Rice: More Than 250 Unexpected Ways to Cook the Perfect Food
The New Complete Book of Pasta

Foreword to the Consumers Union Edition

*T*here are few foods as universally appealing and popular as pasta. It can be prepared as lunch or dinner, as either a side dish or a main dish. Pasta recipes range from simple to elaborate, and the possible combinations of different pastas and sauces number in the hundreds. Pasta can be made to suit just about any and every occasion. Because pasta is so versatile, relatively inexpensive, easy to prepare, and low in calories, Consumers Union is pleased to add *The NEW Complete Book of Pasta* to our list of books on food and cooking topics.

This is a revision and update of the Scotts' original cookbook, which has been in print continuously for the past seventeen years. It provides not only the basics for beginners, but also some challenges for the gourmet cook. With 390 recipes and descriptions of 175 types of pasta, this book is one of the most authentic and comprehensive cookbooks available on pasta.

The Scotts have traveled extensively throughout Italy for many years collecting recipes for American cooks. From the obscure to the great regional classics, from how to make and cook pasta to what sauces work best with various types—fettuccine with shrimp, linguine with asparagus, spaghetti with anchovies, even green noodles with venison—there is a wealth of culinary knowledge here that will appeal to a wide range of tastes.

The NEW Complete Book of Pasta covers everything from the history of pasta to the great variety of soups and sauces that can be served as accompaniments. And it represents what the Italians call *cucina genuina*, truly authentic recipes and advice. (No cold pasta salads or other American aberrations will be found here.) There is some brand information, an explanation of the standards that the authors have set, and lists of ingredient substitutes. (While many recipes may be variations you simply have not thought of before, some of the recipes include obscure ingredients that many stores do not commonly stock.) There are even translations provided for the Italian names of particular dishes. In short, this is the type of book that cooks can simply read and enjoy, in addition to being a practical guide for creating great pasta dishes.

As with all Consumer Reports Books not of our own making, this book is the work of its authors. We emphasize that the authors' opinions are their own and not necessarily those of Consumers Union. In the absence of our own rigorous evaluations of the name-brand products mentioned in this book, recommendations by CU are impossible. We trust you'll use and enjoy the recipes contained herein just the same.

The Editors of Consumer Reports Books

Contents

LAKE ORTA, the island of San Giulio—Piedmont

Introduction

*M*uch has happened to pasta since this book appeared in 1968, most of it good, some of it not so good. As this was the first complete book on the subject published in the United States, it caused some changes in pasta eating and buying patterns.

Prior to the ten years we spent researching and assembling the first edition, pasta in America was called "macaroni," "noodles," or "spaghetti." Mainly, "pasta" was an unused word. The favorite dish here was spaghetti and meatballs in a long-cooked, heavy tomato sauce. Pasta was always served as an entrée, not a moderate first course, as it is usually offered in Italy.

The good result here, we hope in part because of our book, is that Americans stepped out of the old spaghetti rut and began using many varieties of pasta with the recipes that we offered, pairing pasta with other foods and using it properly as a first course. *Pesto*, which we had great fondness for, became the rage; pasta with vegetables became an "in" dish. Such is the power of pasta today that even some aloof French restaurants in Manhattan regularly offer *pasta du jour*, a remarkable accomplishment for a food that the French considered peasant fare and never held in high regard.

In this trail-blazing book we also declared that pasta was one of the most beneficial of all foods, an energy-builder, and that it did not, if used properly, put on poundage. This came as a surprise, for most of us had believed that pasta was fattening. But four ounces of cooked pasta contain just 210 calories, about the same as two small apples. It also contains more protein (13 percent) than potatoes, and four ounces of cooked pasta have all the vitamins and iron recommended for the United States daily allowance for adults.

Pasta also provides six of the eight body-building essential amino acids. The sauces we use on pasta provide the other two amino acids, and sound like a nutritionist's dream of what's good for us: meat, seafood, fresh vegetables, cheese, eggs, and fruit (tomatoes are fruit).

Pasta may lead all foods as a producer of energy. Human energy is fueled by carbohydrates, fat, and protein. Too many Americans, however, have an imbalance in intake, deriving energy from 42 percent fats, 30 percent protein, and only 28 percent carbohydrates.

Many of us, however, are confused by the word "carbohydrates" because there are two types, simple and complex. The simple—table sugar, honey, and other sweets—require no digestion. The simple carbohydrate rapidly floods the body with blood sugar, then vanishes, supplying a quick lift, then a fast drop, which is followed by hunger and mental and physical dullness. These carbohydrates are to be avoided.

Complex carbohydrates, however, require time to metabolize, then release a slow, constant stream of glucose (blood sugar) at the rate of about two calories per minute to fuel the body and brain. This "time-release" energy is necessary for the health of the body; it maintains a carbohydrate reserve and keeps blood-sugar levels stable. On a diet with complex carbohydrates outpointing fats and protein, we do not feel hungry and can sustain physical and mental activity for greater lengths of time.

Today, pasta has become the favorite of many athletes. Calling pasta intake "carbo-loading," they have discovered that the body stores the energy-giving carbohydrate in pasta more readily than any other kind, thus the body can draw upon it for a greater length of time. A majority of the runners in the New York City Marathon eat pasta for two or three days before the contest, and a free pasta dinner for all contestants the night before the race has become a tradition.

We ourselves discovered a long time ago that pasta peels off the pounds, if used properly. What is pasta's magic as a weight remover? No magic at all. It's simply a splendid food offered in many tasty and tempting varieties that acts as a natural appetite suppressant, ensuring that one eats moderately and healthfully. This is what all nutritionists want us to do.

As a team, we're perhaps the embodiment of the profits of pasta. Probably no one has eaten more pasta than we have while we were researching and testing recipes, not only for the original pasta book, but for this revision. With the hundreds of dishes of pasta that we've eaten, neither of us has gained an extra pound.

Without recognizing it as a "diet," we probably knew almost from the beginning, more than two decades ago, that pasta as a dining way of life was ideal. While researching this book, especially in Rome, the friends and acquaintances we admired most were slim, dynamic, elegant people. We followed their example when we dined with them (and forever after) as they ate Italian. This means that they ate wisely and well, the way many enlightened Italians have been doing traditionally for years.

We followed their way of eating and easily maintained the weight that we think best for us—without giving up any of the foods that we like. Fortunately, neither of us likes sweets, the quick calorie builders we decided long ago to do without. So, one battle won: no desserts.

Of course, the key to the diet, as we learned from observation in Rome, is pasta. Our friends *always* began a meal with a *slender two ounces of pasta*, any kind of pasta, with any kind of sauce they wanted. Then followed a modest but balanced meal: a small serving of fish or poultry, or a small steak or chop. Their secret: Pasta satisfied the appetite, making it possible to cut the portions that followed at least by half. By adding a green salad, then fruit for dessert, these Italians not only cut calories drastically, but their intake was also about as healthful as it could be.

And now we reluctantly take a step back from the positive, in dismay at how the popularity of pasta has been perverted by fads that trivialize not only pasta, but classic, basic fine cooking itself.

The food establishment, to keep itself going, thinks it must relentlessly present new tastes and textures to the public, to overcome boredom with the normal techniques, to titillate America's jaded palate.

Result: pasta abuse.

Probably the worst of the many offenses against good taste are the cold pasta salads that are being served in American homes and offered in take-out food establishments. We checked several of the most reputable of these in Manhattan and counted in each more than a dozen cold pasta salads, each more repugnant than the other and all expensive.

In Italy, pasta salads are unknown. Even children there are aware that pasta should never be served cold, and that it is ridiculous to offer a cold pasta with a cold sauce. "They fight with one another," one Italian chef told us. There are classic dishes of hot pasta served with cold sauces, some in this book. But the masters of pasta cuisine laugh when you tell them that America is in the midst of a cold pasta salad fad. It's a joke.

But it's far from a joke when you are proudly offered cold *ziti* with half-cooked, cold vegetables buried in a thick commercial mayonnaise; or pasta, cooked to near-glue, served cold in an "American" cream soup. One of the new specialties in Manhattan is cold *fusilli* covered with a cold, tart mustard-cream sauce, topped with cold, half-raw cubes of eggplant and cauliflower or broccoli flowerets. The take-out shops are touting over-cooked, gummy, precooked pasta in a cold sauce that is to be heated at home, and some restaurants are even offering cold, half-cooked *penne,* dipped in cold tomato sauce and trotted out as cocktail nibbles.

Of course, some of us don't know any better, and others perhaps have forgotten, or never knew, what pasta properly cooked and served tastes like. And when a misguided female restaurant reviewer of *The New York Times* lauds a cold (!) pasta salad in a "French" restaurant, it becomes confusing and difficult indeed for the public to know what is right and what is wrong, even though taste should tell us.

The reaction of a noted Italian restaurateur in Manhattan to one of the popular cold pasta salads there, *tortellini* with *pesto,* sums up our feelings. He called it "outrageous."

Unfortunately, these absurdities continue: In the Midwest one "cook" has become famous for his chocolate pasta! Fresh pasta is being presented in rainbow hues and in foolish flavors. For example, lemon, grapefruit, and orange noodles. In Dallas they're even selling tasteless pasta made from black beans. All sorts of nonsense is being published in the food magazines—mixing grated lemon rind into the pasta dough, also soy sauce, ground nuts, hot peppers, and seafood. In this fresh pasta frenzy it has reached the point where the pasta itself overwhelms the sauce.

One of the cardinal rules of making and cooking pasta is to retain the flavor and personality of pasta properly made with semolina or high-gluten flour. It is a classic food in itself, not to be used as a receptacle for weird ingredients, such as fried, heavily ginger-flavored *linguine* we've seen.

An excellent pasta dish can be simplicity itself—noodles dressed only with sweet butter and cheese. One of the most respected restaurants in Paris serves its popular fricassee of *langoustines* and sole only with buttered noodles. The taste counterpoint is superb. High on the roster of Italy's most famous pasta dishes is *fettuccine Alfredo,* noodles tossed with just butter, cheese, and heavy cream. The list of simple sauces is long. Typical are garlic and anchovies in olive oil, sweet butter with peas or mushrooms, and many more. Pasta can be paired with small amounts of an almost limitless number of classic Italian sauces, with no need or excuse to resort to kitchen buffoonery.

Pasta, the Italians say, is history. And they resent anyone attempting to destroy their history as we currently are doing in the United States.

It's evident that the American food establishment and its magazines, in trying for new gimmicks, have gone from the sublime to the ridiculous in corrupting the classics. For example, soaking prunes in herbal tea,

LORETO, the Santuario della Santa Casa—The Marches

poaching tiny new potatoes in Asti Spumante, making hollandaise sauce with sour cherries, creating overwhelming puréed red pepper sauces, sweet and hot, that are served with just about everything except ice cream. One highly publicized teaching chef was recently heralded here for his originality in lavishly layering *lasagne* with red pepper purée. That brave egg-enriched big noodle never had a chance. It went down, drowning in a sea of pungent pepper without a whimper. The dish should have been called "Montezuma's Revenge."

Happily, however, food fads in the United States, though many, are short-lived. Pasta can take only so much abuse. It is an ancient, world-respected food that cannot be counterfeited for very long. Its classic repertoire will ride out this storm of mediocrity.

We're even being encouraged in this mediocrity, again by the food establishment, to eat pasta any way we please. Sure, we can eat pasta propping it on a spoon, cut it up, or use our fingers—but the masters, the Italians, use just a fork, and that's good enough for us. They claim that "spoon-eating" is for children, amateurs, and people with bad table manners.

Italians with whom we talked in Italy, and here, described the fork method: Place the tines into a few strands of string pasta, spaghetti, *fedelini*, etc., not trying to gather up too large a mouthful. It helps to let the tines of the fork rest against the curve of the bowl or plate, while twirling the fork, then giving it short, quick lifts to avoid gathering too much pasta. Then lift the moderate forkful and enjoy it. These experts also agreed that if the pasta is properly cooked al dente, some of it will dangle, but the fork won't gather too much. But if it is overcooked, too much will easily wrap around the fork, making it more difficult to gather a small amount.

What about the pasta itself? Which is the best? Since first writing this book, we've changed our minds. Then, we lauded fresh pasta, calling homemade better than any other kind. As we look back now, we probably felt that way then because making pasta ourselves was exciting and gave us a feeling, as it was cut or came from the hand-operated machine, that we had mastered the craft. We made it ourselves, thus it had to be the best. We don't feel that way now. Tastes change and experience teaches.

Now, with all pasta a fad in the United States, there are remarkable new machines for the home kitchen that make pasta almost as fast as you can pour in the flour.

We are not enthusiastic about them.

Just before writing these words, we attended the David Frigo family wedding in Waterbury, Connecticut. It was a classic Italian wedding, much good food, music, and dancing, and many old friends were there. At one table sat eight elderly ladies, all born in Italy, and all with precise ideas on pasta. They knew that we had written the first book on pasta in the United States and welcomed us warmly as we joined them at their table.

One lady was talking about the new pasta machine her son-in-law had just bought. "All you do," she snorted, "is put in the flour, oil, water and eggs, press a button and out comes pasta."

"But what pasta!" said another expert. "So soft it cooks in half a minute. You don't watch it you got glue!"

Another at the table spoke about her daughter using a food processor with an attachment to make pasta, ready to cook in ten minutes.

"I don't like to say anything," she said. "That machine was expensive and they're proud of it. But when my husband and I go there for dinner it's all we can do to get the pasta down. Too soft. No character! No flavor!"

Out of this conversation, and the experience of the ladies in making pasta gained during decades of doing it the Italian way, came several positive pronouncements. That formidable table of experts agreed to a woman on the following:

Electric machines that make and cut the pasta fast are taboo.

After the pasta dough is mixed and kneaded and formed into balls, it should rest for at least a half hour; an hour is better. Some of the ladies claimed that resting it overnight is even better, producing a better-tasting, more velvety pasta.

Their main complaints with the electric machines were that not only are they too fast, but also that the manufacturers recommend all-purpose white flour. The ladies insisted that semolina is best, high-gluten unbleached white flour second best. They repeated that speed has no part in producing superior homemade pasta. The dough must be rested, they insisted, before rolling and cutting. They also said that the super-speed machines take all the skill and the pride out of pasta making.

Opinion was divided on how to roll and cut the pasta. Half the ladies were positive that old-fashioned rolling out by hand and cutting by hand is best. "Takes time, sure," said one, "but you must remember that making pasta is an art and a labor of love."

The rest sitting in judgment on pasta on that wedding evening declared that the little hand-operated machines from Italy, especially the Atlas, are excellent. They sent the "rested" balls of pasta through the rollers several times to attain the perfect thinness. Next, some of the ladies dried the thin sheets until they were taut, then cut them into the desired widths on the machine, then dried the pasta for thirty minutes before cooking or freezing it.

We gave them no arguments. They were the real thing, these female *pastaie* who had been making pasta before we were born. Also, we agreed with them. We have used the little Atlas for years and found it the perfect machine. We have also tried the new "fast and easy" machines. It is our opinion also that pasta made the old way is better.

We did have a minor disagreement with the ladies, however, that we didn't mention. A friend showed us how he made pasta with a food processor. He didn't use the pasta attachment but just mixed the dough. The experts might have had some criticism, but we doubt it. Especially after they heard his name, which had a nice Italian ring to it.

In fact, our friend, Bruno Valbona, an executive vice-president with Waring, taught us how to use the Waring food processor (which he perfected) to mix pasta.

His method: He placed the steel knife in the work bowl, then added 2 eggs, 1 teaspoon of salt, 1 teaspoon of olive oil, 4 tablespoons of water, put the top on the work bowl, and mixed the ingredients for 15 seconds. Next, he poured in 1 cup of high-gluten unbleached flour and mixed for 15 seconds. Then, with the machine running, he slowly added another cup of flour, processing the dough until it was a smooth ball. He pointed out that the dough should be smooth, not sticky. If it is sticky, add more flour, carefully, by the single tablespoonful, processing for mere seconds. If it remains sticky, add another tablespoonful.

Bruno Valbona then lightly floured a cutting board, coated the dough ball with the flour to prevent sticking, then wrapped it in plastic and let it rest for thirty minutes. After sprinkling more flour on the cutting board, Bruno divided the ball of dough into 8 equal parts. Using a small hand-operated Italian pasta machine, he set the rollers on the widest setting and ran each piece of dough through the rollers once. He floured the sheets lightly, then sent them through the rollers again. He set the rollers at the next thinner notch, lightly floured the sheets, and ran them through the rollers twice.

Next, he rested a broom handle across the backs of two chairs, covered it with paper toweling, draped the pasta sheets over that, and let them dry until they were taut. He set the pasta machine on the noodle setting and ran all the sheets of dough through. He let the noodles dry for 30 minutes, separating them as they dried. He then cooked the pasta for *1 minute.*

It is difficult to convince most people that fresh pasta cooks very fast and thus can easily become gummy. Even some of the so-called professionals don't seem to realize this. We had dinner at a lauded Italian restaurant in Elmira, in upstate New York, ordered fresh pasta (made with one of the new super-speed machines) with salmon. A mistake. It was so overcooked that if you tried to lift one strand of pasta with a fork, the entire serving lifted from the plate. A gummy mess.

The word, however, is out: "Fresh is best." The fad is in. Not with us. We are convinced that commercial pasta from Italy is superior to most fresh or "homemade" American pasta. It has more flavor and cooks al dente without a lot of pot-watching.

As the ladies at the wedding said, probably the faults in most fresh pasta here have two sources: the fast machines and the use of ordinary white flour. Italy's commercial dry pasta is made with semolina, the heart of durum wheat, which retains its nutty, flavorful personality.

Bearing us out, as this is written, are four of New York City's leading Italian restaurateurs who claim that good commercial Italian dry pasta, such as de Cecco, del Verde, or Siga, are superior to most fresh pastas served or sold in this country. Their quality and flavor are consistent, whereas it is always a gamble with the fresh kind.

In fairness, however, some professional fresh pasta manufacturers in places like New York City do utilize heavy-duty machines in making fresh pasta and use eggs and high-gluten flour. This pasta is excellent. Also, if fresh pasta is purchased in an Italian section of a city, most likely it will be good. All this, however, is only the beginning. It *must* be cooked properly. A very, very short time.

This is not written as a blanket condemnation of fresh pasta! But if one closely examines many food fads, often they are found faulty. We've attempted to point out some of the problems. But what we write is personal (as is this book), merely our own reactions. Readers must make their own decisions.

We hasten to add that in Italy fresh pasta is no fad. It is an art form, the making and the cooking perfection itself. We have, however, encountered fresh *carbonara* outside of Rome (where it is superb) that was quite gummy. We think we found it in Bari, but other than that, all manner of fresh pasta in Italy is superb.

We freely admit that when we decided to write this book more than two decades ago, we didn't realize what a formidable task it would be, finding our way through a unique world of food, learning not only a many-faceted foreign cuisine, but also a culture.

And we didn't know very much about pasta except that we had a passion for it. Maria Luisa's was inherited, Jack's acquired from countless memorable meals with her family. Many trips to Italy made this book possible, and, of course, the kindness and generosity of Italian chefs, restaurant owners, and various friends and families. If we had tried to acquire so many cooking techniques and recipes in France, we would have needed more than persuasion. We would have needed a gun.

This revised edition is strictly Italian, and we have added to it fifty-four new Italian recipes that we have discovered and tested. We have remained true to what the Italians call *cucina genuina,* which means cooking that is genuine, authentic, unadulterated, and natural. This is the standard and pride of "Italian cooking" itself, a term that is actually a misnomer. We've been told many times by chefs and friends in Italy that there really is no such thing as Italian cooking. It is the cooking "of" Italy, the nineteen regions that make up the country. Thus it has unique variety, and there is great loyalty to the distinctive dishes of the Abruzzi (where many claim the best cooks come from, as does Maria Luisa's family), Arezzo, Florence, Lucca, the Piedmont, and other regions. Rome, though, is somewhat like New York City, and its restaurants represent every region and its specialties.

How we conceived the idea of writing this first complete book of pasta remains, to us at least, as interesting now as it was those twenty-five years ago.

THE NEW
COMPLETE
BOOK
OF PASTA

"No man is lonely while eating spaghetti—
it requires too much attention . . ."

CHRISTOPHER MORLEY

ROME, the Bernini Fountain, Piazza Navona

I
A Pasta a Day

*E*very book has its moment of inspiration, often in a conversation, a song, a sight or a memory. This one began in Rome in one of Italy's finest restaurants, George's, where we were sitting with the Italian Tourist Office's United States director and an official of CIT, the leading travel agency in Italy. We were gathered for lunch, talking about a travel book we were researching, just before taking off for an exploratory drive through the little-known southern section of Italy.

The Tourist Office lady had a dish of tuna and white beans to start; the CIT man suggested that we have instead spaghetti *all'amatriciana* and spoke glowingly of that favorite dish of Rome before it arrived, describing it as a sauce of sweet red peppers and ripe tomatoes simmered with young pork cheek, served over *bucatini*. It finally came, hot and sending up steam as we like it, in soup bowls. Before we started, the CIT man straightened in his seat, looked severely at us, and said: "Please, as a favor, do not disgrace the pasta and use a spoon!"

When we told him that we never used a spoon (a lesson taught by our mother and mother-in-law many years ago), he brightened and smiled. "*Grazie*, thank you. I am happy.

"We are proud of our pasta," he said. "Only in this country is it served properly, a delight to the palate, a thing of beauty when it comes to the table with its many shapes and variety of sauces. We make poetry with

CAMOGLI, *Liguria*

our pasta—flowers, stars, seashells, beautiful twirls, and elegant twists."

He stopped then and gave us a searching look. "Did you know, for example, that we can serve a different pasta every day of the year? Without repeating ourselves?"

There it was. The inspiration, even a possible title for this book. A pasta a day! And research has proven the CIT man right, even conservative. Our years of wandering about Italy, fork in hand, have since produced evidence that the Italians probably could serve two different pasta dishes a day without repetition all year long.

Italians do not hold grand opera in higher regard than they do their national dish. They have even raised a museum in its honor. Called the Museo Storico degli Spaghetti, it is located in Pontedassio, not far from the Ligurian Sea and the Italian Riviera. We discovered much about pasta there that should be passed on.

The *museo* is in a huge old house, the family seat of the Agnesis, who, it is believed, began the Italian pasta industry in an old mill in Pontedassio in 1824. Vincenzo Agnesi, the remaining scion of these spaghetti pioneers, spent many years assembling the items in the museum. We spent two days wandering there, taking notes and becoming educated.

A few of the facts we discovered: Pasta was not discovered by Marco Polo in China and brought back to Italy, for *ravioli* was being eaten in Rome in 1284, almost twenty years before Marco Polo's famous travels. *Fettuccine*, that tasty dish of noodles, cheese, butter, cream and raw egg yolk, was not created in Rome by a restaurateur named Alfredo for Mary Pickford and Douglas Fairbanks, but was eaten by the Romans much as it is now in 1200 and was known as *lagano cum caseo*.

In the museum are ancient and modern machines and instruments used in the manufacture of pasta, from long, gleaming Sicilian "knitting needles" used to dry spaghetti in spirals to the mechanical monster, the continuous-extrusion press, that forms and sends out pasta in a swift stream. Paintings are everywhere, etchings, prints—showing pasta being made in huge sheets, peasants dancing in the streets eating it in long streamers from their hands, nobles daintily eating it as it is brought by the servants; cartoons showing foreigners having difficulties (such as winding the strands around their necks) eating pasta. There is a puppet show with Chinese characters in pigtails eating spaghetti while Marco Polo stares in astonishment.

Museum books and ancient documents attest to pasta being one of the oldest and most revered foods, eaten as early as 5,000 B.C. Boccaccio paused in his salacious attack on the Church long enough to create the country of Bengodi where people live on a mountain of cheese and do nothing but make, cook, and eat pasta. Rossini, Rabelais, D'Annunzio, Goldoni rave about pasta each in his own inimitable way; the poet Merlin Cocai created a book of poetry, glowing odes to pasta. We leafed through a cookbook, *De Honesta Voluptate* by Platina, published in 1485, which gave excellent old pasta recipes, plus several intriguing ways to serve those ancient necessities, larks' tongues and hummingbirds' livers.

And for the first time we found, at the museum (and more in Rome), a list of pasta names with English translations. As we had never seen them elsewhere, we thought they were worth recording, even though many of these names are not the ones best known commercially in this country. The illustrated Glossary, which begins on page 36, includes the names on this list, to which have been added many more—translated or described to the best of our ability—of other pastas we have eaten in Italy and as many as we could find of the names that are familiar on the shelves of American grocery stores and supermarkets.

A few times, when in doubt concerning the list, we consulted D. Maldari & Sons in Brooklyn, diemakers for the pasta industry in the United States, men with a vast knowledge of the myriad forms pasta takes. But even these experts couldn't give us a complete list.

"Must be a thousand different shapes," the senior Maldari said. "Who can list all of the ways of the imagination?" Who, indeed, especially of the Italian imagination? There are enough different kinds of pastas to keep most of us busy at the boiling pot for the rest of our lives.

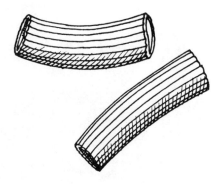

ROME, the Spanish Steps

CHÂTEAU DE ST. PIERRE—Valle d'Aosta

II
Pasta: What Is It?
& A Glossary of
Pasta Names

*B*y now we all know that pasta is the generic term for all the multitude of products made from semolina and water. Semolina is the golden, sugar-fine flour made from the heart of durum wheat. This is the hardest and purest of all wheats.

In the land of its birth, pasta is much more than that. As our CIT travel-agency friend said, "We Italians make poetry with pasta." And indeed they do. Each region of Italy has its special shape, the variations limited only by the imagination. The Romans cut theirs in long strips; the Bolognese like ribbons of various widths; in the south some places specialize in pasta shaped like seashells, others the clam or star shape; in Naples they prefer the "little worms," *vermicelli;* in Sicily, spirals dried on knitting needles are popular.

In addition to taste, pasta passes another test of all excellent foods—it is pleasing to the eye. Its graceful twirls and twists, slender reeds, shells, butterflies, and ribbons appeal to other than chefs and diners. One of the most successful window displays that Tiffany's, the famed jewelers on New York's Fifth Avenue, ever had was one that used pasta as its theme. Every window had it, hanging from the ceiling suspending a diamond ring; piles of it, looking like wheat sheaves, displaying a single watch; *rigatoni* and *ditalini, linguine* and *bucatini, fettuccine* and sphaghetti were arranged in patterns that stopped passersby in their tracks. We saw the windows many years ago; never had the imagination of the Italians in designing their pasta forms offered a more glittering showcase.

But we still prefer to admire pasta at the table. Unless it is made at home, all first-class pasta is made the same way: just a healthy mixture of fine semolina and water (eggs are added for noodles and many *pastine,* the tiny pastas used in soups), kneaded into a smooth dough that will pass through dies (pierced metal discs). As the dough goes through the dies, it comes forth as solid rods, spaghetti. When a steel pin is placed in the center of each die, the dough emerges as hollow rods known as macaroni. For the short elbow style, a notched pin is used, allowing the dough to move through more quickly on one side, curling it somewhat.

The long strands of spaghetti and macaroni are placed on racks and put in drying ovens. The shorter varieties go on trays, then into drying cabinets. Pasta is not baked. It is slowly dried while filtered air constantly passes over it. Timing is all important. If it dries too quickly, then it breaks easily; if it dries too slowly it may spoil.

Egg noddles are made the same way except that, rather than the dough passing through dies, it is pressed through rollers in sheets, then cut into the desired shapes.

No matter what the form, pasta emerges as an almost magic substance that has the ability to carry and pass on a range of other flavors that is remarkable. A commercial tomato-grower near Pompeii pulled this power of pasta into perspective for us. "Pasta," he said, "absorbs and magnifies anything it is mated with. Even a simple thing like olive oil becomes magnificent when warmed and tossed with pasta. . . ."

Right. But pasta achieves these results by taking many forms and by being used in many ways. The subject of how pastas are used in cooking can be confusing. For our purposes, we take the complication out of pasta dishes by separating them into categories and then noting how these overlap.

For instance, a first group of four categories includes pastas that are . . .

> . . . *boiled,* and served with all manner of sauces, such as spaghetti, *linguine,* etc.
> . . . *boiled,* too, are noodles such as *fettuccine,* but usually tossed with simple sauces
> . . . *baked,* with their sauces, such as *lasagna* or *ziti*
> . . . *stuffed,* first, then boiled and sauced, such as *ravioli;* or sauced and baked, such as *cannelloni*

The baked and stuffed-baked categories above are a special group unto themselves, *pasta in forno,* which means that this pasta is not usually served

CAMPITELLO DI FASSA, in the Dolomites—Trentino-Alto Adige

on the plate and the sauce then added, as with most of the others, but is a dish cooked in the oven (or partly cooked in the oven; the pasta itself is parboiled before the dish is assembled and baked). *Lasagne* is the queen of this variety. *Pasta in forno* is important because it is about the only pasta the Italians, who know how to handle it better than anyone else, consider an entrée or main course.

Or, a different kind of distinction can be made by placing pastas in just two classifications . . .

> . . . *pasta in brodo,* pasta in broth; in other words, soups
> . . . *pasta asciutta,* literally "dry" pasta, but simply meaning all the pastas *not* served in broth; in other words, all the pastas in the four initial categories

Pasta in brodo is an important classification because of the wide range of sizes and shapes made to be used just in broth. Dies for at least eighty-four shapes are available to American manufacturers. These pastas run from tiny golden kernels and *pastine* much smaller than a grain of rice to snails just under the size of a golf ball. Cockscombs, sparrows' eyes, stars, shells, butterflies, nuts, cloverleaves, tubes, sausages, baby chicks, wheels, little hats, flowers, horseshoes, umbrellas—the list is limitless. They are usually served in a rich chicken broth. Often only the pasta floats in the clear broth; sometimes vegetables and meat are added. Most of us are familiar with the thick, lusty meal-in-itself *minestrone.* This is *pasta in brodo,* despite the fact that in addition to curved tubular pasta it also has tomato, beans, meat, and sometimes potatoes.

Pastas used for *pasta asciutta* are not quite so fanciful but they still have a large range of sizes and shapes, and it is with these that the huge repertory of pasta sauces are served.

You can now start all over again with *pasta asciutta* and divide *it* into two categories . . .

> . . . *pasta fresca,* which is fresh or homemade pasta
> . . . *pasta secca,* which is dried or commercial pasta

Fresh pasta, at least in Italy, is usually made at home, although it can be purchased in many shops. It can run to any shape or size the cook knows how to make, or has the equipment to make—spaghetti, noodles, *cannelloni, ravioli,* just about anything. *Ravioli* are always *pasta fresca* and are best homemade. Technically, they should be stuffed with a mixture of vegetables, cheeses, and eggs. If they are filled with meat, they are larger, often round, and become *agnolotti. Pasta fresca* is often used for *pasta in forno.*

Pasta secca, that is, all the commercial dry pastas we usually buy, can run from the thickness of a hair to the size of your thumb, can be flat like *linguine* and *fettuccine* (our favorite), thick and grooved like *rigatoni*, curled, twisted, or just smooth and straight, and these all come in several thicknesses, as does spaghetti.

Both *pasta secca* and *pasta fresca* are used *in brodo*.

Finally, in connection with meal planning and the way that Americans will use this book, pasta recipes can be classified—in a non-Italian way and depending on the circumstances—into first course and entrée, both of which should be labeled *use your better judgment*.

You will see on reading some of these recipes that it is not those for *pasta in forno* exclusively that have the hearty ring of a main dish. Some others are so clearly entrées that the recipes specifically state this. But then still others, with elaborate sauces or numerous ingredients, are more ambiguous—substantial dishes that, as first courses, certainly will serve at least six people or even more if the entrée to follow is also substantial. Though we consider almost all pasta dishes as first courses in spirit, we do not always go on to the conclusion that an entrée *must* necessarily follow. A modest dish of pasta, salad, cheese, and fruit are quite enough for most of us, at luncheon, supper, or at times of weight-watching in general. Consider, if you will, that such a meal is to have only a first course and no entrée, and you will still be serving pasta as it should be.

Though this is a heretical American view, we would even suggest that *The New Complete Book of Pasta* is one of the best possible places to look for interesting recipes when you want to plan very small and simple meals—and that for this purpose many of the very easy recipes made with few ingredients can even be the best.

A GLOSSARY OF PASTA NAMES

This glossary is an informal affair, designed to help you find your way around the tangle of pasta terminology but by no means claiming to be the authoritative last word on the subject. It is, nevertheless, a larger compilation of terms than we have yet seen in any one place.

The list has been assembled from four sources and it can be used as a dictionary to look up any pasta word you find in this book and a good many more besides. First, we have included the entire translated list that we found at the Museo Storico degli Spaghetti in Pontedassio. Just a few of these pastas we have never seen, and this fact is indicated by an asterisk preceding their names. These are not used in the recipes in this book. Most of the items on the Pontedassio list, however, are available in this country, or counterparts are available that are easy to recognize.

Second, all the pastas we have used in the book are listed here. Many, though well known, were not on the museum list. Wherever necessary, the English titles of the recipes give an informal literal translation of the Italian name of the pasta used. But some clarification is often needed in addition, so this Glossary provides a description when the literal translation cannot do the job. All the pastas used in the recipes are available in this country, though it is a question, as explained below, whether you will always find them sold under the same names.

Third, some of the most-used pastas do fall into definite categories, such as spaghettis, macaronis, noodles, which have variations in size, length, surface texture, etc., that can be quite systematically classified. We have turned for this information to the catalog of one of the largest suppliers of the dies that American manufacturers use in making pastas. The die manufacturer has neatly summarized the categories and suggested an orderly Italian nomenclature, which we repeat here, for most of their possible variations. Not all these variations are in fact produced, but they could be.

There is no guarantee that the American pasta brands will use this nomenclature, however. Each manufacturer has his own idea of how to explain the nature of the product to his buying public. "Non-skid spaghetti" proved to be one salesman's idea of how to identify *fusilli*—a description neither accurate nor appetizing but it must be admitted it does stick in the memory. We have listed here hardly any of these highly variable American terms. Happily, though, the pasta manufacturers *do* use much Italian nomenclature, if not in very standardized fashion. Differences in size in one product, such as the several sizes of spaghetti, they indicate by numbers, but as these are not the same for every brand, we have not referred

BAGNAIA—Latium

to them here. However, when you find a pasta you like, those numbers are worth remembering for future reference.

Besides the basic forms of pastas, there are all sorts of unclassifiable shapes which the pasta industry refers to, somewhat helplessly, as "specialty products." They are not necessarily obscure; some, such as pasta shells, are well known indeed. We have listed many here by their Italian names.

The selection of pastas available varies widely from one part of the country to another. In fact, it even varies disconcertingly from one Italian specialty shop to another in the same city. Nevertheless, nowadays, any self-respecting supermarket carries two or three dozen or more different pastas and noodles. You may not always get exactly what you want, but you cannot often complain of lack of variety. Our fourth source of information for this glossary was an all-day shopping trip to the downtown Italian section of New York City, where the grocery stores carry what may very well be the widest selection of pastas, both American and imported, to be found in the country. Here we unearthed many more names, often for pastas we already knew by other names. The glossary points out many of these duplications to you and lists names found usually only on imported brands for which there are nevertheless counterparts in American brands.

Which brings us to the most important use of this glossary. Each recipe in this book calls for a particular pasta. It is the one which in size, shape, thickness, texture is the best suited to the particular sauce and method of cooking and serving. But this is not to say that *no* other pasta will do, let alone that the name has to be exactly the same. The point is to know what the pasta called for is like, and then to find a counterpart or an approximation if exactly that pasta by exactly that name is not to be found.

The illustrations in the Glossary are drawn life size. They show forty widely available shapes, some of which can have more than one name (in which case we give you a cross-reference). None of the many long straight pastas are illustrated, but the listings explain the variations in their dimensions. Armed with this information, you should be able to tell what you are looking for for any given recipe. Then you should certainly be able to find either the right pasta by some name or a similar one that will do quite as well.

Acini di pepe "peppercorns"—(for soup)

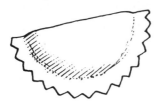

Agnolotti round *ravioli* filled with meat; they are also made as semicircles, like tiny turnovers. Though these should be made fresh (see page 59), there are good frozen brands in some specialty shops.

*Alpini "mountains" or "Alpines" (for soup)

Amorini "little cupids" (for soup)

Anelli "rings" (for soup)

Anellini "little rings" (for soup)

Anellini rigati "grooved rings" or "gears" (for soup)

Arancini "little oranges" (for soup)

Avena "oats" (for soup)

Bavette translated as "steel castings" in the list at the Italian spaghetti museum, this is an oval (rather than round) spaghetti, thinner than *linguine* (which is also oval). See *Linguine.*

Bavettine very narrow *linguine*

Bocconcini "small mouthfuls"; this pasta is quite a mouthful, being a grooved tube ½ inch in diameter and 1½ inches long before it is cooked. It is similar to *rigatoni.*

Bows the American versions of these are usually made of egg-noodle dough and there are many sizes. *Farfalle* ("butterflies") are the Italian version, likely to be plain, not egg, pastas, also of many sizes.

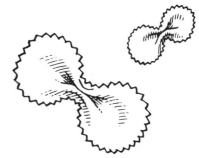

Bucati "with a hole"; an adjective applied to some pierced or hollow pastas

Bucatini pierced hollow pasta, like macaroni, but thinner than spaghetti; see Macaroni

Cannelle "small reeds" or "pipes," i.e., hollow. This is, however, quite a large pasta; see Macaroni.

Cannellini "tiny reeds"; a small version of *cannelle*

Cannelloni "large reeds," i.e., large and hollow, though *cannelloni* are usually flat squares of pasta rolled around a stuffing. To make, see pages 57 and 58.

Canneroni "large reeds"

Canneroni lisci "large smooth reeds"; see *Zitoni,* to which these are similar

Canneroni rigati "large grooved reeds"; see *Zitoni rigati,* to which these are similar

Cannolicchi small pasta tubes

*****Cannoni** "cannons" or large tubes

Capelli d'angelo "angel's hair" (for soup); also used now as a first-course pasta to toss with a sauce.

Capellini "fine hairs"; very fine pasta, as fine as soup noodles but round. See Spaghetti.

Cappelletti "little hats" that are stuffed; to make, see Index

Cappelli di pagliaccio "clown's hats" (for soup)

Cappelli di prete "priests' hats"

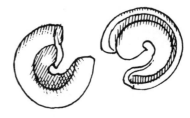

Capelvenere "maidenhair fern"; fine noodles for soup

Cavatelli a short curled noodle; to make, see page 384. The Italian commercial version illustrated here is like a narrow, ripple-surfaced pasta shell. The American commercial version is larger and less well shaped.

Chicchi di riso "grains of rice"; see also *Orzo*

Chiocciole "snail shells"; see *Lumache*

Chitarra see Spaghetti *alla chitarra*

Conchiglie "conch shells"; these are usually called simply "shells" and are the same as *maruzze* (see). They are often made grooved (*rigati*). See also Giant shells.

Conchigliette "tiny shells"; *maruzzelle* is another diminutive for the same thing. *Conchigliette piccole* is a term for very tiny shells for soup.

Coralli "coral"; one of several names for very small pasta tubes used in soup. There is also *corallini*, even smaller, and both versions are also made *rigati* (grooved). See *Tubettini*, which is very similar.

*Cravatte "bow ties"

Creste di galli "cockscombs"

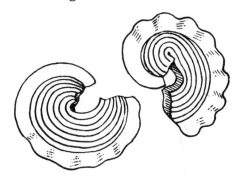

*Datteri "little dates"

*Di natali Christmas pasta

*Di natali rigati grooved Christmas pasta

Ditali "thimbles"; macaroni cut in short lengths, even shorter than elbow macaroni, to which it is related.

Ditalini "little thimbles"; small macaroni cut in very short lengths; often used in minestrone.

Elbow Familiar to all in the term "elbow macaroni," elbow pastas are small semicircles that can be made of any of the hollow tubular pastas.

The die manufacturer lists almost all the macaronis in elbow form, some in large as well as small semicircles. The diameters range from the size of spaghetti to over ½ inch . . .

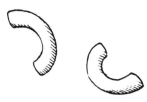

Elbow *bucatini*
Elbow *perciatelli*
Elbow *maccheroncelli*
Elbow *mezzanelli*
Elbow *mezzani* or macaroni
Elbow *ziti*
Elbow *zitoni*

These are followed by grooved (*rigati*) forms, of which, theoretically, there could be more than those listed . . .

Elbow *mezzanelli rigati*
Elbow *mezzani rigati*
Elbow *ziti rigati*
Elbow *zitoni rigati*

Combining the number of dies for elbow and elbow-*rigati* pastas, in both small and large semicircles, these 11 names could account for 28 products, providing the pasta manufacturer does not invent still more sizes for the semicircles!

In actual practice, not too many elbow names are used, but the American passion for elbow macaroni per se has led the Italian importers to use the English word elbow on their packages of this pasta.

*Elena named after an Italian queen, Elena

*Elettrici rigati "grooved electric wire"

Farfalle "butterflies"; usually called "bows" in this country. There are many variations in size and design. American bows are likely to be made of egg rather than plain pasta dough.

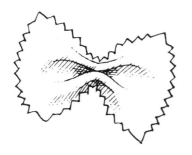

Farfallette "little butterflies"

Farfalline "tiny butterflies"

Farfalloni "big butterflies"

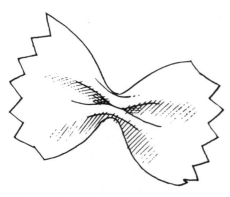

*Favoriti "favorites"

Fedelini "the faithful," according to the museum list; this is one of the thinnest of the spaghettis, thinner than *vermicelli*

Fettuccine "small ribbons"; one of the best-known Italian noodles (the other is *tagliatelle*). Commercially, they are sold both as straight rods and loosely bent and curled, as illustrated. They are about ¼ inch wide. *Fettuccine* are often made fresh; see pages 57 and 58. Directions for how wide to cut them vary in recipes for homemade *fettuccine*.

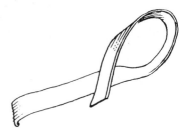

Fettuccelle "little ribbons"; a narrow version of *fettuccine*

Fettucce "ribbons"; the widest of this noodle family, about ½ inch

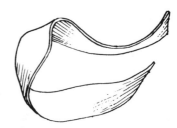

Fettucce riccie "curly ribbons"; noodles with a rippled edge. See *Riccie*, and see *Margherita* which is about the same as *fettucce riccie*.

*Fiorentini small pasta of Florence

Foratini "small pierced" pasta (for soup)

Foratini fini "tiny pierced" pasta (for soup)

Funghini "little mushrooms" (for soup)

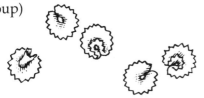

Fusilli "twists"; spaghetti twisted like a corkscrew in a long form. Quite different but given the same name is a tight short spiral that looks like a machine part; this version is given yet another name, *rote,* or "wheels."

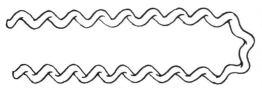

Fusilli bucati "twists with a hole"; i.e., *fusilli* made of thin macaroni

Gemelli "twins"; these look like two short pieces of spaghetti twisted together like a rope. An Americanized name for them is "twists Napoletani."

Giant shells these are very popular in this country and are served stuffed. They come grooved *(rigati)* and plain. Italian words for shells are *conchiglie* and *maruzze.*

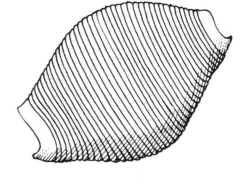

Gnocchi "dumpling"; there are Italian dishes in which this word does indeed mean a type of dumpling. But it is also used by Italian manufacturers as a pasta name, and variations of the name apply to quite different pastas.

Gnocchi itself is used for a pasta similar to *cavatelli. Gnocconi* looks like a short piece of *mafaldine.* (See illustrations under these names.)

Gnocchetti "small dumpling"; some short forms of pasta tubes may have their names changed to *gnocchetti* if they are cut even shorter. An example is *canneroni lisci* (see), which also has a *rigati* (grooved) form. These become *gnocchetti lisci* and *gnocchetti rigati* when they are cut about 1½ inches instead of 2 inches long. *Mezzi gnocchetti lisci* is the same tube cut about ½ inch long. All these tubes are roughly the diameter of *zitoni* (see).

Gnocchetti di ziti these are shorter forms of cut *ziti* (see illustration under *Ziti*) and there can be four: *gnocchetti di ziti,* both smooth and *rigati,* only about ½ inch long and very like *ditali* (see illustration under *Ditali*); and *gnocchetti di ziti lunghi* ("long"), also both smooth and *rigati,* about an inch long.

Lancette   "small spears" (for soup)

Lasagne   a word, according to the Italian spaghetti museum list, that means "pots" (derived from the Latin *lasanum*). Be that as it may, *lasagne* is the familiar, very wide flat pasta used most often in baked

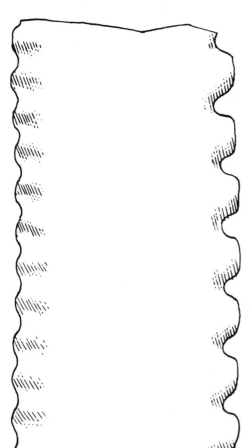

dishes. To make, see pages 57 and 58.

Lasagne ricci   *lasagne* with one or two sides "curly" or rippled, sometimes called *lasagne riccie un lato* if rippled only on one side; see *Riccie.* Ripple-edged *lasagne* is often sold without the word *riccie* appearing on the label at all.

Lingue di passeri   "sparrows' tongues"; similar to *linguine* but a little bigger (see below)

Linguine   "small tongues"; this is really a spaghetti, but it has the shape of a narrow, thick noodle. The American manufacturer's dies produce *linguine* that are actually oval rods, a sort of flattened spaghetti. He gives these products (which are all long) the following names, ranging from quite fine to somewhat oversize . . .

> *Bavettine*
> *Bavette*
> *Linguine*
> *Lingue di passeri*

With variations in die sizes, these 4 names can actually cover 6 sizes of oval-rod pastas.

Linguine fine   a smaller version of *linguine*

Lisci   "smooth"; the adjective applied to pastas made with a smooth surface to distinguish them from the same pastas also known in grooved (*rigati*) versions

Lumache   "snails"; a shell shape, of which there are several sizes

Lumachine "small snails"

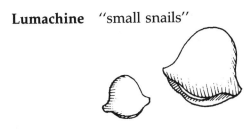

Macaroni our general term for hollow or pierced pasta products. The possibilities range from a macaroni no larger than spaghetti to *tufoli*, a very large tube, a good inch in diameter, which is served stuffed, somewhat like *manicotti* or *cannelloni*. The die manufacturer gives them these names . . .

Spaghetti *bucati*
Bucatini
Perciatelli
Maccheroncelli
Mezzanelli
Mezzani or *Maccheroni*
   (see below)
Ziti
Zitoni
Occhi di lupo
Cannelle
Tufoli

Pastas by these 11 names can most of them be made with dies of several different sizes, for a possible total of 20 sizes of hollow pastas.

Through sizes as large as *ziti* or *zitoni*, some brands, especially the Italian, are made long like spaghetti. The very thick ones are cut shorter. However, for all except the thinnest hollow pastas, short lengths (1 to 2 inches or sometimes more) are the ones you are most likely to find. The American brands sometimes call them "cut to cooking size." Some of these short forms are often curved rather than straight; see *Magliette* and Elbow. They are also made with surfaces grooved rather than smooth (see *Rigati*).

In addition, there are numerous other Italian names for hollow pastas of various sizes and length that are listed throughout this glossary.

Maccheroni the Italian spelling of macaroni; the diminutive for a smaller size is *maccheroncelli*. See also *Mezzani*. You will often find these in either long or short forms without a distinction being made in the names ("*tagliati*" would indicate the short form).

Mafalda or **Mafalde** a broad noodle rippled on both edges; *mafaldine* is the diminutive for a smaller version. See also *Riccie*.

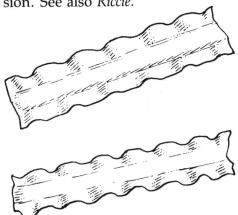

Magliette "links"; the word is used for rather short and slightly curved sections of pasta rods whose names indicate the original long forms, such as . . .

Magliette mezzani "medium links"; curved sections of medium-size macaroni

Magliette rigate "grooved links"; curved sections of grooved pasta tubes

Magliette spaccate "split links"; curved section of split pasta tubes

However, the total number of pastas that could be cut and curved in *magliette* form as suggested by the die manufacturer is much more imposing than the few above that we have most often used. They are all based on macaroni, i.e., hollow forms, from a thickness of less than ¼ inch up to a diameter of about 1 inch . . .

Magliette maccheroncelli
Magliette mezzanelli
Magliette mezzani
Magliette ziti
Magliette zitoni
Magliette occhi di lupo
Magliette cannelle

Pastas by these 7 names can most of them be made with dies of more than one size, for a total of 14 sizes of *magliette* pastas, and then the entire list can be repeated grooved (*rigati*). The *rigati* forms can be made on so many sizes of dies that there is a conceivable total of 28.

But finally, note that the word *magliette* is often omitted in the naming of both American and Italian pasta brands. The reason may be that in actual manufacture the straight short forms of hollow pasta tend to come out of the dies not really straight but also slightly curved, so that the distinction between straight and curved becomes largely theoretical. At any rate, you will often see pastas that certainly look as if they should qualify as *magliette* referred to merely by their basic names.

Manicotti "small muff," i.e., a tube. However, *manicotti* is usually fresh homemade pasta cut into large flat squares and rolled around a stuffing; to make, see pages 57 and 58.

A commercial form of *manicotti* is a giant tube, at least 4 inches long, over 1 inch in diameter, with the ends cut on the diagonal. The tube is often grooved. See *Mostaccioli rigati,* as this form of *manicotti* is just like it in oversize form with oversize grooves.

Margherita "daisy"; this does not look like a daisy, however. It is a moderately narrow noodle rippled along one side, similar to *fettucce riccie.*

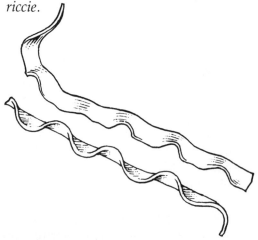

Margheritine "small daisy"; this does look a little like a flower. See *Funghini; margheritine* is almost exactly the same shape and about three times the size.

Maruzze "seashells"; there are at least 7 sizes, including the giant shells that are served stuffed. See Giant shells. And see *Conchiglie*; these are the same thing as *maruzze* and there are several names for the several sizes.

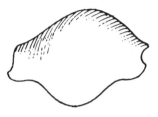

Maruzzelle "small seashells"

Maruzzine "tiny seashells"; the smallest of the pasta shells

Mezzani "medium"; this word is often used for the standard middle size of macaroni, or *maccheroni*. You will find both long and short forms by the same name.

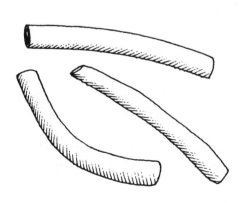

Mezzani tagliati medium-size macaroni cut into short lengths; *tagliati* is often left off the name of the pasta

*Millefiori "one thousand flowers"

Mille righe "one thousand stripes"; see *Rigatoni*, as the two are almost identical. This pasta is cut a little shorter (about 1½ inches) and has finer grooves.

Mostaccioli "small moustaches"; but these do not really look like moustaches. They are medium-size pasta tubes, 2 inches or so long, with diagonally cut ends. See also *Penne*, which are the same thing.

Mostaccioli rigati "grooved small moustaches"

Mostacciolini "tiny moustaches"; see also *Pennine*

Mughetto "lily-of-the-valley" (for soup)

*Napoleoni "Napoleons"

Nastrini "ribbon" or "tape"; the name is not very descriptive, as this pasta is a small bow with a zigzag edge all the way around, like American egg bows. See also *Farfalle*.

Nocciole "hazelnuts"; a shell shape of which there are several sizes as well as *rigati* (grooved) forms

Noodles there are many names for noodles of many widths, manufactured or homemade. The range of widths available commercially goes from less than ⅛ inch to over 1 inch, and the die manufacturer gives them these names, with corresponding English terminology . . .

Trenettine	Extra fine
Trenette	Fine
Fettuccelle	Medium
Fettuccine	Medium
Fettucce	Medium
Lasagnette	Broad
Lasagne	Extra broad

Lasagne, of course, is also made much wider than the inch or so the die manufacturer suggests when it is used for baking. Starting with *fettuccelle*, noodles may be rippled on one or two sides; see *Lasagne* and *Mafalda*, and see *Riccie*. See *Tagliatelle* for another important noodle family.

The 7 names above cover 14 sizes of dies with which noodles can be made and even more widths than that are surely made. In addition, noodles are sold as long straight rods, in folded form, and loosely bent and curled. The width of the noodle has more bearing on the texture and flavor of the cooked pasta than the form in which it is packaged. In theory, noodles are always made with egg dough, which makes a definite difference in flavor.

Occhi di lupo "wolf's eyes"; these are large tubes; see Macaroni

Occhi di passeri "sparrows' eyes"; tiny circles (for soup)

*****Occhi di trota** "trout's eyes"

*****Ondulati** pastas "that wave"

Orzo "barley"; small pasta that looks more like rice and is cooked in much the same way (see page 234)

*****Panierini** "small baskets"

Pappardelle broad noodles; in Italy this noodle is often served with hare.

*****Parigini** small pasta of Paris

Pasta fresca fresh pasta or pasta dough; to make, see page 61

Pasta fresca all'uovo fresh pasta or pasta dough with egg (for noodles); to make, see page 57

Pasta grattugiata grated fresh pasta (for soup); to make, see page 98

Pasta verde green pasta or pasta dough; to make, see page 60

Pastina "tiny dough"; very small pasta for soup. The labels, American and Italian, usually recommend it for baby food as well, but don't let that put you off.

Penne "pens" or "feathers"; pasta tubes cut diagonally at both ends, like a quill pen, into short lengths. See *Mostaccioli*, which are the same thing. Most of the *penne* family is also made *rigati* (grooved).

Pennine small *penne*; there are also *pennette*, which are quite tiny

Pennone large *penne*

Perciatelli "small pierced" pasta; long, hollow like macaroni, and about twice the thickness of spaghetti. See Macaroni.

Perciatelloni a larger version of *perciatelli*, it is about equivalent to a slim macaroni such as *maccheroncelli* or *mezzanelli*

Perline microscopici "tiny pearls" (for soup)

Pipe see *Lumache; pipe* are not quite the same thing, but they are very similar. There are *lisci* (smooth) and *rigati* (grooved) forms.

Pulcini "little chickens" (for soup)

Quadrettini "small squares"; flat, like noodles. Other forms of the word are *quadrucci* and *quadratini*.

Ravioli the well-known pasta squares, stuffed with eggs, vegetables, or cheese; to make, see page 59. See also *Agnolotti*.

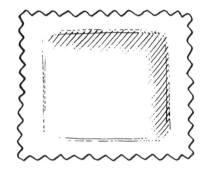

Raviolini small *ravioli*

Reginini "little queens"; small short pasta tubes

*Rex "king"

Ricci if you come across this, it will look like the short spiral form of *fusilli*. See *Fusilli*.

Riccie "curly"; the adjective applied to noodles of various widths when one or both sides are wavy or rippled. The ripple-edged noodle family is large, including widths from about ¼ inch to 1¼ inches, rippled on one side only, 4 names cover 11 possible widths . . .

Fettucelle riccie
Fettucce riccie
Lasagnette riccie
Lasagne riccie

Un lato, meaning "one side," can be added to these names to distinguish them from the noodles rippled on *both* sides. The latter the diemaker lists in widths from about ½ inch to about 3 inches. Five names cover 9 sizes . . .

> *Mafaldine*
> *Mafalda*
> *Lasagnette riccie*
> *Lasagne riccie*
> *Lasagne large riccie*

All these pastas are long. The illustration shows only fragments, but full width; the larger is *lasagne large riccie*, the smaller is *mafaldine*.

Riccini another type of small "curl" or twisted pasta, this one is shown in a grooved (*rigati*) form

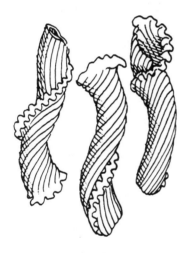

Ricciolini "little curls"

Rigati "grooved"; the adjective applied to various pastas when their surfaces are grooved or ridged. Hollow pastas, pasta shells (nut and conch), and some decorative soup pastas are made *rigati*.

The die manufacturer lists for hollow or macaroni pastas, ranging from less than ¼ inch to over 1 inch in diameter . . .

> *Perciatelli rigati*
> *Maccheroncelli rigati*
> *Mezzanelli rigati*
> *Mezzani rigati*
> *Ziti rigati*
> *Occhi di lupo rigati*
> *Cannelle rigati*
> *Rigatoni*

The pastas by these names can be made on so many different sizes of dies that there is a theoretical total of 41 grooved, hollow pasta forms. And then, this list is only for the straight and more or less long forms of *rigati* pastas; see *Magliette* and Elbow for others.

Seashells (*maruzze* is one name) can be made *rigati* in at least 7 sizes, nut shells (*nocciole*) in 4.

Rigatoni "large grooved" pasta tubes, actually the largest of all except for commercial *manicotti*

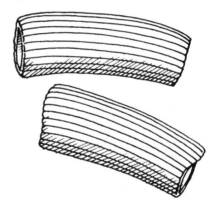

Risino "tiny rice" (for soup)

*Rosa marina "rose of the sea"

Rote "wheels," complete with hub, spokes, and grooved rim; there are also square wheels! However, the same name is used for an entirely different form, a spiral also called *fusilli;* see *Fusilli.*

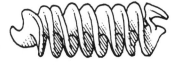

Rotelle "small wheels"

Rotini "tiny wheels"; you may also find *rotelline,* which are very small and used in soup

Salamini "tiny sausages" (for soup)

semi di mela "apple seeds" (for soup)

Semi di melone "melon seeds" (for soup)

Shells see *Conchiglie, Maruzze,* and Giant shells

Spacemen and astronauts believe it or not, there are such, obviously aimed at the juvenile trade. They serve fairly well as a substitute for pasta wheels; see *Rote.*

Spaghetti "a length of cord or string" is the metaphor that describes the most famous pasta of all; it is a solid round rod, as distinguished from the macaronis (round but hollow), *linguine* (solid but flattish or oval), and noodles (flat).

The list of spaghettis for which American pasta manufacturers can buy the dies, ranging from fine as a hair to slightly oversize is . . .

Capellini
Fedelini
Vermicelli
Spaghettini
Spaghetti
Spaghettoni

Pastas by these 6 names can each be made with dies of several different sizes, for a total of 16 sizes of solid-rod round pasta. These are all made long; the die manufacturer suggests only one short and probably rare form, elbow spaghetti.

In addition to the straight-rod form, the very thin spaghettis (*capellini, fedelini, vermicelli*) may be found in folded form similar to the folded forms of noodles. American manufacturers give these such names as "*vermicelli* clusters."

Spaghetti alla chitarra "guitar-string" spaghetti. In reality a long, thin-cut noodle, it may be rolled into a nest, a variation of the folded spaghettis mentioned above. You may find this pasta called *maccheroni alla chitarra,* but it is nevertheless as thin as the one called spaghetti. A wire cutter that looks very like a musical instrument is used to make it.

Stelle "stars" (for soup)

Stellini "little stars" (for soup); you may also find this spelled *stellette*

Stivaletti "little boots" (for soup); a small elbow macaroni

Stortini "small crooked" pasta (for soup); these look a little like tiny wriggling fish

Tagliatelle a word derived from the verb *tagliare*, "to cut"; there is an entire family of these noodles which is really no different from the *fettuccine* family except that this first one, *tagliatelle*, is wider, about ¾ inch in the homemade version (see pages 56–58). The flat pasta called *lasagnette*, which name some manufacturers use, is a noodle about this same width.

The 4 names in the family, progressing from ¾ inch to ⅛ inch, are...

> *Tagliatelle*
> *Tagliolette*
> *Tagliolini*
> *Tagliarini*

Tagliati "cut"; an adjective applied to short versions of some pastas

Tortellini "small twists"; to make these stuffed pastas, see page 59. Some specialty shops carry good frozen brands and dried *tortellini* are

also made, but these are not very satisfactory.

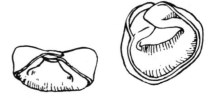

Trenette narrow noodles; see Noodles

Triangoli "triangles"; flat, like noodles

Trifogli "cloverleaves" (for soup)

Tripolini little pasta bows, named in honor of the conquest of Tripoli

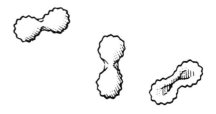

Tubetti "little tubes"; these are very short as well as small. You may also find *tubetti lunghi* ("long") which are 1-inch lengths of slim macaroni; there is a *rigati* (grooved) form of these.

Tubettini "tiny tubes"; a smaller version of *tubetti* for which there are also long and/or grooved versions

Tufoli very large pasta tubes; they are served stuffed

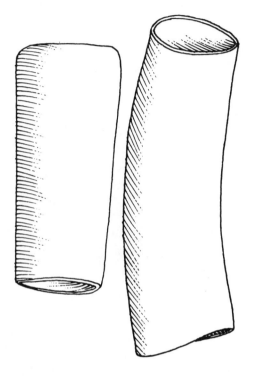

Vermicelli "little worms"; a very thin spaghetti. Like a number of the thin pasta products, *vermicelli* are sold not only as straight rods but also in folded or "cluster" form.

Vongole "clam shells"

Vongolette "little clam shells"

Ziti "bridegrooms"; a large macaroni, really a tube. See Macaroni. This word alone means the long form, as long as spaghetti. *Ziti tagliati* ("cut") is the correct name for the short form illustrated. This is the form you are most likely to find, but very often the qualifying *tagliati* is left off the name. American brands sometimes say "cut in cooking lengths" on the package. Long *ziti* are often broken before they are cooked.

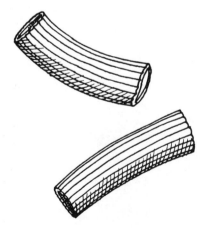

Ziti rigati "grooved bridegrooms"; a version of *ziti* with ridges

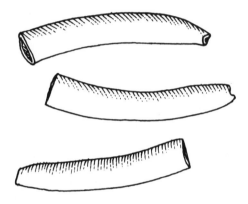

Zitoni "husky bridegrooms"; a large version of *ziti* that also has a *rigati* form

AMALFI, the Cathedral of Sant' Andrea—Campania

III
Pasta: How to Make It, How to Cook It

*B*ooks and recipes probably have instructed you to use four quarts of boiling water for a pound of pasta, stir with a spoon, drain in a colander, usually rinsing in cold water afterward. We believe all of this to be wrong, designed to convert pasta into a gooey mess, and so do the professional Italian chefs we have turned to for advice and technique.

Never use a spoon for stirring pasta while it is cooking. A spoon brings it together, and togetherness is not part of pasta cookery. Separate but equal is the way here. Use a wooden fork and gently separate the strands as they cook. A successful dish of pasta begins in the pot of water in which it is boiled.

Providing it is a *good* pasta. So let us start with the pasta itself, then take it in steps until it reaches your table.

As most commercial pastas are made with semolina, it is virtually impossible to get a bad one, but some are better than others, and a few American manufacturers are producing so-called "starch-free, instant-cooking" varieties. We say beware of these. But some made-in-America pastas are fair, even though we have found the imported ones superior, both in flavor and in standing up to cooking without becoming too soft too fast. Most better stores carry at least one of the imported brands. We mention names of imported pastas that we like in the Introduction.

Some of the best pasta we've had was in San Marzano, not far from Pompeii, the area of small green farms where most of Italy's plum tomatoes are grown commercially. This pasta was noodles, *tagliatelle*, made by the lady of the house that morning before lunch. They hung drying, like strips of beaten gold, on a wooden rack in the kitchen. The sauce was made of tomatoes and basil from the garden, simmered in olive oil and seasoned with freshly milled black pepper. It was superb.

We had gone to San Marzano to look at the plum-tomato gardens (and to see Pompeii) and now sat in the kitchen sipping a glass of Lacrima Christi (tears of Christ), a fine white wine grown on slopes not far from old Pompeii. We watched, fascinated with this woman's skill, far above what we ever could accomplish.

The Technique of Making Pasta Fresca

She sifted 4 cups of semolina flour onto a large slab of marble in the center of the kitchen table; using two fingers, she made a well in the center, its bottom about halfway down into the mound of flour. Into this went 4 lightly beaten eggs, 1½ teaspoons of salt, 2 teaspoons of olive oil, and 2 of warm water, the liquid added gradually to make the dough soft enough to handle. Flexing her fingers into it, she first used just her right hand until the flour, eggs, and oil were well mixed into a ball. Then she removed the dough, wiped the marble clean, floured it lightly, and placed the dough ball back and began kneading with vigor, slapping it and pressing it down with the heel of her palms until it was smooth. We timed this operation. It took exactly 10 minutes.

"Now I let it rest," she said, placing a large bowl over the well-kneaded pasta ball. "I don't know why," she said, as we went into the garden to pick the plum tomatoes and the basil, "but by the time we get back into the house, that dough will be ready to roll. Covering it makes it much easier."

Using a broom handle, cut to a 3-foot length (we use a tapered pastry roller), she then rolled out the pasta, after first dividing the large ball into four pieces. This was done only after that all-important slab of marble had been cleaned again and lightly floured. This expert lady was a large, well-formed woman with lots of strength, and she rolled that pasta dough out into much thinner sheets than we could have.

Next she took a sharp knife and cut the sheets into strips ¾ of an inch wide. About 1 pound of these she placed on a clean white cloth to dry for lunch, the rest she hung on the wooden rack for *pasta secca*—to dry long enough so that it didn't need refrigeration or have to be used immediately. The noodles on the cloth dried in exactly 1 hour, then went into a huge 12-quart pot of boiling water.

That was the method, which we have yet to see improved, and here are the ingredients again. They make 1½ pounds or so.

PASTA FRESCA ALL'UOVO

4 cups semolina flour
4 fresh eggs, lightly beaten
1½ teaspoons salt
2 teaspoons olive oil
2 teaspoons warm water

There are good reasons for using semolina flour. It makes a tastier pasta that also holds up better in the cooking. But if you can't get it in a specialty shop or an Italian grocery store, don't fret. Ask for an unbleached, high-gluten flour.

Do not use "self-rising" flours and avoid the new miracle flours, the so-called "instantized" flours. There is no such thing as instant pasta.

The thing to remember in kneading the pasta is, if the flour doesn't mix or hold together as you knead, add more liquid, slowly; or, if the dough is too soft, then add more flour—but either way, easy does it. Add small amounts of liquid as you mix the dough, or correspondingly, if it becomes too soft, add small amounts of flour to bring it back into form.

From this very dough made by the wife of that tomato-grower at San Marzano can come a variety of fresh pastas. We make from this same recipe *manicotti, fettuccine, lasagne, cannelloni,* and *tagliatelle.*

After the dough is rolled and before drying it, it must be cut. Rather than cutting long strips from the spread-out sheets, there is a quicker and more effective way of doing this: The original well-kneaded ball of dough has been divided into 3 or 4 pieces and each one rolled into a sheet as thin as you can make it, paper-thin. As we discussed in the Introduction, there are excellent hand-operated machines for this. Now roll up or fold each sheet into a long roll. Then cut the roll crosswise, making strips any width you wish, depending upon what you are going to use them for. The strips may then be very gently unfolded and cut into special lengths if that is required. Or lightly toss the cut noodles to unfold them. *Note:* In the Introduction we describe the method of mixing the dough in a food processor.

To Cut Manicotti: Cut the sheets of dough into 3-inch squares. Dry on cloth or floured board, covered with a cloth, for 1 hour. (See Index for fillings.)

To Cut Fettuccine: Cut rolled sheets of dough into ¼-inch strips. Unfold and dry for 1 hour, covered.

To Cut Lasagne: Cut dough into strips 2 inches wide, 4 to 6 inches long, depending on how broad you want this noodle. Dry for 1 hour, covered.

To Cut Cannelloni: The dough for this should not be any thicker than ⅛ inch, even thinner if possible; cut into 4- or 4½-inch squares. Dry for 1 hour, covered. Then cook 5 squares at a time, popped into 5 quarts of boiling water, for 4 minutes. Remove with a slotted spoon, and drain well on absorbent cloth (See Index for fillings.)

To Cut Tagliatelle: These were the noodles, ¾ inch wide, prepared by the wife of the tomato-grower. They may be cut from rolled sheets of dough. *Tagliarini* are the smallest version of this noodle, cut ⅛ inch wide.

POMPEII, the Via di Mercurio—Campania

If you want to experiment, and this adds to the pleasure of making your own pasta, make the noodles wider, smaller, longer, shorter. But whatever you do dream up, the Italians have probably been there before you.

PASTA FRESCA FOR RAVIOLI AND TORTELLINI

This dough is handled a little differently. The ingredients below make about 1 pound of dough.

3½ cups semolina flour (see page 57)

1 teaspoon salt

2 eggs, lightly beaten

1 tablespoon olive oil

      and/or

2 tablespoons warm water

Sift the flour onto the board or marble slab, sprinkle in the salt, make a center well, and add the eggs and oil gently so that they remain in the well. Now gradually mix well, kneading into a soft smooth dough, slowly adding drops of warm water to soften it if necessary. Knead from 5 to 10 minutes, long enough to have a smooth elastic dough; cover with pan or bowl for a half hour.

To Shape Ravioli: (See Index for fillings.) Reflour the board. Cut the dough into 2 sections, roll out each section to no more than ⅛ inch thick, and cut into 3-inch strips as long as the sheets. Place teaspoons of the filling 2½ inches apart on this long strip. Cover with a similar 3-inch-wide strip of dough, pressing the dough firmly around each spoonful of filling. Using a pastry wheel or a *ravioli* cutter, cut into 2- or 3-inch squares, depending upon how large you want the *ravioli*. They should dry, covered with a cloth, for at least 1½ hours before cooking.

To Shape Tortellini: This is done somewhat differently from *ravioli*. The dough is cut into 2-inch circles (with a glass or cookie cutter), the filling is placed atop, and each one is folded to form a half circle. Press the edges of each half circle firmly together, then bend it, seam side out, to form a ring, and press together firmly the overlapping points of the original half circle. *Tortellini* are a Bolognese specialty, and local legend has it that they resemble the navel of Venus, copied by a lusty innkeeper who sneaked a look. The legend is a good clue to the correct shape, for proper *tortellini* should look like large, well-formed navels.

A word of caution regarding *ravioli,* or any of the pastas that are to be filled. After you have rolled the dough and cut it into strips, place the filling on it immediately before the dough has dried. Dried dough is difficult to press into shape. Spoon the filling in position and form the dough over and around it, according to what you are making. Place the filled pasta on a clean white cloth, cover with another cloth, and then let it dry for a half hour.

PASTA VERDE

This recipe makes a little more than 1 pound of green noodles.

  ¾ pound cleaned fresh spinach
  4 cups semolina flour (see page 57)
  2 eggs, lightly beaten
  1 teaspoon salt

Cook spinach without water, well covered, until tender. Drain well, pressing out *all* the water. Then force through a sieve or purée in a food mill or food processor.

Sift the four onto a board or marble slab, make the center well, and add the beaten eggs, the salt, and finally the spinach. Now knead until the dough is well mixed. Knead for 15 minutes until it is smooth, adding water if it is too dry or flour if too soft. Separate the smooth ball of dough into 3 sections. Then, using preferably a 2-foot tapered pastry rolling pin, flatten each piece, rolling it and pressing it into extremely thin sheets, ⅛ inch or thinner, if possible. To make cutting easier, these sheets can now be gently folded into long rolls, which can then be cut straight across into ⅓- or ¼-inch strips. The noodles should then be unfolded and dried on a clean white cloth for 1 hour before cooking.

All of the foregoing *paste fresche* are made with eggs; thus they are noodles. The following is a recipe for fresh pasta without eggs, in the manner of the commercial dry pasta, except that this one will not be hard and dry and it will be tastier.

PASTA FRESCA

3 cups semolina flour (see page 57)
1 teaspoon salt
2 tablespoons olive oil
1 cup warm water

Sift flour onto board, make center well, and add salt, olive oil, and small amount of water. Slowly mix, bringing flour from around edges, kneading together. Add more water if needed; continue kneading until dough is formed into a smooth ball. Cover dough with a bowl and let it rest for 10 minutes. Now reknead until dough is smooth and very elastic. Re-cover with bowl for 15 minutes, then divide dough ball into 3 pieces, and roll into ⅛-inch sheets. Cut strips into desired widths, or press through the small pasta machine (described on page 17) that has dies for making fresh spaghetti or other forms. Dry for 1 hour before cooking.

Do not worry when you are making homemade pasta if it seems too soft, or too hard, to handle; a little more water or more flour will take care of it.

Caution: We repeat. Fresh pasta cooks much more quickly than dry, so be especially careful; test it often or it will get too soft.

From our pokings and peerings among the pots and pans in many restaurant kitchens in several Italian cities, we have discovered that most professional chefs handle pasta about the same way. We made a survey of ten restaurant kitchens in Rome, watching pasta being cooked and served. Almost to a man, the chefs went about it this way:

The pasta was boiling merrily in a large, deep pot. The waiter would come, the chef would take a long fork and dip out the pasta, shaking it and holding it over the pot until most of the water had dripped off. Then he dropped it into a warm, rimmed soup bowl. Next he spooned from another pot the correct sauce and placed it on top of the pasta, without mixing. Then the waiter hurried off so that the dish would be hot when placed before the customer. There was a variation on this theme, with the chef sometimes using a huge warm bowl on the back of the stove to place the pasta in. He added butter and tossed the pasta in the bowl before giving it to the waiter. In three kitchens the chefs did this, then grated cheese over it, tossing cheese, butter, and pasta together, then forked out the correct amounts into the warm bowls held by the waiters. The sauce always went on last, just a large spoonful in the center atop the pasta.

When we asked about the technique of forking the pasta directly out of the boiling water, one chef said: "This way the pasta stays hot longer, it is very lightly covered with moisture which keeps the strands separate. Each strand of pasta keeps its own personality and doesn't become dry. That is the danger; dry pasta is sticky pasta. Draining it in a sieve or colander also bunches it, can make it dry and sticky. Rinsing does the same thing. Most of this hot water comes off before I fork the pasta into the plate or mixing bowl, yet each strand is coated enough so that it is protected against the next strand, won't stick to it. Also that slight amount of water on each piece helps in the mixing when the diner puts pasta and sauce together."

This chef, at one of the great restaurants of Italy, did not mix together pasta and sauce, coating each strand as many of us believe is necessary. We asked why.

"Here in Rome," he said, "we seldom mix the pasta and sauce. Too much sauce destroys the flavor of the pasta, makes it heavy. Let each one mix to his own desire and demand."

Much of this is against long-stated so-called rules of pasta cookery, but it is the expert's way, and we have found through trial and error and much ruined pasta that it is the best way. For home direction there are just a few steps to follow for cooking either fresh or dry pasta.

HOW TO COOK PASTA

At least *seven quarts* of water should be used for one pound of pasta. The water should be in a very deep pot, so the pasta has space to swim without the strands or pieces being forced against one another. *Two tablespoons* of salt should be added—after the water is sharply boiling, and at the instant *just before* the pasta goes in. We have discovered that if the water and salt boil together for long, the pasta will have a disagreeable odor, oddly like that of carbolic acid.

ORTA, the Town Hall—Piedmont

VENICE—*Venezia Euganea*

Let us repeat that, because we are not going to say it very often again: *For 1 pound of pasta, use 7 quarts of water and 2 tablespoons of salt.* This is the rule unless the recipe specifies otherwise, and we are not going to list water and salt every single time pasta is cooked in this book because our publisher told us this redundant information would add at least twenty-five pages to the book. Look this up in the Index if you forget on what page you read it.

Note another technique to prevent pasta from sticking, a familiar one which the chefs also use—especially for fresh homemade pastas or for the large ones that are most inclined to stick—add a tablespoon of olive oil to the boiling water.

Now, to keep the water at this boiling rate and temperature, having added the salt, turn up the heat, then gently add the pasta (without breaking!), and push it down until it is all submerged. As stated before, use a wooden fork to stir, separating the strands or the pieces as they cook. Continue this. Gently does it.

Now the timing. There are several schools of thought on this: Some books have time charts for each type; others say a flat number of minutes. The professionals use only one test: the tooth. One pasta chef who has been standing over his pots for forty years told us that he keeps a small bowl on the back of the stove with a dollop of sauce in it. Every few seconds, after the first three minutes, he forks out a strand or a piece of pasta and dips it into the sauce and tastes it. He cautioned that the various types take different times, saying that *capelli d'angelo* (angel's hair) are so fine that he cooks them exactly two seconds. "The big ones you don't have to watch too carefully before the first three minutes, but the smaller they are, the more caution. Spaghettini and *vermicelli* we often test twelve times while they are cooking. *Rigatoni* perhaps only four times."

So it isn't just "place in boiling water and cook" for a certain number of minutes as directions on many a package of pasta state. It is test and test—to the tooth, al dente, for that is what this means. When ready, again according to our chef friends, the pasta should be biteable and have no flavor of flour—then it is done, al dente.

We like our pasta just a bit softer than al dente—a shade—still firm and chewy, however, but not *quite* so underdone as some Romans like it.

Our testing method might not work for most. We use a medium wineglass of Chianti for spaghetti, a half for *vermicelli*, a glass and a half for *perciatelli*. We time our pasta by drinking the glass of wine. But this has taken much wine and much practice. We never bolt it. But on several occasions when we were cooking big *ziti* and *rigatoni*, we were reeling a bit before we pronounced the pasta properly cooked. So our recommendation, at least in the beginning, is to follow the example of the pros—test it against the tooth. It is the safest, most effective way.

We differ slightly from the professionals in the handling of pasta, but the theory and result remain the same. We, too, think that rimmed soup bowls or heat-holding ramekins are the best serving dishes, always hot, always individually served.

We keep a large ceramic bowl on the back of the stove, with fresh unsalted butter in it. As it warms, the butter melts, ready for mixing. (Another method: If you like to mix butter with pasta—it adds much flavor—before saucing and serving, shave it into the cooked pasta, don't throw it in in a lump. Shaving the butter permits the pasta to absorb it more quickly.)

But usually, we fork the pasta from the boiling pot into the warm bowl with the butter (one half a quarter-pound stick for a pound of pasta), letting the water drain off into its cooking pot before each forkful goes into the bowl. When it is all in the warm mixing bowl, we mill two turnings of pepper into it, toss it gently with wooden fork and spoon, being careful not to bruise it. Then, using a cylinder grater, we grind in Asiago or Parmesan cheese and toss again (three pieces of cheese each about the size of a walnut for a pound of pasta). Now the pasta is placed in the individual hot bowls, and a heaping spoonful of sauce goes over it (use a large kitchen spoon, or the one with which you are stirring the sauce), and it is brought to table piping hot. (Sometimes pasta and sauce *are* first tossed together; the recipe will say.)

A quarter of a pound of pasta is *more* than enough for each serving. At the elbow of each guest we place a small cylinder type of cheese grater, should he (or she) want more cheese. The test of good pasta is that each guest will eat all he has been given and will look as if he wants more—which he shouldn't get, for, properly, another course follows.

Back to cooking techniques: These must be tempered with common sense. The fork-from-pot method can be used with the stranded pastas, *linguine, vermicelli,* spaghetti, the flat noodles, *fettuccine, tagliatelle,* etc. But with the shells, or *rigatoni, tufoli, ziti, lasagne,* broken or already cut to cooking length, we suggest removing them with a slotted spoon, or a big flat, perforated skimmer, or go to the colander if you must; then into the warm bowl on the back of the stove—without rinsing—or, for baked pastas, directly into the casserole for the covering of sauce before the dish enters the oven.

It is our belief that the stranded pastas, those without holes or a bore, absorb or soak up sauce only from the outside, and thus can best be mixed to the taste of the diner by himself. But pasta with crevices, holes, and flutes benefits from being well mixed with the sauce before serving, offering a taste delight that only this type can: sauce on the outside, the inside, in the grooves and fluted surfaces.

Also, the dishes that depend upon cream and vegetables should be mixed well before serving, always adding a spoonful of peas, or mushrooms, or whatever the main ingredient is, on top just before bringing to the table.

PASTA CHEESES FOR GRATING

A chapter on the methods of pasta cookery cannot be complete without a word on cheese. Good, aged cheese is as important as a fine grade of pasta: There are three, in our opinion, which should be mentioned first that properly are to be grated and mixed with pasta: Asiago, Parmesan, and Pecorino Romano. Asiago is a *Grana* type of cheese, originating in the province of Vicenza. Properly aged (it should be a golden color, hard, and at least three years old before it is used with pasta), Asiago is nuttier and has more flavor than either Parmesan or Romano. It is also less expensive. But it is also more difficult to obtain. The best we have had is produced by the Frigo family, which has been working with Asiago for six generations, an Asiago superior even to that made in Italy—it is made by the Frigos here in the United States, in Wisconsin. It is most easy to get from: Frigo Food Products, Inc., 46 Summer Street, P.O. Box 446, Torrington, Connecticut 06790. Once you've used golden, aged Asiago with pasta, you are hooked. You will use no other. But if you can't find it, aged Parmesan is the first choice. This should be at least two years old. It is a popular cheese and more easily obtainable.

Let us say it again, for it makes all the difference: As in wine, age is important in pasta cheese. And it should be Italian, or at least made by Italians, for no one else has mastered the art of making Asiago, Parmesan, and Romano. There are American and South American substitutes. But they are just that, substitutes. The good stores are honest about pasta cheeses; quite often their reputations depend upon it, especially if they have many discerning customers. An aged Parmesan isn't white, but faintly yellow—and very hard. It should taste slightly sweet, slightly nutty, and it should not be salty. The best of the Parmesans is Parmigiano Reggiano (*Grana*), made the same way as it was in the tenth century. This is a finely textured, golden cheese that is always properly aged. Other very dependable brands are Polenghi, Galbani, and Locatelli.

Near PESARO, on the Adriatic—The Marches

Romano is white, somewhat salty in flavor, and sharp; proper Parmesan is none of these. Some dishes call for one or the other, but we have found that even if a recipe does call for straight Romano, flavor is always enhanced by using half Parmesan. Cheeses under two years of age are not yet grown up enough to do anything good for your pasta. Young cheeses are all right for oven pasta dishes that are long-baking and have other flavor-adding ingredients. (Also, for baked pastas and for stuffed ones, other types of cheeses are often required. These are specified in the relevant recipes.)

The important thing to remember is that the cheese should always be freshly grated; never buy it already grated; it quickly loses its snap, picks up an almost sawdusty flavor, and does nothing for your dish.

And while we are on the subject of cheese, it is never (in Italy) added to pasta with seafood. Why, we've never been able to determine, but the rule is just. We tried *linguine* (this is nearly always teamed with seafood; why, again we couldn't find out) and white clam sauce in Taranto, and with the waiter glaring, grated some cheese over it. It didn't add anything and detracted from the seafood flavor, which is delicate and shouldn't be tampered with.

The subject of Italian grating cheeses cannot be brushed off with our saying that only three are worth consideration. Asiago, Parmesan, and Romano are our favorites, thus we mentioned them first. But there are several more which should be grated over pasta and sampled so that you can come to your own conclusions. *Ricotta Siciliana* is a soft, spicy, aged cheese, especially good over very thin pasta such as vermicelli. *Caciocavallo* is a grating cheese with a powerful personality, perhaps too powerful. *Pepato* comes impregnated with whole black peppercorns and is excellent grated over simple pasta dishes that need some such special authority. *Ragusano*, if you can get it, comes close to rivaling Parmesan; it is Sicilian, made from cow's milk, spicy, but also rich and nutty. *Pecorino di Tavola*, somewhat sharp, is very good with the old favorite, baked macaroni and cheese. *Incanestrato*, impressed with a braided basket design, is bitey, "different," and excellent. All are authentically Italian and deserve a trial mating with your pasta.

EQUIPMENT

Tools and cooking utensils are also important. Chefs have taught us that the enameled cast-iron pots from France and Belgium are not only handsome, heavy, and serviceable, but perfect for pasta because they are good conductors and hold the heat so long. They are also excellent should you want to store leftover pasta and sauce in the refrigerator, for they have snug-fitting covers that prevent the food from picking up odors. We have them in various sizes, but the 10-quart pot receives the most use for boiling pasta, giving it enough water and plenty of room to swim.

Again going to the chef's system, we use copper pans for our sauces. They are the best conductors of heat, spreading it evenly. And a gas stove (chefs use nothing else) is preferable, for no matter what those who use electric ranges tell you, gas is the heat that can be properly controlled at all times.

For removing the pasta from the pot there are "spaghetti forks" for sale in many markets, double forks on one handle, designed to lift stranded pasta easily from boiling water and to hold it firmly while the water is shaken off. A slotted spoon and a large skimmer are excellent for performing the job with other types, *ravioli*, etc. A wooden spoon should be used for mixing sauces and *only* a wooden fork for stirring the pasta while it cooks.

Other tools: a 20-inch-square pastry board or marble slab; a 2-foot tapered rolling pin; a glass container marked for measuring in both ounces and cups; the usual nest of measuring spoons, ranging from ¼ teaspoon to a tablespoon; and a wire whisk for mixing and blending.

Mouli makes small cylindrical cheese graters that can handle a lump of freshly cut cheese easily and take all the labor from the job. This firm also manufactures a parsley mincer which is effective for that so-often-chopped item and will mince other herbs, and onions, too. For garlic *that is to remain in the sauce*, a garlic press is indispensable. You should also have carbon-steel knives (no chef ever uses a stainless-steel knife)—a paring knife, a filleting knife, and a big chef's knife for chopping and mincing.

If you are going to try homemade pasta, there are machines available in several sizes and prices with dies and cutting blades that will neatly shape your spaghetti or cut your noodles after you have properly prepared the dough. There are also *ravioli* cutters, and special *ravioli*-form trays, and various other cutters for pasta. Italian specialty shops have all of the items mentioned here except the pots and pans. A little thought regarding the proper tools to do the job will pay dividends in efficiency, cut down time and labor—and produce better pasta.

If you have difficulty finding the various pastas suggested in this book, or imported ingredients, or cooking equipment, or the tools and gadgets to shape and cut homemade pastas, the Italian *drogheria* and *salumeria* (grocery and delicatessen) which has solved all these problems for us is Frigo Food Products, 46 Summer Street, P.O. Box 446, Torrington, CT 06790, mentioned earlier. They mail promptly to any place in the United States.

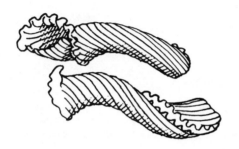

ATRANI, on the Amalfi Drive—Campania

IV
Basic Sauces & Some Special Sauces

Writing a cookbook on pasta develops into a devious enterprise. At first glance, if you like to cook, it seems an interesting project, its one obvious but unreal hazard the fact that you may put on weight if you test every recipe (though we have *not* put on weight while testing). But when you get into the organization, then the actual doing, the cooking, and testing, suddenly comes an overwhelming realization: A book on pasta is virtually a book on Italian cookery. The meats, fish, fowl or other elements that form the base of the sauce, and which are often served *after* the pasta, require dexterous know-how in preparation. Therein lies the deviousness: In the pages of a pasta cookbook lies information on many forms of cooking. Thus, when you cook hare for a *fettuccine* sauce, the inspiration first comes with the proper preparation of the hare.

This holds true for everything from a pig's foot to a mussel. Master the art of making a proper pasta sauce, and you are a long way toward mastering the art of Italian cooking—acknowledged by some experts as being the best in the world. After all, the Italians brought the fork to France and fathered modern cookery during the Renaissance.

We are of the school that firmly believes that sauces should carry delicate flavor and that no one ingredient in them should dominate or overwhelm. (As previously stated, we also are very much "anti" tomato paste in anything.) Thus we are wary of any recipe that lists "a cup of olive oil" or one that blithely suggests "a bunch of garlic" or "twelve garlic cloves."

PAESTUM, the Temple of Neptune—Campania

Largely, these are untested recipes and if one follows them, they prove to be an assault on the stomach. We remember when a national magazine brought out its beautifully illustrated cookbook, and we eagerly tried the white clam sauce for *linguine*. This book was of the "cup" school. The clams were drowned in olive oil and garlic, with the result that when you ate the pasta with "clam" sauce, all you tasted was olive oil and garlic; the subtle flavor of the clams didn't have a chance.

So, go carefully. Recipes are usually written to serve four or six people, which should involve an absolute maximum of one or one and a half pounds of pasta. Rarely should any such recipe need more than one clove of garlic; be suspicious if it calls for more than two. Olive oil should be used sparingly too. Two tablespoons are quite a lot for a pound of pasta; three tablespoons plenty, and four, time to be wary. And use good oil. A sauce is only as good as its ingredients.

Virgin olive oil, the first pressing (the food establishment is now stressing in its usual excessive way "Extra Virgin Olive Oil!" We find that virgin is fine and even less than virgin perfectly okay), is the best and, especially for Italian food, Italian olive oil is the first choice. The oil should not be too heavy or have too penetrating an olive flavor. It should be light gold-green and have little odor. Through trial and error we have found that Francesconi is our first choice, Berio second, Bertolli third; next Sasso, Pastene, and *Madre Sicilia*. There is no need to buy blindly in olive oils. All reputable stores (especially Italian) have some of those listed above. In our opinion, if you try to economize in buying olive oil, you are taking a chance.

In America many have the misconception that all Italian pasta sauces are made with tomato. Nothing could be further from the truth. There are many excellent sauces that have tomato as a base, and they are among our favorites, but the range of flavors, colors, and ingredients of pasta sauces is restricted only by the imagination. The Italians can whip up a delicious sauce with just butter and cauliflower, or a touch of olive oil and a few clams, and there are few tastier sauces than that made only with puréed fillets of anchovies.

However, in order not to frighten you off, let's start with something familiar, a simple tomato sauce that can be a basic sauce for any pasta and will be so called. This is a sauce often used to cover the meat for the main course while it cooks, the meat giving the sauce much added flavor, the sauce helping fix this flavor and also moistening the meat—each giving strength to the other.

To Prepare Fresh Tomatoes

You will be doing this often. It depends on the recipe whether they are seeded and diced or put through a food mill. They must always be peeled. To do this, plunge them briefly into boiling water and they will be easy to peel. To seed plum tomatoes, cut out the small core at the stem end with a pointed knife, and deseed the tomato by holding it in one hand and squeezing (the seeds, or most of them, pop out). Other varieties usually have to be cut in half before the seeds can be squeezed out. When a recipe calls for the fresh tomatoes to be put through a sieve or food mill, this will dispose of the seeds. (If you wonder why you are sometimes told to deseed tomatoes even though the *sauce* is later put through a sieve, this is because the seeds may give a bitter taste to the sauce as it cooks. This isn't necessarily true, but with certain types of tomato it is.)

POMMAROLA

Basic Tomato Sauce

Always in a tomato sauce we prefer ripe, fresh tomatoes, but they are seasonal, and the best canned plum tomatoes are excellent.

3 pounds very ripe plum tomatoes,
    peeled, seeded, and diced, or 9 cups of canned tomatoes
    (two 2-pound, 3-ounce cans)
1 garlic clove
2 tablespoons good olive oil
1 teaspoon salt, or to taste
A liberal amount of milled black pepper
    (preferably the black Indian Telli-
    cherry peppercorn, the world's best)
1 tablespoon dried sweet basil

For this we prefer to peel, seed, and dice the tomatoes, but you can also grind them in a food mill or push them through a sieve, which will remove the seeds. If canned tomatoes are used, just put them through the food mill, depulping and deseeding.

Peel garlic, cut into 3 pieces, and put in deep frypan with the olive oil. Simmer over a low flame until the garlic is brown (don't burn). Press the pieces of garlic flat in the pan and swish them around in the oil; then remove and discard them.

Now, in a swift, definite movement (don't pour in slowly or the oil will flare and geyser over the stove), dump the bowl of tomato into the pan. Add the salt and pepper and the dried basil. Keeping the flame low, stir the sauce frequently with a wooden spoon until it is well blended and bubbling. Keep the flame low for 10 minutes, then raise slightly, enough so the sauce is cooking well, but not bubbling so much that it is throwing tomato all over the stove. Continue to cook and stir in the uncovered pan until the water has evaporated and the sauce thickens. The right test here is to taste it. If it has body and flavor and isn't watery, then it is ready. Time is usually 30 minutes. The recipe makes 7 cups. This is a sauce that you can use for any pasta. It is light, tasty, and has a fresh flavor.

Note: Seven cups is, obviously, quite a lot of sauce. Two cups is what we usually allow to serve six people. The point is that, for certain simple sauces such as this one, it is no more trouble to make a big batch than a small one, *and*, again important, tomato sauces freeze very well. So why not use enough ingredients so that you will have sauce for the freezer that you can just pull out some other time when you need a quick dish of spaghetti?

For a number of the sauces in this chapter, the quantities given are large. They are the ones that we consider freeze particularly well, and several have multiple uses, so it is really simpler to make the one large batch rather than to go through the whole thing several times in small batches. Freeze the sauce in pint (2-cup) containers.

Now, to start you off in style on the theory of the dual use of a sauce—for the main dish of a meal as well as the first-course pasta—we are inserting here an unusual recipe that properly belongs in the chapter on meat. The basic tomato sauce, after being used as an ingredient of this recipe, becomes quite transformed and does for the spaghettini on which it is first served something that the original version could not have done. It is, in fact, an entirely new sauce and has meanwhile contributed mightily to the beef roll that is to follow—an excellent illustration of the importance of sauce to Italian cookery.

The beef roll is the creation of an old family friend, Catherine Spadaccino, a kitchen wizard. We've sat and watched this masterpiece develop several times in her kitchen in Danbury, Connecticut. Hers is one of the most impressive ground-meat dishes in the Italian repertoire, cleverly teaming beef, eggs, excellent cheese, and tangy sausage. And sauce. It is an unusual company dish and interesting to prepare. Don't get discouraged as you read. This is a project, but it is not a difficult dish. Just follow directions in steps.

CATHERINE SPADACCINO'S FOGGIA BEEF ROLL

5 pounds top-round steak, ground
2 cups dry bread crumbs
4 leaves of fresh basil, chopped
1 tablespoon chopped fresh Italian
    parsley
7 fresh eggs, beaten
1 cup coarsely grated Romano cheese
1½ teaspoons salt
1 teaspoon freshly milled black pepper
1 tablespoon olive oil
4 four-inch Italian sweet sausages
4 hard-cooked eggs
4 slices of provolone cheese
4 cups Basic Tomato Sauce (page 76)
1 teaspoon sugar
¼ teaspoon ground cinnamon
½ teaspoon dried oregano
1 pound spaghettini
Butter
Asiago or Parmesan cheese

In a bowl, blend together beef, bread crumbs, basil, parsley, beaten eggs, ½ cup of the Romano, salt, and pepper. Spread the tablespoon of olive oil onto the waxed paper, board, or table where you will make the roll. Reserve 1 cup of the meat mixture for patching the roll later, which it may need. Place the rest of the meat mixture on the oiled board. Flatten out (rolling pin helps) into a large round medallion ½ inch thick.

Broil the sausages. Place them whole on the flat meat; place hard-cooked eggs between and surround with the slices of provolone. Sprinkle the remaining ½ cup of grated Romano over everything; mill on more black pepper, sprinkle on more salt. Now carefully roll the meat until you have a firm, tubular roll. If there are holes or open places, patch them with the cup of ground meat that you saved. Now slide the roll into an oiled open pan or casserole; bake it uncovered in a 400° F. oven until it is firm and brown, about 45 minutes.

Meanwhile, in a saucepan heat basic tomato sauce, thicken with 2 tablespoons of drippings from meat pan, stir, and simmer 10 minutes. Lower oven heat to 300° F. Cover the roll with the tomato sauce; lightly sprinkle with sugar, cinnamon, and oregano. Bake meat roll and sauce together for 30 minutes, spooning sauce occasionally over meat as it simmers. Then remove meat to a hot platter and let set, to become firm and slightly cooled for easier slicing. Serves 6 to 8.

Shortly before the meat is done, cook the spaghettini. When the pasta is al dente, remove with the fork-from-pot method, place in warm bowl with butter and grated cheese, and toss. (The correct way to do all this is explained in How to Cook Pasta on pages 62–66.) Serve with a spoonful of sauce over each individual serving.

Here is a particular secret of pasta: With this dish of spaghettini topped with the piquant sauce, you get the full flavor of the tomato, the meat, and the subtle seasonings, and together they herald the triumph to come— the meat roll, which arrives at the table whole, is carved before the guests, and displays, when it is sliced, the colorful pattern of hard-cooked eggs, sausages, and melted cheese centering each slice. The remaining sauce is brought in a bowl for guests to spoon over the sliced meat. It is the sauce that makes a success of the whole meal, not merely of one or the other course.

The uninitiated may imagine that, once they have learned to make and cook pasta, all that a pasta cookbook can then tell them is how to make pasta sauces. This is too simple a view, as the preceding recipe for the Foggia Beef Roll has shown. Nevertheless, it is true that you will encounter an uncommon number of sauces in this book, so this separate chapter of sauces may seem redundant. However, it contains the basic ones that need to be isolated because they are repeatedly called for later. And the remainder, though some are specifically mentioned again only a few times, have been chosen to make here a group that will give you a foretaste of the immense variety of pasta sauces to come. They include a few classics that are so famous that one would tend to call them also "basic" sauces, and a few unusual ones to whet your appetite to read on.

FILETTO DI POMODORO

Neapolitan Light Tomato Sauce

This is a favorite sauce with the "like-it-light" people in the Naples region. Simple and savory, it is also versatile, can be cooked quickly, and goes well with any form of pasta. Many Italian restaurants, and the few good ones in this country, consider this a summer-Sunday sauce. That day they make it fresh; they make the pasta fresh, too (usually a noodle), toss it with butter and cheese, and spoon filetto di pomodoro *over the individual dishes or bowls of pasta. Enough to make you say, "Ever on Sunday!" If we were restricted to one sauce, this, or the white-truffle-and-butter (page 368), would be the one we would choose. The reason: simplicity and flavor. One of the virtues of Italian cookery is this simplicity, and it is that very asset, in our opinion, that lifts it above any other.*

4 heaping tablespoons of minced pros-
    ciutto fat (if unavailable use bacon)
2 tablespoons olive oil (the best you
    can buy)
1 tablespoon butter
3 large white onions, chopped
4 large fresh basil leaves, minced, or 1 ta-
    blespoon dried sweet basil
10 very large ripe plum tomatoes, peeled
    and diced, or 9 cups (two 2-pound 3-
    ounce cans) Italian plum tomatoes,
    put through a food mill
Freshly milled black pepper
½ teaspoon salt, or to taste

In a saucepan, over medium heat, sauté the finely minced prosciutto fat in the oil and butter until it is crisp, but not overly brown. Add the onions and basil. Simmer for 6 minutes. Add the tomatoes to the pan and stir everything well with a wooden spoon; simmer for 20 minutes, stirring frequently. Mill in a generous amount of pepper, add the salt, and stir well. Raise heat, stir, and cook off any excess water from tomatoes. Makes 7 cups.

MARINARA SAUCE

We first had marinara sauce made on a boat anchored off Taranto in southern Italy. Cooked by fishermen, who daily still tow their nets into the sea, and over a charcoal brazier on deck, this tomato sauce was ready in twenty minutes. Fishermen never have the sauce plain; they use it as a quick and piquant base in which to cook the ocean harvest. That day we stirred in a handful (a large fisherman's hand) of tender baby squid. They also drop in small fish, shrimp, clams, mussels, snails—most anything that comes from the sea. We are not certain that marinara is connected with or derived from the sea or marine; but we are certain that the fishermen's way improves it. As you'll see, marinara, the light, quick sauce, is an inspiration, even without help from the sea.

2 tablespoons olive oil

2 small white onions, chopped

2 small carrots, scrapd and chopped

1 garlic clove, minced

Liberal amount of milled black pepper

18 medium-size very ripe plum tomatoes, peeled, seeded, and diced, or 9 cups (two 2-pound 3-ounce cans) plum tomatoes

1 teaspoon salt, or to taste

3 tablespoons butter

¼ teaspoon dried hot red pepper

One of the virtues of a marinara sauce is that it is so quick and easy to prepare, and light. In a deep saucepan, over medium heat, sauté in the oil the onions, carrots, and garlic until onions are soft. Mill in the black pepper and add the tomatoes. Stir the sauce well, add the salt, and cook, uncovered, for 20 minutes. Now push the sauce through a food mill. It will emerge velvety. Melt butter in the pan and add the strained sauce. Stirring often, cook over medium heat for 15 minutes. For extra personality, at this stage stir in the hot red pepper. Makes 7 cups.

BEEF SAUCE

2 garlic cloves, minced
2 tablespoons olive oil
2 tablespoons butter
1 pound beef chuck, ground twice
1½ teaspoons salt, or to taste
Liberal amount of milled black pepper
2 cups beef stock or bouillon
1 tablespoon chopped parsley

In a deep saucepan over medium heat, sauté garlic in oil and butter until soft. Stir in beef, breaking it up with a wooden spoon; add the salt and pepper, and cook for 15 minutes. Stir in beef stock and simmer, uncovered, for 10 minutes. Add parsley, stir, and serve. Makes about 3 cups.

BOLOGNESE SAUCE

We discovered this sauce after a wild-boar hunting trip in the Apennines, when we went to Bologna to taste civilization again. We had it, just a spoonful over some light, marvelous **tortellini***, and sat in the restaurant until we finally wheedled the chef, who was also the owner, into giving us the recipe. We were eventually lucky enough to be invited into his kitchen to watch him prepare it. It is one of the most famous of pasta sauces and has many variations, but we believe this is the classic one.*

3 tablespoons chopped bacon
3 tablespoons butter
4 tablespoons chopped prosciutto
2 small white onions, chopped
2 small carrots, scraped and chopped
2 celery ribs, scraped and chopped
½ pound beef chuck, chopped
½ pound veal, chopped

¼ pound lean pork, chopped

1 cup Chicken Broth (page 96)

1 cup dry white wine

3 large ripe tomatoes, peeled, seeded and
  diced or 2 cups (one 1-pound can)
  Italian plum tomatoes

1 teaspoon salt

Liberal amount of milled black pepper

1 clove

⅓ teaspoon grated nutmeg

2 cups hot water

½ pound mushrooms, sliced

3 raw chicken livers, chopped

¾ cup heavy cream

In a deep saucepan, over medium heat, cook bacon in butter until soft; add prosciutto and simmer for 2 minutes. Add onions, carrots, celery; cook until soft. Stir in the beef, veal, and pork; simmer until half done, the beef pink. Then stir in the broth and wine, raise heat slightly, and cook until sauce thickens, stirring constantly. Blend in the tomatoes (if canned, first put through strainer or food mill). Add salt, pepper, clove, nutmeg, stir in well, and taste for correct amounts. Blend in hot water, cover pan, and simmer over low heat for 1 hour, raising cover and stirring frequently. Now blend in the mushrooms and the chicken livers. Raise heat slightly and cook, uncovered, for 5 minutes. Just before using the sauce, blend in the heavy cream, stirring the mixture well. Makes about 5 cups.

HAM SAUCE

½ pound sliced raw ham, diced (prefera-
    bly prosciuttini or prosciutto)
3 tablespoons butter
1 tablespoon olive oil
1 cup Chicken Broth (page 96)
½ teaspoon salt, or to taste
Liberal amount of milled black pepper
2 tablespoons freshly chopped parsley
2 cups heavy cream

In a saucepan, over medium heat, sauté ham in butter and oil until crisp.
Stir in broth, salt, and pepper and cook, uncovered, for 15 minutes. Add
parsley, stirring well. Cook for 10 minutes, until sauce begins to thicken,
then stir in heavy cream. Makes about 3 cups.

BÉCHAMEL SAUCE

6 tablespoons butter
4 tablespoons flour
1 teaspoon salt
Milled pepper
2½ cups milk, warmed
Pinch of grated nutmeg

In a double boiler melt the butter; add the flour as butter melts and stir
smooth as you sprinkle in the salt and mill in the pepper. When mixture
is golden and velvety, *slowly* stir in the warm milk, stirring constantly, and
stir for 15 minutes, until sauce is thickened and of smooth consistency.
Taste for flavor; add more salt or pepper if needed and stir in the pinch of
nutmeg. Makes about 2½ cups.

TAORMINA—Sicily

MORNAY SAUCE

6 tablespoons butter
1½ tablespoons sifted flour
2 cups milk, warm
1 teaspoon salt
Milled black pepper
2 egg yolks
6 tablespoons grated Asiago or Romano cheese

In a saucepan, over medium heat, melt butter; stir in flour to make a smooth paste. Slowly add the warm milk. Simmer and stir for 5 to 10 minutes, until sauce thickens. Keep the flame low and your spoon busy or sauce will burn. Season to taste with salt and pepper. Beat egg yolks; remove sauce from stove and stir in the egg yolks and cheese. Stir well and quickly. Makes about 2½ cups.

MUSHROOM AND CHEESE SAUCE

5 tablespoons chopped shallots
8 tablespoons butter
1 pound fresh mushrooms, chopped
7 tablespoons flour
2½ cups milk, warmed
2 cups heavy cream, warmed
1 cup grated Gruyère cheese
1 cup grated Asiago or Parmesan cheese
1½ teaspoons salt
Much milled black pepper

Sauté the shallots in the butter in a deep saucepan until soft. Add mushrooms and simmer for 10 minutes, stirring often. Blend in the flour, the milk, and the cream, stirring constantly until sauce is smooth and thickened. Add the cheeses, season with salt and pepper, and stir well until all ingredients are perfectly blended. Makes about 4½ cups.

SALSA ALLA MERETRICE

Harlot's Sauce

This is a sauce reputed to have been created by the prostitutes of Naples, possibly because it can be prepared quickly and beween assignments. It was first served to us in the private dining room of that splendid Roman hotel of our friend Alberto Wirth, the Victoria.

2 garlic cloves, minced

2 tablespoons olive oil

8 anchovies, cut into pieces

4½ cups (one 2-pound 3-ounce can) plum
    tomatoes, put through food mill

8 stuffed green olives, sliced

8 pitted black olives, sliced

1 teaspoon capers

1 teaspoon dried sweet basil

¼ teaspoon dried hot red pepper

VAL DI FASSA —Trentino-Alto Adige

In a saucepan, over medium heat, sauté garlic in the oil until soft; add the anchovies. When anchovies have broken apart, add the tomatoes; simmer for 10 minutes. Blend in olives, capers, basil, and red pepper. Simmer in uncovered pan for 20 minutes, or until sauce has thickened. Serve on *vermicelli*, among other pastas. See page 138 and page 346. Makes about 4 cups.

SALSA D'OLIO, AGLIO, ED ALICI

Olive Oil, Garlic, and Anchovy Sauce

Although this sauce appears in several other places in somewhat different versions, the principle of blending the hot-oil sauce with the pasta is the same for each of them—and it is tricky. If the sizzling oil is mixed with the cooked pasta too fast, it will make the pasta gummy.

¾ cup fine olive oil, in all
4 garlic cloves, halved
2 cans (2 ounces each) anchovy fillets
4 tablespoons butter
Freshly milled black pepper

Heat ½ cup of the oil in a saucepan over medium heat; brown garlic in this, being careful not to burn it. Discard garlic. Stir in one 2-ounce can of anchovies, and break them up with a wooden spoon as they cook. Simmer over low heat until anchovies become a sauce. Drain the second 2-ounce can of anchovies, cut one third of them into small pieces, and set these and the whole fillets aside. Just before serving the pasta, add the cut-up anchovies to the hot sauce. Place the drained pasta in a warm bowl in which butter has been melted, toss pasta well, coating each strand. (This prevents the hot oil in the sauce from cooking the pasta further and making it gummy.) Mill in pepper. Now add the hot anchovy sauce, a spoonful at a time, tossing carefully after each spoonful. (This spoon-by-spoon technique also prevents the pasta from gumming.)

Meanwhile, you have heated the remaining 4 tablespoons of olive oil in a small saucepan. Now, using a fork, quickly run the remaining whole anchovy fillets through the hot oil. Arrange 2 over each individual dish of pasta, and serve immediately. This sauce is sufficient for 1½ pounds of pasta to serve 8.

Note: You will see oil remaining in the bowl in which you mixed the pasta. Leave it there. The pasta has enough after the mixing; more would make it too oily.

SALSA D'ARAGOSTA ROSSA

Red Lobster Sauce

We've had many rave letters on this classic sauce!

    1 live lobster (1 pound)
    3 tablespoons olive oil
    1 bottle (8 ounces) clam juice
    1 whole white onion, peeled
    1 celery rib
    4 cups Marinara Sauce (page 81)

Rinse the lobster well in cold water. A half inch down on the underside of the head, pierce it with a rigid, sharp pointed knife. When the lobster is motionless, split it from that point down to the tail. Remove the solid dark green string in the tail. Separate claws and tail from the body. Heat the oil in a frypan and place the pieces of lobster, still in the shell and undersides down, in the oil. Cook over medium heat until shell gets red, or for about 10 minutes, turning often. Pour in clam juice, add onion and celery, cover pan, and simmer for 10 minutes.

Prepare the marinara sauce in a large saucepan. Remove onion and celery from the lobster pan and discard them. Add lobster and its liquid to the marinara sauce. Stir well, and simmer, uncovered, for 20 minutes, lifting the lobster pieces from the pan frequently to drain the liquid in the shells into the sauce. When the sauce has thickened, stir, then remove from heat. Remove lobster meat from shells, discard shells, and put lobster back into the sauce.

This sauce is served on *linguine,* among other pastas. Spoon liberal amounts of sauce over each portion and center a piece of lobster meat atop the pasta in each dish. Makes about 4½ cups.

SALSA CON LE VONGOLE IN BIANCO
White Clam Sauce

Americans know this sauce perhaps as well as any except the tomato-paste-ridden "meat sauce" of our misguided restaurants. White clam sauce, too, is usually abused, being made with far too much garlic and oil. See page 156 for a new sauce we've perfected.

FETTUCCINE CON PARMIGIANO E BURRO
Fettuccine with Parmesan and Butter

Freshly grated cheese and butter, with the addition of milled black pepper, are the classic and incomparable "sauce" for a variety of pastas but best of all for fettuccine. *The recipe is given on page 374, in the chapter called Particular Pastas where we have included a special section on this most particular of pastas and several variations on the butter-and-cheese theme.*

SALSA VERDE
Green Sauce

¾ pound sweet butter
1 tablespoon olive oil
½ garlic clove, minced
2 small white onions, minced
Salt and pepper to taste
2 cups finely chopped Italian parsley (use
    only Italian parsley)

Combine butter and oil in pan over low heat. When butter is melted, stir in garlic and onions and sauté until onions are soft. Add salt and pepper. Stir in parsley quickly. Pour over cooked drained pasta, toss until well mixed, and serve immediately. Makes enough for 1½ pounds of pasta to serve 8 people as a first course.

BOLOGNA, *the Neptune Fountain—Emilia-Romagna*

PESTO ALLA GENOVESE

Since this remarkable recipe appeared in the United States, much has happened to it. Some of it good, much of it bad. The good part is that it has become a favorite, the bad that it is now used cold on pasta and other salads, on fish, chicken, and roasts, so carelessly that it overwhelms other food, especially delicate fish. The people in Genoa who invented it would be aghast, even at the way we use it with pasta.

Note: It should be used *only* on *hot* pasta or lightly spooned into a lusty soup such as *minestrone.*

Pesto has such a powerful personality that the Genovese suggest putting just a light spoonful or two on a serving of pasta. Also, they often toss the pasta in butter first, lightly sprinkle it with cheese, then add the *pesto.* Too often, in fact, usually, in the United States pasta is literally drenched with *pesto,* which destroys the flavor of the pasta itself and gives the dish a bitter taste. "Too much," the Genovese say, "is too bad."

In Genoa, we are told, some purists still make *pesto* the old way, making a paste of the ingredients in a mortar and pestle, thus the name. We tried it that way several times, then gratefully went to the blender.

Now the food processor rules supreme, handling *pesto* superbly. In the blender there is much stopping and scraping down. Not with the processor; seconds do it.

2 cups fresh basil leaves

½ cup Italian parsley

½ cup grated Asiago or Parmesan cheese

½ cup grated Romano cheese

12 blanched almonds

1 tablespoon *pignoli* (pine nuts)

12 blanched walnut halves

1 garlic clove

3 tablespoons butter

½ cup olive oil

1 pound *fettuccine* or *trenette,* cooked in
    boiling salted water until al dente,
    drained (see below re adding hot
    pasta water to the *pesto* mixture)

It isn't necessary to use *pignoli* (they're very costly), or even almonds. Walnuts alone do the job nicely. If using just walnuts, double the amount.

Place all ingredients, except the olive oil and pasta, in a blender or food processor. As you blend or purée, slowly add the olive oil. Process or blend into a smooth paste. Place this *pesto* sauce (or the amount you will use) in a warm bowl on the back of the stove.

After the pasta has cooked, before it is drained, add 2 tablespoons of the hot water in which the pasta cooked to the bowl with the *pesto*. Stir, blending well. Serve the drained pasta (like the Genovese, we first toss it with soft butter) in hot soup bowls, lightly sprinkled with grated Asiago. Dollop a moderate amount of *pesto* atop. Each diner mixes it to his or her liking.

Note: We usually make a double batch of *pesto*. It freezes very well. We have kept it for one year frozen in glass jars. Flavor and brilliant green color stayed intact. Serves 6 to 8 for a first course.

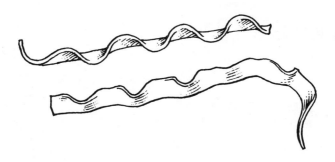

V

Soups: Pasta in Brodo

Good food like good music brings back memories that make life worthwhile. It takes a soup, for example, to make us remember Pisa, and Lord Byron, probably the world's most dashing poet. It was many years ago when we entered Pisa early one winter, with a cold rain blanking out the landscape, the usually dignified and impressive cathedral square dark and deserted, the only living object a cat so wet that it looked as if it hadn't yet grown hair, the entire city with its ancient buildings seeming a place from another time from which all life had fled.

We hurried into a small restaurant not far from number 11 Lungarno Mediceo, a dank, gray sixteenth-century palace. Byron had lived here while he wrote *Don Juan,* and probably had gotten inspiration at times in a tiny restaurant much like the one we entered.

We got more than inspiration. We got warm; a bowl of soup not only brought us quickly to life, but gave that dark old city new dimension. Our *pasta in brodo* was *occhi di trota* (trout's eyes), small tubes of pasta, many upended in the rich broth, the openings like staring eyes; nuggets of beef, flecks of fresh parsley, and slivers of carrots made it a soup to remember. We can almost hear the sound of trumpets and envision the medieval pageantry that once was Pisa when we think back on its sight and its smell, the savory, steaming stuff sending its scent throughout the little *trattoria* as the waiter brought it to our table. We walked out into the rain new people, and the city now became romantic, not old and dismal.

Soup does have this way of renewing the spirit. Even Napoleon is sup-

PISA, The Tower and the Cathedral—Tuscany

posed to have said, "Soup makes the soldier." There is no doubt that it makes the meal.

Note: If you cannot find the various pastas such as *anellini* (little rings) or *semi di melone* (melon seeds) and many of the others in your neighborhood, then use the easy-to-come-by varieties such as *pastina, tubettini, ditalini.* We indicate here the pastas originally used in the recipes that were given to us or that we gathered in Italy. The unusual shapes do add appeal to the soup—the little cockscombs, the small sausages, the tiny nuts and rice. But if you can't get to an Italian store to buy them, then most any of the small soup pastas can be substituted.

BRODO DI POLLO

Chicken Broth

The *brodo,* the broth for your pasta, can be prepared in several ways. Personally we prefer chicken broth, using a fat, yellow-skinned stewing chicken, two carrots, an onion, two celery sticks (with tops), a half handful of fresh parsley, freshly milled black pepper, three teaspoons of salt. Simmer the chicken and vegetables, completely covered with cold water, in a covered 10-quart pot until tender. Then remove the chicken (for other meals), leave the cover off the pot, and simmer the stock until it is reduced by at least half. We then strain it, pour it into proper containers, and freeze it. Thus we always have the makings for *pasta in brodo,* a great wintertime dish, an unusual first course any time.

We have discovered that chicken wings can always be purchased at a reasonable price. We often substitute these for the stewing chicken. The broth isn't quite so rich, but it is excellent.

BRODO DI MANZO

Beef Broth

Beef is handled much the same with a couple of innovations. We use shin, shank, stewing beef, chuck clod. Remove the beef when tender, but not overcooked and stringy, and reduce broth. Stock is reduced to evaporate some of the water, giving the soup more body and much more flavor. When the beef is cooled, we cut it into small nuggets, about the size of a five-cent piece, and place them in the broth. Both go into a bowl, then into the refrigerator overnight. By morning a thick coat of fat has formed on top. This is removed, the broth is rewarmed and strained. Then, with the meat equally divided, it is placed in containers and popped into the freezer.

Contrary to some beliefs, in our opinion freezing does not detract from the flavor.

If making homemade broth seems too time-consuming, canned College Inn chicken broth and beef broth are both quite acceptable.

When you are ready for *pasta in brodo*, the next steps are simple. But don't start off the wrong way, as many do, by cooking your pasta in the broth at the beginning. This clouds it and is only done with certain particularly fragile pastas. Much of the appeal of *pasta in brodo* is the appearance of the rich, clear broth floating the golden pasta. Cooking the pasta in the broth destroys much of this.

Cook your pasta, just as you do for any other dish, in a large quantity of briskly boiling water, but this time without salt, as the broth will be sufficiently seasoned. Remove the pasta when it is *firmer* than al dente, definitely on the chewy side. Drain it, then add it to the warm soup and simmer for 5 minutes. We like to add thinly sliced fresh vegetables, carrots, onions, sometimes a tablespoon of fresh peas, for the 5 minutes of simmering, then bring the *pasta in brodo* to table with a spoon of fresh minced parsley floating on it, and we often grate Parmesan on it just before serving.

ACINI DI PEPE STRACCIATELLA
"Peppercorns" with Chicken Broth and Eggs

2 quarts Chicken Broth (page 96)
½ cup *acini di pepe* or other very small
    soup pasta
3 eggs
½ cup chopped Italian parsley
½ cup grated Asiago or Parmesan cheese

Reserve 1 cup of cool broth. In a heavy pot, over medium heat, bring all but the reserved cup of broth to a boil. Add the pasta and cook 5 minutes, or until the pasta is just al dente.

In a bowl, combine and beat together the cup of cool broth, the eggs, parsley, and cheese. Pour into the hot broth, stirring constantly, and, stirring vigorously, simmer 2 or 3 minutes. Taste for seasoning. Serves 4 to 6.

Additional cheese may be served at the table.

SALAMINI IN BRODO
"Tiny Sausages" in Broth

2 quarts clear Beef Broth (page 96)
¾ cup *salamini*
⅓ cup grated Parmesan cheese
1 tablespoon chopped Italian parsley

In a large pot, bring the broth to a simmer. In another pot, cook the *salamini* al dente; drain. Add to broth. Serve in hot soup bowls, sprinkled with cheese and parsley. Serves 4 to 6.

BRODO CON PASTA GRATTUGIATA
Broth with Grated Pasta

½ recipe Pasta Fresca all'Uovo (page 96)
3 quarts Chicken Broth (page 96)
2 tablespoons chopped Italian parsley
½ cup grated Parmesan cheese

Prepare the dough; let it rest in kneaded ball for 10 minutes; then grate it into pieces, using the flat type of grater. Reflour your pastry board; dry the pieces of grated pasta on it for 40 minutes. In a large pot, bring the chicken broth to a boil; reduce heat and add the pasta gratings; simmer for 10 minutes. Stir in the parsley; simmer for another 5 minutes. Serve in hot soup bowls with Parmesan sprinkled atop. Serves 8.

ANELLINI CON ZUPPA DI BUE E LEGUME

"Little Rings" with Beef Vegetable Soup

⅓ cup *anellini*
1 small white onion, chopped
2 small carrots, chopped
3 tablespoons cooked lima beans
¼ pound beef chuck, ground
2 quarts Beef Broth (page 96)
½ teaspoon salt

In a pot, cook *anellini* in plenty of boiling water less than al dente; drain. Add vegetables (except beans) and raw beef to simmering beef broth; cook until carrots are tender. Stir in the drained pasta and lima beans and sprinkle in the salt; simmer for 5 minutes. Serve in hot soup bowls. Serves 4 to 6.

ZUPPA DI RISINI ED UOVO CRUDO

Soup with "Tiny Rice" and Raw Egg

2 quarts rich Chicken Broth (page 96)
¾ cup *risini* (tiny rice) or other tiny soup
    pasta
6 very fresh raw egg yolks
Grated Asiago or Parmesan cheese

In a pot, bring the broth to a boil; add the *risini*, reduce heat, and simmer 5 minutes, or until the pasta is al dente. Serve at the point of boiling in hot cups and drop an egg yolk into each. Allow to rest for a minute or two to slightly set the yolk. Pass the cheese at the table. Serves 6.

SPAGHETTINI ED UOVA IN BRODO ALLA MARIA

Spaghettini and Eggs in Broth alla Maria

½ cup 1½-inch pieces of spaghettini
2 quarts Chicken Broth (page 96),
   brought to a boil in a large pot
3 eggs, beaten
⅓ cup grated Romano cheese

Cook spaghettini al dente; drain. When chicken broth is boiling, stir in spaghettini. Remove from fire and blend in the beaten eggs, stirring rapidly until the eggs float in shreds. Ladle into warm soup bowls. Sprinkle Romano atop each serving. Serves 4 to 6.

ZUPPA DI BUE CON SPAGHETTINI

Spaghettini with Beef Soup

1 recipe Beef Sauce (page 82)
2 egg yolks
2 cups heavy cream
2 quarts Beef Broth (page 96)
½ cup 1½-inch pieces of spaghettini

Prepare beef sauce. Place eggs in a very large bowl and beat with whisk, slowly adding the cream and the beef broth, blending well. Stir this into the beef sauce, which should be simmering. Cook the spaghettini al dente, drain, and stir into the beef soup, mixing everything well. Simmer for 4 minutes. Serve in hot soup bowls. Serves 8.

ZUPPA DI CAPELVENERE E FUNGHI
"Maidenhair Fern" and Mushroom Soup

2 quarts Chicken Broth (page 96)
⅓ cup chopped carrots
⅓ cup chopped celery
2 tablespoons chopped shallots
1 teaspoon salt
8 small mushrooms, sliced
¼ pound *capelvenere*

In a large pot, bring the broth to a simmer, add the carrots, celery, shallots, and salt, and simmer for 10 minutes. Stir in the mushrooms and *capelvenere*, stirring mixture well with a wooden fork. Cook for about 10 minutes. These fine noodles cook quickly, and the vegetables should be on the crunchy side, not overdone. Serves 4 to 6.

ZUPPA DI PASTA E PREZZEMOLO
A Pasta and Parsley Soup

2 tablespoons butter
1 tablespoon olive oil
1 medium-size onion, finely chopped
2 medium-size potatoes, coarsely grated
½ cup chopped Italian parsley
1 bay leaf
¼ teaspoon dried thyme
2 quarts rich Chicken Broth (page 96)
¾ cup finely broken up string pasta or a
    small soup pasta
Salt and freshly ground black pepper to
    taste
3 tablespoons soft butter
¾ cup grated Asiago or Parmesan cheese

In a large heavy pot, over medium heat, heat the butter and oil. Add the onion and cook 2 minutes, or until soft. Do not brown. Add the potatoes, half of the parsley, the bay leaf, thyme, and broth. Bring to a simmer, cook for 5 minutes. Stir in the pasta and cook for 3 minutes (depending on the type of pasta) until it is just al dente. Remove and discard the bay leaf. Taste, then add salt and pepper, if needed.

Just before serving in hot bowls, stir in the soft butter and ¼ cup of cheese. Serve with the remaining parsley sprinkled over individual servings. Pass the remaining cheese at the table. Serves 4 to 6.

ZUPPA DI SCAROLA E VERMICELLI ALLA MARIA
Maria's Escarole and Vermicelli Soup

½ cup 1½-inch pieces of *vermicelli*
1 head of young escarole, cut into bite-
    size pieces
2 tablespoons chopped carrot
2 quarts Chicken Broth (page 96)
½ teaspoon salt
Milled black pepper

Cook *vermicelli* less than al dente; drain. In a pot, simmer escarole and carrot in chicken broth seasoned with the salt for 20 minutes. Add the pasta and simmer for another 3 minutes. Mill in black pepper, stir well. Ladle into hot soup bowls. Serves 6.

ZUPPA DI SCAROLA CON FUNGHINI E PISELLI
Escarole Soup with "Little Mushrooms" and Peas

2½ cups dried whole peas
2 quarts water
2 white onions, chopped

4 tablespoons chopped prosciutto fat
2 tablespoons olive oil
1½ tablespoons rice flour
1½ teaspoons salt
Liberal amount of milled black pepper
1 head of escarole, chopped or shredded
½ cup *funghini*

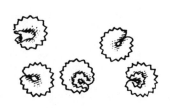

Cover the peas with water and bring to a boil. Remove from fire, let soak for 45 minutes, and drain. Place the drained peas in a large pot and add the 2 quarts of water; cover pot and simmer for 1 hour. In a saucepan, over medium heat, sauté onions and prosciutto fat in the oil until onions are soft and fat is golden brown; blend in the rice flour and stir. Add mixture to the pot of peas; sprinkle in salt and mill in pepper to taste. Stir in escarole and simmer, uncovered, for 20 minutes. Cook the *funghini* al dente; drain. Stir into soup pot, simmer for 5 minutes, and serve. Serves 4 to 6.

ZUPPA DI BROCCOLI ALLA ROMANO

Broccoli Soup Roman Style

2 white onions, minced
1 garlic clove, minced
4 thick slices of prosciutto, diced
1 tablespoon olive oil
Liberal amount of milled black pepper
1 bunch of broccoli
¼ pound salt pork, diced
2 tablespoons butter
5 cups Chicken Broth (page 96), heated
½ cup 1½-inch pieces of spaghettini
¼ cup grated Romano cheese

PALERMO, detail of the Cathedral—Sicily

In a large pot, sauté onions, garlic, and prosciutto in the oil until soft. Mill in pepper and stir in water to cover. Simmer with the pot covered for 20 minutes. Use just the tips of the broccoli; wash them, barely cover with water, and cook al dente. In a saucepan, over medium heat, sauté the diced salt pork in the butter until crisp. Stir in the drained broccoli and simmer for 5 minutes. Add to the onions, garlic, and prosciutto mixture, blending well. Stir in the chicken broth. Do not cook further; broccoli tips should be firm and intact. Cook spaghettini al dente in plenty of boiling salted water; drain. Gently stir into the soup. Serve in hot soup bowls with Romano sprinkled atop. Serves 4 to 6.

ZUPPA DI PISELLI E CAPELLI D'ANGELO

Fresh Green Peas and "Angel's Hair" Soup

3 slices of *pancetta* or bacon, chopped

2 tablespoons olive oil, optional

1 small onion, finely chopped

1 garlic clove, minced

2 cups tiny shelled fresh peas

½ teaspoon sugar

2 quarts rich Chicken Broth (page 96)

2 cups broken-up *capelli d'angelo,* or other very, very fine string pasta

Salt and freshly ground black pepper to taste

1 cup grated Asiago or Parmesan cheese

In a heavy pot, over medium heat, cook the *pancetta* until golden and crisp. Remove with a slotted spoon and drain on paper towel. Reserve. If there are not 2 tablespoons of fat in the pot, add enough olive oil to make up that amount. If there are more than 2 tablespoons of fat, pour off all but that amount. Add the onion and garlic and cook until soft, about 2 minutes. Do not brown.

Stir in the peas and sugar and enough of the broth to barely cover the peas. Cook until the peas are tender. Pour in the remaining broth, bring to a boil, add the pasta, and cook until al dente (about 30 seconds). Taste and add salt and pepper, if needed.

Ladle the soup into hot bowls and sprinkle on some cheese and some of the crisp *pancetta*. Serve remaining cheese at the table. Serves 4 to 6.

ZUPPA DEL VILLAGGIO CON CAPELLINI
Soup of the Village with Fine Vermicelli

 1 pound leeks, sliced thin (white part only)
 4 tablespoons butter
 1 teaspoon salt
 3 quarts Chicken Broth (page 96)
 3 small potatoes, diced
 ½ small cabbage, parboiled for 15 minutes and chopped
 ¼ pound *capellini*
 ¼ pound Asiago cheese, grated

In a large pot, sauté the leeks in the butter, add salt, and simmer until soft. Stir in chicken broth, potatoes, and cabbage. Simmer, uncovered, for 1 hour, or until potatoes are soft but not mushy. Add the *capellini* directly to the broth; cook for 2 minutes. Serve in hot soup bowls with Asiago sprinkled atop. Serves 6 to 8.

MINESTRA DI FORATINI FINI E CAVOLFIORE
Soup of "Tiny Pierced" Pasta and Cauliflower

 1 medium cauliflower
 3 shallots, chopped
 1 cup chopped lean pork
 3 tablespoons olive oil
 1 large ripe tomato, peeled and diced
 2½ quarts Chicken Broth (page 96), warm

1 teaspoon salt
Milled black pepper
¼ pound *foratini fini*
⅓ cup grated Parmesan cheese

Wash cauliflower, cut off leaves, then break into flowerets. Soak the flowerets in a bowl of salted water for 15 minutes; drain. In a pot, over medium heat, sauté shallots and pork in the oil until shallots are soft and pork almost crisp. Blend in tomato and 1 cup of the chicken broth; add salt and pepper and break up the tomato with a wooden spoon as it cooks. Simmer for 15 minutes, uncovered. Stir in cauliflowerets and remaining broth and simmer for 25 minutes, uncovered, stirring gently often. Cook the *foratini fini* less than al dente; watch carefully, as they cook quickly. Drain, add to cauliflowerets and broth, and simmer for 5 minutes. Serve in hot soup bowls with Parmesan sprinkled atop each serving. Serves 6.

MINESTRA MARITATA

Sicilian Sausage Soup

2 tablespoons olive oil
¼ pound sweet Italian sausage, removed
   from its casing
2 garlic cloves, finely chopped
2 quarts Chicken Broth (page 96)
3 tablespoons Marinara Sauce (page 81)
½ cup coarsely chopped, cooked Swiss chard
½ cup coarsely chopped, cooked Savoy cabbage
½ cup *orzo*, cooked al dente, drained
Salt and freshly ground black pepper to taste
Freshly grated Asiago or Parmesan cheese

In a heavy pot, over medium heat, heat the olive oil and cook the sausage and garlic for 10 minutes, stirring and breaking up the sausage with a fork. Add the broth, marinara sauce, Swiss chard, cabbage, and pasta, blending well. Bring to a boil; stir. Taste and season with salt and pepper, if necessary. Ladle into hot soup bowls and serve immediately. Pass the cheese at the table. Serves 4.

MINESTRA CON PESTO
Soup with Pesto

3 tablespoons butter
4 tablespoons minced salt pork, blanched
    in boiling water for 2 minutes, well drained
½ head of 1½-pound Savoy cabbage,
    trimmed and shredded
1 cup fresh string beans, cut into ½-inch pieces
2 medium-size potatoes, cut into ½-inch cubes
1 medium-size onion, finely chopped
1 large leek (white part only), thinly sliced
2 quarts Chicken Broth (page 96)
Salt and freshly ground black pepper to taste
¼ pound fresh spinach, trimmed, stems
    discarded, and chopped
1 cup broken-up string pasta (spaghetti,
    linguine, trenette, etc.)
½ cup Pesto alla Genovese (page 92)
Freshly grated Asiago or Parmesan cheese

In a large heavy pot, over medium heat, melt the butter. Add the salt pork and cook for 3 minutes, or until golden. Lower heat; add cabbage, string beans, potatoes, onion, and leek and cook, covered, stirring occasionally, for 10 minutes. Add the broth, cover, and simmer for 30 minutes, or until the vegetables are just about tender. Taste and season with salt and pepper, if necessary. Add the spinach and pasta and cook, uncovered, until the pasta is al dente (the time depends upon the pasta). Stir in the *pesto* and cook, stirring, for 1 minute to blend.

    Serve in hot bowls and pass the cheese at the table. Serves 6 to 8.

VALTOURNANCHE—Valle d'Aosta

ZUPPA DI PERLINE MICROSCOPICI
E CAVOLO ROSSO

Soup of "Tiny Pearls" and Red Cabbage

¼ pound lean pork, finely minced

¼ pound Canadian bacon, minced

1 white onion, chopped

3 tablespoons butter

6 very ripe plum tomatoes, peeled and diced

1 teaspoon salt

Milled black pepper

1 small firm red cabbage, chopped

3 quarts Chicken Broth (page 96)

4 tablespoons *perline microscopici*

¼ cup grated Asiago cheese

In a pot, over medium heat, sauté pork, bacon, and onion in butter until onion is soft; stir in tomatoes and salt and mill in pepper. Simmer for 20 minutes, stirring and breaking up tomatoes with a wooden spoon as they cook. Add the red cabbage; simmer for 15 minutes. Blend the whole mixture with simmering chicken broth, cover, and cook for 45 minutes. Stir in the *perline microscopici* and simmer, uncovered, for another 10 minutes. Serve in hot soup bowls with Asiago sprinkled atop. Serves 8.

SEMI DI MELA CON PURÉ DI CAROTE

"Apple Seeds" with Puréed Carrot Soup

¼ pound butter

1 pound carrots, scraped and chopped

4 onions, chopped

1 teaspoon salt, or to taste

1 teaspoon sugar

2 quarts Chicken Broth (page 96)

2 tablespoons chopped parsley

½ cup *semi di mela*

½ teaspoon minced chervil

Melt two thirds of the butter in a large pot; stir in carrots, onions, salt, and sugar; simmer until carrots are soft, about 20 minutes. Add 1 quart of warm chicken broth, stir in the parsley, and bring to a boil. Reduce heat and simmer, uncovered, for 30 minutes. Push the contents through a sieve, return to the pot, and add the rest of the broth. Simmer, uncovered, for another 15 minutes. Cook the *semi di mela* al dente; drain. Add to the broth and simmer for 3 minutes. Take from the fire; stir in the remaining butter and the chervil. Serve in hot soup bowls. Serves 4 to 6.

NOCCIOLE CON PURÉ DI POMODORO

Pasta "Nuts" with Puréed Tomato Soup

¼ pound butter

3 white onions, chopped

1 garlic clove, minced

1 *bouquet garni* of parsley, thyme, and bay leaf

2 pounds ripe tomatoes, peeled, diced, and drained

1 teaspoon salt

1 teaspoon white pepper

2 quarts Beef Broth (page 96)

½ cup *nocciole*

Butter

Melt butter in a large pot; stir in the onions and garlic and simmer until onions are soft. Add the *bouquet garni*, the tomatoes, the salt, and white pepper. Simmer for 25 minutes, stirring often and breaking up the tomatoes with a wooden spoon. Add 1 quart of beef broth; simmer for 30 minutes. Remove and discard the *bouquet garni*. Push the contents of the pot through a sieve. Return the puréed mixture to the pot and simmer for 10 minutes, adding the remaining broth as the soup cooks. Cook the *nocciole* al dente, drain, and stir into the soup. Simmer for 4 minutes. Serve in hot soup bowls, dotted with butter. Serves 4 to 6.

CAPPELLI DI PAGLIACCIO CON ZUPPA DI RAPE

"Clown's Hats" with Turnip Soup

2 small white turnips, peeled and diced
½-pound chunk of lean smoked bacon,
  chopped
2 tablespoons butter
2 tablespoons olive oil
2 quarts Beef Broth (page 96)
1 tablespoon chopped Italian parsley
⅛ teaspoon dried rosemary
1 teaspoon salt, or to taste
⅓ cup *cappelli di pagliaccio*
Milled black pepper
⅓ cup grated Parmesan cheese

In a saucepan, over medium heat, sauté turnips and bacon in butter and oil until bacon is soft and beginning to crisp. In a large pot, bring broth to boil and stir in turnips and bacon. Add parsley, rosemary, and salt; simmer, uncovered, for 35 minutes. Cook the clown's hats less than al dente, drain, and stir into soup pot. Mill in black pepper, stir well, and simmer for 5 minutes. Serve in hot soup bowls with grated Parmesan sprinkled atop each serving. Serves 4 to 6.

ZUPPA DI CAPELLINI E ZUCCHINI

Fine Vermicelli and Zucchini Soup

1 medium zucchini, diced
2 tablespoons butter
2 tablespoons olive oil
1 teaspoon salt
Liberal amount of milled black pepper
2 quarts Chicken Broth (page 96)
2 eggs, beaten

¼ cup grated Asiago cheese
1 tablespoon chopped Italian parsley
2 fresh basil leaves, chopped
¼ pound *capellini*

In a pot, over medium heat, sauté zucchini in butter and oil for 10 minutes; sprinkle with salt and pepper. Add the broth, stir well, and simmer, covered, for 25 minutes. Place eggs in bowl and beat with a whisk, blending in cheese, parsley, and basil. Cook *capellini* al dente; watch carefully, as they are very fine and cook rapidly. Drain, stir into egg mixture, and add all to soup pot. Remove from fire, blend well with wooden fork. Serve in hot soup bowls. Serves 4 to 6.

ZUPPA DI MUGHETTO CON PESTO

"Lily-of-the-Valley" Soup with Pesto

⅓ recipe Pesto alla Genovese (page 92)
3 tablespoons olive oil
¼ pound shell beans, shelled
¼ pound spinach, washed and chopped
¼ pound beets, washed and diced
2 white onions, chopped
1 leek, chopped
3 medium potatoes, peeled and diced
1 small cabbage, shredded
1½ teaspoons salt, or to taste
Liberal amount of milled black pepper
4 quarts water
½ cup *mughetto*

Prepare the *pesto* and put aside. Heat the olive oil in a 6-quart pot over medium heat and slowly add all of the vegetables, stirring them into the oil. Cook for 15 minutes, stirring often. Add the salt and pepper and the water; cover the pot and simmer for 1½ hours. Remove the cover and stir

in the *mughetto*, which has been cooked al dente and drained; add the *pesto*, stirring it in well. Simmer for 5 minutes. Serve in hot soup bowls. Serves 4 to 6.

ZUPPA DI DITALINI E FAGIOLI FRESCHI
"Little Thimbles" and Fresh Lima Bean Soup

    4 tablespoons olive oil
    3 tablespoons butter
    2 white onions, chopped
    1 celery rib, chopped
    2 cups (one 1-pound can) plum tomatoes
    1½ pounds fresh lima beans, shelled
    2 quarts Chicken Broth (page 96)
    ¼ teaspoon dried sweet basil
    1 heart of romaine lettuce, shredded
    1 teaspoon salt, or to taste
    Liberal amount of milled black pepper
    ⅓ cup *ditalini*
    ⅓ cup grated Romano cheese
    ⅓ cup grated Parmesan cheese

In a pot, over medium heat, in the olive oil and butter sauté onions and celery until onions are soft. Stir in tomatoes and simmer for 15 minutes, breaking them up with a wooden spoon as they cook. Blend in lima beans and broth and simmer, covered, for 45 minutes or until lima beans are tender. Add basil and the shredded lettuce; sprinkle in salt and pepper. Cook *ditalini* al dente, drain, and stir into the soup. Simmer for 5 minutes, uncovered. Mix the two cheeses and pass at table with soup, which has been served in hot bowls. Serves 4 to 6.

ASSISI, the Basilica of San Francesco—Umbria

ZUPPA DI CECI ALLA TOSCANA
Chick-Pea Soup Tuscan Style

    1 pound *ceci* (chick-peas)
    1 teaspoon salt
    2 sprigs of rosemary, wrapped and tied
        in cheesecloth
    1 garlic clove, minced
    4 anchovy fillets, drained
    2 tablespoons olive oil
    2 tomatoes, peeled and diced
    2 quarts Chicken Broth (page 96)
    ½ cup *conchigliette* (tiny shells)

Soak the *ceci* in water for 3 hours. Drain, place in a saucepan, and cover
with fresh cold water. Add the salt and the rosemary. Cover and simmer
for 40 minutes, or until *ceci* are tender. Discard the rosemary and put *ceci*
and liquid through a food mill. In a large pot, sauté the garlic and anchovies in the oil until smooth and well blended. Stir in the tomatoes and
add the hot chicken broth. Simmer, uncovered, for 25 minutes. Blend in
the puréed *ceci*. Cook *conchigliette* al dente separately; drain. Stir into the
soup; simmer for 5 minutes. Serve in hot soup bowls. Serves 4 to 6.

ZUPPA DI ORZO E FEGATINI
"Barley" Soup with Chicken Livers

    2 tablespoons butter
    6 chicken livers, trimmed and chopped
    1 small garlic clove, minced
    2 quarts Chicken Broth (page 96)
    ¾ cup *orzo* or other small soup pasta
    Salt and freshly ground black pepper to taste
    2 tablespoons chopped parsley
    1 cup grated Asiago or Parmesan cheese

PISA, the Baptistery—Tuscany

In a frypan, over medium heat, melt the butter. Add the livers and garlic and cook for 2 minutes, or until the livers are brownish but still have a pink tinge to them. Set aside.

In a heavy pot, bring the broth to a boil. Add the pasta and cook for 5 minutes, or until al dente. Stir in the chicken livers and any butter in the pan. Taste before adding salt and pepper. Sprinkle each serving with parsley. Pass the cheese at the table. Serves 6 to 8.

ZUPPA DI SEMI DI MELONE

"Melon Seeds" Soup

2 small white onions, chopped
1 garlic clove, minced
1 large celery rib, chopped
2 tablespoons olive oil
3 quarts Beef Broth (page 96), simmering
    in a large pot
1 cup cooked *ceci* (chick-peas)
1 cup shredded cabbage
4 large tomatoes, peeled and diced
⅓ cup *semi di melone*
⅓ cup grated Parmesan cheese

In a saucepan, over medium heat, sauté onions, garlic, and celery in the oil for 5 minutes, and add to the simmering beef broth. Add *ceci*, cabbage, and tomatoes. Cover the pot and cook for 25 minutes. Cook *semi di melone* separately al dente, drain, and add to soup pot. Simmer for 5 minutes. Serve in hot soup bowls with Parmesan sprinkled atop. Serves 6.

ZUPPA DI ZUCCA E PASTA FINE FINE ALLA MODENA

Pumpkin Soup with a Very Fine Pasta

5 tablespoons butter

1 medium-size onion, coarsely chopped

1 garlic clove, chopped

1 celery stalk, scraped and coarsely
   chopped

½ teaspoon salt

¼ teaspoon freshly ground black pepper

1 bay leaf

4 cups Chicken Broth (page 96)

2 cups cubed (½ inch) fresh pumpkin
   (the kind you use for jack-o'-lanterns)

½ cup milk and ½ cup heavy cream, or
   substitute 1 cup half-and-half

2 cups cubed cooked chicken

½ teaspoon (or to taste) nutmeg

1 cup broken-up very fine pasta (the
   finest you can find, such as *capelli
   d'angelo*)

½ cup finely chopped fresh spinach

In a large pot, over medium heat, melt 3 tablespoons of butter. Add the onion, garlic, and celery, and cook 2 minutes. Do not brown. Add the salt, pepper, bay leaf, broth, pumpkin and cook, partially covered, about 25 minutes, or until the pumpkin can be mashed against the side of the pot. Remove and discard the bay leaf. Purée the soup in a blender or food processor.

Return purée to the pot. Stir in the milk and cream, chicken, and nutmeg. Cook for 2 minutes. Add the pasta and cook for 1 minute, or until the pasta is just al dente. Taste for seasoning. Stir in the spinach and remaining butter and serve. Serves 6.

TRIFOGLI CON COTECHINO E LENTICCHIE
"Cloverleaves" with Sausage and Lentils

½ pound dried lentils, soaked in water 5
   hours
1 small *cotechino* sausage
2 teaspoons salt
2 tablespoons olive oil
2 small white onions, chopped
1 tablespoon flour
Milled black pepper
2 cups Chicken Broth (page 96), warm
½ cup *trifogli*

Drain the lentils and place in a large pot with the whole sausage. Cover with water, add 1 teaspoon of the salt, cover, and simmer for 1½ hours, or until lentils are tender. Heat the olive oil in a saucepan and sauté the onions in it until soft. Stir in the flour, remaining salt, and the pepper. Slowly add the broth, stirring the mixture into a smooth sauce. Add this to the lentils and stir in well. Cook the *trifogli* al dente, drain, and stir into the lentil pot. Remove the skin from the sausage and cut sausage into rounds; then quarter the rounds. Serve lentil soup in hot soup bowls with 4 pieces of sausage in each bowl. Serves 4 to 6.

ZUPPA DI TUBETTI E LENTICCHIE

"Little Tubes" and Lentil Soup

½ pound dried lentils
3 quarts water
1 leftover ham bone
1 teaspoon salt
Milled black pepper
2 small white onions, chopped
2 celery ribs with leaves, chopped
3 tablespoons olive oil
⅓ cup *tubetti*

Soak the lentils in water for 5 hours; drain. Place lentils in a large pot with the water, the ham bone, salt, and pepper; simmer for 1½ hours. In a saucepan, brown onions and celery in 2 tablespoons of the oil; stir into soup pot. Simmer for 20 minutes, uncovered. Cook *tubetti* in plenty of salted water al dente; drain and add to soup, stirring in well. Blend in the remaining oil and mill in more black pepper. Remove ham bone; dice its meat and return this to the soup. Serve in hot soup bowls. Serves 4 to 6.

FLORENCE, the Ponte Vecchio—Tuscany

VERMICELLI CON CIAVATTONI E COTICHE

Vermicelli with White Beans and Pork Rinds

½ pound dried white beans
2 quarts water
1 teaspoon salt
½ pound pork rinds, cut into strips
8 ripe tomatoes, peeled and diced
Milled black pepper
3 tablespoons chopped pork fat or ham
    fat
2 tablespoons olive oil
1 garlic clove
½ cup white wine
⅓ cup 1½-inch pieces of *vermicelli*

Soak the beans covered with water for 3 hours; drain. Place in a large pot with the 2 quarts of water, salt, pork rinds, half of the tomatoes, and some pepper. Simmer, covered, for 1½ hours. In a saucepan, sauté the chopped pork fat in oil. Add the garlic and cook until pork and garlic are soft. Mill in some pepper and blend in remaining tomatoes and the wine, breaking up tomatoes with a wooden spoon as they cook. Simmer for 20 minutes, then stir the pork mixture into the bean pot, blending well. Cook slowly, uncovered, for 15 minutes, stirring often and taking care not to break up the beans. Cook *vermicelli* al dente; drain, stir into bean pot, and simmer for 3 minutes. Serve in hot soup bowls. Serves 4 to 6.

MINESTRA DI VERDURA E PROSCIUTTO

Vegetable and Ham Soup

½ pound lima beans, shelled
2 celery ribs, scraped and chopped
1 head of escarole, chopped
¼ pound spinach, chopped
6 small beets, diced
1½ teaspoons salt
Milled black pepper
2 tablespoons olive oil
2 white onions, chopped
1 carrot, scraped and chopped
3 tablespoons minced ham fat
½-pound slice of ham
1 pig's foot
¼ teaspoon dried marjoram
½ cup *cannolicchi* (small pasta tubes)
⅓ cup grated Parmesan cheese

In a large pot, place the lima beans, celery, escarole, spinach, beets, salt, and pepper. Add enough water to cover the vegetables; cover the pot. Bring to a boil, then reduce heat, and simmer for 10 minutes. In another very large pot, heat the oil and sauté onions and carrot in it until onions are soft. Stir in the minced ham fat, add the ham and pig's foot, mill in pepper, and add the marjoram. Simmer for 15 minutes. Then add the water from the vegetable pot and all the vegetables from that pot. Simmer all together, covered, until pig's foot is tender to the fork, about 40 minutes. Remove the pig's foot and ham slice, dice both, and return them to soup pot. Cook the *cannolicchi* less than al dente, drain, and stir into soup pot. Simmer for 5 minutes, uncovered. Serve in hot soup bowls with Parmesan sprinkled atop. Serves 6.

MINESTRONE ALLA CONTADINA

Countrywoman's Minestrone

½ cup dried kidney beans

½ cup dried lentils

1 large white onion, chopped

½ pound salt pork, diced

2 tablespoons olive oil

2 cups (one 1-pound can) Italian plum tomatoes

Milled black pepper

1 teaspoon salt

1 small firm cabbage, cored and chopped

2 carrots, scraped and cut into small bite-size pieces

2 leeks, cut into ½-inch pieces

4 quarts Beef Broth (page 96)

2 tablespoons fresh peas

1 medium zucchini, cut into small bite-size chunks

3 small potatoes, diced

½ cup *ditali* ("thimbles")

½ cup grated Asiago cheese

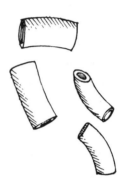

Soak kidney beans and lentils in water for 5 hours; drain. In a saucepan, over medium heat, sauté onion and salt pork in the oil until onion is soft and salt pork nearly crisp. Add tomatoes and break up with a wooden spoon; mill in black pepper and add the salt. Place beans, lentils, cabbage, carrot, and leeks in a large pot with the beef broth. Simmer until vegetables are half done and beans and lentils are still firm, about 25 minutes. Stir in peas, zucchini, potatoes, and tomato-onion-salt-pork mixture. Mill in more black pepper and simmer until beans, lentils, and vegetables are tender. Cook *ditali* al dente, drain well, and stir into the bean pot. Simmer for 5 minutes. Serve in hot soup bowls with Asiago grated atop each serving. Serves 6 to 8.

Note: If more liquid is needed, add small amounts of hot water, stirring it in well.

Near CAMPITELLO, the Dolomites—Trentino-Alto Adige

RAVIOLINI IN BRODO

1 recipe for Pasta Fresca for Ravioli (page 59)
½ cup ricotta cheese, drained
½ cup grated Parmesan cheese
2 egg yolks
1 tablespoon chopped Italian parsley
4 quarts Chicken Broth (page 96)

Prepare dough and roll into sheets as for *ravioli*. Mix the cheeses, egg yolks, and parsley, blending well. Place teaspoons of the cheese filling 1 inch apart on 1 sheet of the dough; cover with the other sheet of dough, pressing it around each mound of filling. Using a pastry cutter, cut 1-inch squares, rather than the usual 2-inch, since these are to be used in soup. Press the edges of each square again to make sure they are sealed. Dry for 25 minutes. Bring half of the chicken broth to a simmer. Drop 6 *raviolini* at a time into the broth and cook for 6 minutes. Remove them with a slotted spoon onto paper towels to drain. Continue until all are cooked. In another pot bring remaining broth to a boil. Ladle it into individual soup bowls and float 6 *raviolini* in each bowl. Serves 4 to 6.

ZUPPA DI PESCE CON STIVALETTI

Fish Soup with "Little Boots"

2 pounds cod fillets
2 pounds whiting
2 pounds porgies, rockfish, or any inexpensive fish
3 tablespoons butter
3 tablespoons olive oil
4 celery ribs, chopped
4 onions, chopped
2 leeks, diced
2 carrots, chopped
4 ripe tomatoes, peeled and diced

1½ teaspoons salt
Milled black pepper
½ teaspoon dried rosemary
½ cup *stivaletti*

Have the fish cleaned and scaled. In an 8-quart pot, heat the butter and oil; sauté celery, onions, leeks, and carrots in it until soft. Stir in tomatoes and season with salt and pepper and rosemary. Simmer for 15 minutes. Fill pot with hot water, bring to boil, reduce heat, cover, and simmer for 20 minutes. Add the whole fish and the fillets. Simmer, uncovered, for 20 minutes. Remove the cod fillets while still firm to use for second course. Strain remainder through sieve, forcing fish, vegetables, and stock through. Now bring this strained soup to a boil; stir in the *stivaletti* and cook, uncovered, al dente. Serve in large soup bowls. The hot cod fillets follow, as entrée, drenched with melted butter and accompanied by boiled potatoes and a green salad. Serves 6.

ZUPPA DI GAMBERI CON AVENA

Shrimp Soup with Pasta "Oats"

2 tablespoons olive oil
2 tablespoons butter
2 carrots, scraped and chopped
2 celery ribs, scraped and chopped
2 basil leaves, chopped
1 tablespoon chopped parsley
2 white onions, chopped
1½ teaspoons salt
Liberal amount of milled black pepper
2 dozen fresh shrimp in their shells
2 quarts Chicken Broth (page 96)
½ cup dry white wine
½ cup Marsala
⅓ cup *avena*

In a large pot, heat the oil and butter and sauté the carrots, celery, basil, parsley, and onions in it. Sprinkle in the salt and some pepper and simmer for 10 minutes. Add the shrimp in their shells and the chicken broth; simmer, covered, for 10 minutes. Uncover and add the white wine and Marsala, stirring in well. Remove shrimp, peel, cut each one into 3 pieces, and return to pot. Cook the *avena* al dente; stir into the soup. Simmer 3 minutes. Serve in hot soup bowls. Serves 4 to 6.

ZUPPA DI GAMBE DI RANOCCHI

Frogs' Legs Soup

    4 tablespoons olive oil
    2 garlic cloves, minced
    1 tablespoon chopped parsley
    1 carrot, chopped
    1 celery rib, chopped
    2 small white onions, chopped
    3 fresh basil leaves, minced
    24 frogs (or substitute fresh or frozen sea-
        food, such as shrimp, crabs, etc.)
    8 very ripe tomatoes, peeled and diced
    2 quarts water
    2 tablespoons dried mushrooms
    ¼ pound *capelli d'angelo* ("angel's hair")

Heat the oil in a large pot and sauté the garlic, parsley, carrot, celery, onions, and basil in it until onions are soft. Remove hind legs from the cleaned and washed frogs and set aside. Place the rest of the frogs in the pan with the sautéed vegetables and brown; turn often so frogs do not stick to the pan. Add the tomatoes and increase heat until the mixture comes to a boil. Stir well, reduce heat, and add the water. Simmer until the meat begins to separate from the bones. Put everything through a sieve, pressing through so that only bones remain in the sieve. Return the soup to the pot; simmer frogs' hind legs in this until tender, about 10 minutes. Take meat from bones, dice, and return to the soup. Stir in the mushrooms and simmer, uncovered, for 10 minutes. Bring soup to a boil and remove from fire. Stir in the *capelli d'angelo*. This pasta is so fine that it cooks in seconds, so it is not necessary to replace the pot on the stove; stir everything well and serve in hot soup bowls. Serves 4 to 6.

ZUPPA DI SALSICCE E CRAVATTE

Sausage Soup with "Bow Ties"

½ pound dried white pea beans
3 quarts Chicken Broth (page 96)
3 tablespoons olive oil
4 four-inch-long hot Italian sausages
3 potatoes, diced
1 carrot, scraped and chopped
1 small white onion, chopped
1 celery rib, scraped and chopped
4 ripe tomatoes, peeled and diced
1½ teaspoons salt, or to taste
Milled black pepper
½ cup *cravatte*

Soak the beans in water for 3 hours; drain. Place in a large pot, cover with 2 quarts of the broth, and simmer for 1½ hours, or until beans are almost tender but still firm. Heat the oil in a large saucepan; add the sausages, pricked with a fork, and brown. Stir in the potatoes, carrot, onion, celery, and tomatoes; sprinkle with salt and mill in black pepper. Simmer for 15 minutes, then stir in the remaining broth and simmer, uncovered, for 20 minutes. Add this to the bean pot, stirring in well. Cook the *cravatte* al dente, drain, and stir into the bean pot. Simmer, uncovered, for 5 minutes. Serve in hot soup bowls with the sausage in slices, 4 slices to each bowl of soup. Serves 4 to 6.

PASTINA ALLA TOSCANA

1 pound beef round
5 medium chicken livers
2 small white onions, minced
2 tablespoons olive oil
2 tablespoons butter
1 tablespoon minced Italian parsley
2 fresh basil leaves, minced
4 very ripe tomatoes, peeled and diced
1½ teaspoons salt, or to taste
Milled black pepper
3 quarts Chicken Broth (page 96), warm
¼ pound fresh spinach, chopped
¼ pound escarole, chopped
3 tablespoons *pastina* (small pasta for
   soup)

Cut the beef into pieces half the size of your thumbnail; chop the chicken livers. In a large pot, over medium heat, sauté the beef and livers with the onions in the oil and butter for 15 minutes. Stir in the minced herbs and the tomatoes, breaking up the tomatoes with a wooden spoon as they simmer. Sprinkle on the salt and the pepper. Simmer for 30 minutes, uncovered, stirring often. Now add the warm chicken broth and stir in the chopped spinach and escarole. Simmer for 20 minutes. Stir in the *pastina* and simmer for another 5 minutes. Serve in hot soup bowls. Serves 6.

VERMICELLI ALLA SALVATORE

3 veal sweetbreads
4 chicken livers
5 tablespoons butter
2 eggs
Juice of ½ lemon
1 teaspoon salt, or to taste
Liberal amount of milled black pepper
1 tablespoon chopped Italian parsley
⅛ teaspoon dried sweet basil
2 quarts Chicken Broth (page 96)
⅓ cup 1½-inch pieces of *vermicelli*
⅓ cup grated Asiago cheese

Near L'AQUILA, wheat harvest—Abruzzi

In a small pot, parboil the sweetbreads; remove the skin and membranes and dice the sweetbreads. Chop the chicken livers. In a saucepan, over medium heat, sauté the sweetbreads and livers in butter for 8 minutes. In a large bowl, beat the eggs with a whisk; blend in lemon, salt, pepper, parsley, and basil. Slowly stir in all of the broth. Pour into a large pot and stir in the sweetbreads and livers. Simmer for 20 minutes, stirring often. Cook *vermicelli* less than al dente; drain, add to the soup pot, and simmer for 3 minutes. Pass the Asiago. Serves 4 to 6.

ZUPPA DI POMODORO CON POLPETTINE DI VITELLO

Tomato Soup with Veal Meatballs

3 tablespoons butter
2 tablespoons minced ham fat
1 carrot, scraped and minced
1 white onion, minced
1 celery rib, scraped and minced
1 tablespoon minced Italian parsley
2 pounds plum tomatoes, peeled and diced
3 quarts Chicken Broth (page 96)
2 slices of bread without crusts
1 cup milk
½ pound veal, ground twice
1 shallot, minced
2 egg yolks, beaten
1 teaspoon salt, or to taste
Pinch of grated nutmeg
4 tablespoons flour
⅓ cup 1½-inch pieces of *vermicelli*

Heat 2 tablespoons of the butter in a large pot, stir in ham fat, and cook until soft. Then add the carrot, onion, celery, and parsley; simmer for 10 minutes. Stir in the tomatoes, blend in half the broth, cover the pot, and simmer for 1 hour.

Meanwhile, prepare the meatballs. Soak the bread in milk; press out the liquid, then mix bread with the veal in a bowl. In a saucepan, melt the remaining butter and sauté the shallot in it until tender. Add the shallot and butter, the beaten egg yolks, and the salt and nutmeg to the bread and veal. Blend everything well. Form into meatballs the size of marbles.

Bring the remaining broth to a simmer. Roll the meatballs in the flour and drop them into the broth. Cook for 10 minutes. Strain the vegetable mixture and return it to its soup pot. Then stir meatballs and their broth into the pot. Cook the *vermicelli* al dente in plenty of boiling water; drain well. Stir into the soup and simmer, uncovered, for 3 minutes. Serve in hot soup bowls with 6 meatballs in each bowl. Serves 4 to 6.

ZUPPA DI CIMA ALLA GENOVESE CON LINGUINE FINE
Genoese Veal Soup with Fine Noodles

This is a famous soup from Genoa that first requires that you prepare cima, *a stuffed breast of veal.*

½ pound lean pork, ground
¼ pound prosciutto, minced
4 slices of bread, soaked in milk, then
    squeezed dry
1 tablespoon grated Parmesan cheese
1 tablespoon minced pistachios
2½ teaspoons salt
Liberal amount of milled black pepper
Pinch of grated nutmeg
5 eggs, in all
3-pound breast of veal, boned
1 large carrot, chopped
1 large onion, chopped
1 bay leaf
1 tablespoon minced fresh marjoram
¼ pound *linguine fine*, broken into 2-inch pieces

In a large bowl, place the pork, prosciutto, bread, Parmesan, pistachios, 1½ teaspoons of the salt, some pepper, the nutmeg, and 3 of the eggs. Blend all together well to make a filling. Spread the breast of veal flat; spoon the filling over the veal. Fold the meat over, sewing it together to seal in the filling completely. Then tie with string. Place the roll in a 6-quart pot and cover with water. Stir in the carrot, onion, bay leaf, and remaining teaspoon of salt. Cover the pot and simmer for 1½ hours, or until breast is tender. Remove to a platter and place a heavy weight atop to press the meat into its flat Genoese shape.

Add the marjoram to the liquid remaining in the pot in which the veal cooked. Simmer this broth, uncovered, for 20 minutes. Add the *linguine fine* directly to the pot; cook al dente. Beat the 2 remaining eggs and stir them into the broth; bring it to a boil. Remove from the heat and ladle soup quickly into hot soup bowls. Serve the *cima,* sliced thin, as the entrée, accompanied by a vegetable. Serves 4 to 6.

ZUPPA DI POLLO CON STELLINI

Chicken Soup with "Little Stars"

1 stewing chicken trussed
½ cup diced okra
2 cups (one 1-pound can) Italian plum to-
    matoes
1 onion, chopped
2 celery ribs, scraped and chopped
Salt and pepper
⅓ cup *stellini*

In a large pot, cover chicken with water and simmer for 3 hours; take from pot and dice meat. Return chicken meat to pot; stir in vegetables. Season and simmer for 25 minutes. Cook *stellini* al dente; drain, blend with soup. Serves 4 to 6.

VENICE—Venezia Euganea

PICCIONE BOLLITO CON ARANCINI

Boiled Pigeon with "Little Oranges"

2 pigeons (or substitute a fat stewing
    chicken)

8 quarts water

2 large carrots

2 large celery ribs with leaves

1 large onion

6 peppercorns, cracked

1 tablespoon salt

⅓ cup *arancini*

1 tablespoon chopped Italian parsley

In a large pot, put the pigeons in the water with all of the ingredients except the pasta and parsley. Simmer, covered, for 4 hours, or until birds are tender. Remove pigeons, cool, and dice meat from the breasts. Cook remaining stock in the uncovered pot until it is reduced by half. Strain; push vegetables through sieve; return vegetable purée and diced pigeon to the strained stock and simmer for 10 minutes. Cook *arancini* in boiling salted water until al dente, drain, and add to soup pot; simmer for 5 minutes. Serve in hot soup bowls topped with chopped parsley. Serves 4 to 6.

ATRANI—Campania

VI
Seafood with Pasta

Pasta and seafood is to us a dawn sea. It is the little Sicilian fishing port of Licata, a small boat chugging through the darkness as we went netting sardines with three fishermen years ago. It is little boats with bobbing lanterns that send spots of shimmering light; it is dawn coming over the island in staggering waves of light that fall upon the dark sea, making it clear blue and the hauled-in nets of fish a flashing sheet of silver.

But even more than that, it is perhaps the best breakfast, certainly the most unusual, that we have ever had—on a beach, as the sun became warm, and the fish and the pasta cooked.

As we anchored, one fisherman filled an old black pot with seawater and put it over a brazier. Driftwood was gathered, the fire built, the pot boiled merrily. Another fisherman, using a small instrument like a button-hook, inserted it in the mouth of each sardine and pulled innards and bones out. When four dozen were ready, they went into another pot, with olive oil, on the brazier over the driftwood fire.

The pasta, a pound of *linguine*, was ready in eight minutes; so were the fish that literally had jumped from the sea into the pot. We sat on the shore and ate that famous dish of Sicily, *pasta alle sarde*, the *linguine* mixed with a bit of the oil that the fish had cooked in, fresh fennel leaves rubbed through the hands over it, some *pignoli* nuts added, black pepper milled over, and then each person received six crisp, golden sardines on top of his pasta. As we touched a fish, its delicate white meat spilled onto the *linguine,* we twirled it with several strands, and washed it down with one of the best white wines we have tasted, the cold crisp Sicilian Corvo.

That was our introduction to that creative combination—pasta and seafood. Today, probably because of those early circumstances, it still remains our favorite. Surrounded as she is by the sea, Italy makes quite a thing of pasta and myriad creatures from the ocean, and the farther south you go, it seems to us, the more unusual and superb the combinations become. Everything from a sardine to a squid lends its personality.

VERMICELLI ALLA MERETRICE

Harlot's Pasta

The recipe for Salsa alla Meretrice, which is used on other pastas too, is on page 87. For this dish, cook 1 pound of vermicelli *al dente; watch carefully, as they are fine and cook quickly—6 minutes could do it. Drain the* vermicelli. *Serve in hot soup bowls, with a lavish spooning of sauce over each serving. Do not toss, as this is a fragile pasta and too much forking can make it sticky. Serves 4 to 6.*

Pastas with anchovies, or other seafood, that are not, strictly speaking, seafood dishes, are . . .

Maria Limoncelli's "Sparrows' Tongues" (or spaghetti) with Anchovies, page 336.

Linguine with Eggs and Anchovies, page 334.

Bucatini with Anchovies and Mushrooms, page 301.

Baked Stuffed Tomatoes Sicilian Style (with sardines), page 360.

"Tiny Tubes" and Salmon Pie, page 363.

FETTUCCE E PESCE

Wide Fettuccine with Fish

2 tablespoons olive oil
3 small white onions, chopped
1 garlic clove, minced
1 small red pepper, cored and chopped
1 small green pepper, cored and chopped
1 can (2 ounces) anchovies, chopped
Liberal amount of milled black pepper
2 cups Basic Tomato Sauce (page 76)
½ teaspoon dried tarragon
2 medium cod or haddock fillets, cut into
bite-size pieces
1 pound *fettucce*

Heat the oil in a heavy pot. Add onions, garlic, peppers, and anchovies with their oil; mill in black pepper. Sauté until vegetables are soft. Stir in the tomato sauce, then add the tarragon and the pieces of fish. Simmer, uncovered, until fish is just tender but not falling apart. Cook the *fettucce* al dente, drain, and toss gently with half of the fish sauce, using wooden forks. Serve in hot bowls with the remaining sauce atop each serving. Serves 4 to 6.

LINGUE DI PASSERI CON BACCALÀ

"Sparrows' Tongues" with Dried Cod

It is the rare Italian market here or abroad that doesn't have dried, heavily salted cod the length of your arm, stacked just inside the entrance like cordwood. Cod treated like this lasts indefinitely and was the old-world way of preserving heavy catches for future meals. In their usual imaginative way the Italians created a number of dishes from the fish. Baccalà teamed sometimes with pasta, sometimes with polenta, is a tart and tasty dish usually served during the Christmas holiday season.

3 pounds dried cod

⅓ cup flour

1 tablespoon olive oil

3 tablespons butter

2 garlic cloves

Liberal amount of milled black pepper

3 mint leaves, chopped

3 basil leaves, chopped

½ teaspoon capers

4 pitted large black olives, sliced

3 cups Marinara Sauce (page 81)

1 pound *lingue di passeri*

Soak the cod in cold water for 24 hours, changing water at least 6 times. Just before beginning the recipe, wash the cod once more in cold water. Drain and remove skin. Cut it into 1-inch pieces and dredge in flour. Heat oil and butter in a heavy skillet. Add fish and garlic and brown, removing garlic when it turns golden and turning fish so it will brown on both sides. Mill in black pepper; stir in mint and basil leaves, capers, olives, and marinara sauce. Simmer for 20 minutes uncovered. Cook *lingue di passeri* al dente, omitting salt from water since cod is salty; drain. Toss with half of the cod and marinara sauce and serve in hot bowls. Spoon remaining sauce and cod on top. Serves 6.

TAGLIARINI CON BACCALÀ

Baked Noodles with Dried Cod

1 medium-size dried cod

3 tablespoons olive oil

Liberal amount of milled black pepper

1½ cups heavy cream

1 pound *tagliarini*

3 tablespoons butter

Soak the cod for 24 hours, rinsing and changing the water 6 times. Drain cod, cut into pieces, and boil for 20 minutes. Drain, and remove skin and bones. With a blender or food processor blend cod into a paste, slowly stirring in olive oil and milling in black pepper. Continue until mixture is a smooth creamy paste. (Use olive oil sparingly.) When cod is smooth, whip the heavy cream until it is stiff and blend the fish paste into it. Cook *tagliarini* al dente; no salt is needed; drain. Toss with the cod and whipped cream, blending well. Place in a buttered casserole or baking dish and dot with the butter. Bake in a preheated 400° F. oven for 20 minutes, until bubbling and brown. Serves 4 to 6.

BAVETTINE CON INVOLTINI DI PASSERINO

Bavettine with Rolled Flounder

3 tablespoons lemon juice

6 small flounder fillets

1 teaspoon salt

Milled black pepper

3 tablespoons butter

½ cup clam juice

1 small white onion, minced

¾ cup white Chianti

1 tablespoon chopped parsley

2 cups (one 1-pound can) Italian plum tomatoes, pushed through food mill

1 pound *bavettine* (very narrow *linguine*)

Sprinkle lemon juice over the fillets; season with salt and pepper; roll and tie fillets so rolls will not open when cooking. Melt butter in a saucepan, add fish rolls, and brown over medium heat. Stir in the clam juice, onion, wine, parsley, and tomatoes. Cover the pan and simmer for 15 minutes, turning rolls once carefully to avoid breaking. Remove fish rolls to warm platter; continue to cook sauce, uncovered, until thickened and smooth. Cook *bavettine* al dente; drain. Place 2 ounces of *bavettine* in each of 6 warm soup bowls. Untie fish rolls and place one atop each serving of pasta. Put 2 large spoonfuls of sauce over each serving. Serves 6.

PORTOFINO—*Liguria*

QUARESIMI CANNELLONI

Lenten Cannelloni

1 pound haddock fillets

2½ cups milk

1 bay leaf

9 tablespoons (1 stick plus 1 tablespoon)
   butter

1 medium-size onion, finely chopped

3 tablesoons chopped Italian parsley

½ teaspoon salt

¼ teaspoon freshly ground black pepper

¼ cup heavy cream

1 cup grated Fontina cheese

1 recipe of *Pasta Fresca all'Uovo* (page 57)

4 tablespoons flour

Salt and freshly ground black pepper to
   taste

1 uncooked lobster tail (shell removed),
   cut into small pieces

½ cup grated Asiago or Parmesan cheese

In a saucepan, over medium heat, combine the haddock, milk, and bay leaf and bring to a simmer. Lower heat and cook until the fish flakes with a fork (about 10 minutes). Remove from the milk (saving the milk for the sauce), drain, and cool. Strain the milk. Mash the fish and reserve.

In a frypan, over medium heat, heat 2 tablespoons of the butter and cook the onion until soft. Do not brown.

In a bowl combine and blend well the mashed fish, onion, parsley, the ½ teaspoon of salt and the ¼ teaspoon of pepper, the cream, and one third of the Fontina cheese. Taste for seasoning. Set aside.

Roll out the pasta and cut into 4-inch squares. Cook a few squares at a time in boiling salted water for 3 minutes. Do not allow them to sink to the bottom or stick together. Drain and dry on absorbent cloth. Spoon some filling on one third of each square and roll into a cylinder. Arrange the cylinders, side by side, seamside down, in a buttered shallow baking dish.

In a saucepan, over medium heat, melt 4 tablespoons of butter. Stir in the flour and cook, stirring to a smooth paste. Gradually stir in the milk the fish was poached in and cook, stirring into a smooth sauce. Add the remaining Fontina cheese and stir until the cheese has melted. Taste for seasoning, then add salt and pepper. Stir in the lobster pieces. Cook 1 minute.

Spoon the sauce over the *cannelloni*, sprinkle with Asiago or Parmesan, and dot with the remaining butter. Place in a preheated 375° F. oven for 10 minutes, or until thoroughly heated, the top golden, and sauce bubbling. Serves 6.

Note: Commercial *manicotti* can be substituted for the *cannelloni*.

TAGLIATELLE CON SGOMBRO ALLA GENOVESE
Noodles with Mackerel Genoese Style

2 tablespoons olive oil

2 tablespoons butter

2 shallots, chopped

3 tablespoons white wine

3 medium-size mushrooms, sliced

½ teaspoon salt, or to taste

Liberal amount of milled black pepper

3 anchovies, diced

½ recipe Basic Tomato Sauce (page 00)

2 fresh mackerel fillets, cut into 2-inch
   pieces

1 pound *tagliatelle*

Heat oil and butter in a saucepan, stir in the shallots, and simmer until soft. Stir in the wine and mushrooms, the salt, pepper, and anchovies. Simmer, uncovered, until anchovies have melted into the sauce. Stir in the tomato sauce, blending well, and simmer, uncovered, for 15 minutes. Add mackerel pieces and simmer, uncovered, for 15 minutes, until fish is tender. Cook *tagliatelle* al dente, with only 1 tablespoon of salt in the water; drain. Serve in hot soup bowls with the fish-tomato sauce liberally spooned atop. Serves 4 to 6

SPAGHETTI CON TRIGLIE ED UOVA

Spaghetti with Red Mullet and Eggs

2 red mullets, filleted
½ teaspoon salt, or to taste
1½ cups white wine
1 recipe Béchamel Sauce (page 85)
3 hard-cooked eggs, chopped
3 tablespoons chopped parsley
½ tablespoon chopped fresh mint
1 pound spaghetti

Place the fish fillets in a saucepan, sprinkle lightly with salt, and cover with the wine. Simmer for 10 minutes, breaking up the fish as it simmers with a wooden spoon and making sure any bones are removed. Prepare the Béchamel sauce; bring to a simmer. Drain fish and add it to the sauce. Stir in the hard-cooked eggs, parsley, and mint. Simmer, uncovered, for 10 minutes. Cook spaghetti al dente, drain, and add directly to the sauce in the saucepan. Toss well and serve immediately in hot soup bowls. Serves 4 to 6.

FETTUCCINE CON PESCI PERSICI ALLA FIORENTINA

Baked Fettuccine with Perch Florentine

1 recipe Béchamel Sauce (page 85)
12 small fillets of ocean perch
1 teaspoon salt, or to taste
Milled black pepper
2 cups white wine
3 pounds spinach
1 pound *fettuccine*
4 tablespoons grated *Ragusano* cheese

FLORENCE, the Duomo—Tuscany

Prepare Béchamel sauce and keep it warm. Wash and dry fillets and place them in a saucepan; sprinkle with salt and pepper and cover with wine. Simmer for 15 minutes or less, being careful to keep the fish intact. In a small pot, cook the spinach in a small amount of salted water, drain well, and chop. Arrange a layer of the spinach in a baking dish. Cook *fettuccine* al dente; drain. Arrange a layer of the noodles atop the spinach. Add a layer of fish, then repeat the layers of spinach, noodles, and fish. Pour the warm Béchamel sauce over all; sprinkle liberally with grated *Ragusano.* Bake in a preheated 400° F. oven for 20 minutes, or until top is bubbly and brown. Serve 2 fillets per person atop a mound of noodles and spinach. Serves 6.

ZITI TAGLIATI CON SALSA DI SARDE

"Short Bridegrooms" with Sardine Sauce

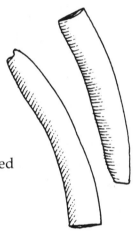

    2 tablespoons butter
    2 tablespoons olive oil
    2 small white onions, minced
    2 fresh basil leaves, minced
    4 medium-size very ripe tomatoes, peeled and diced
    1 pound fresh sardines, cleaned and cut
        into 2-inch pieces
    ½ teaspoon salt
    Liberal amount of milled black pepper
    ½ cup clam juice
    6 large black olives, sliced
    1 tablespoon *pignoli* (pine nuts)
    1 pound *ziti tagliati*

Heat butter and oil in a saucepan and add onions, basil, and tomatoes. Simmer until onions are soft. Add the sardine pieces, breaking up tomatoes and sardines with a wooden spoon as they cook. Sprinkle in salt and pepper and add the clam juice, a tablespoon at a time, stirring it in well. Simmer, uncovered, until the sauce is smooth and not watery. This should take about 25 minutes. Stir in the olives and the pine nuts; simmer for 10 minutes, uncovered. Cook the *ziti tagliati* al dente, drain, and place in a large hot bowl. Pour in half of the sardine sauce; toss well but gently with wooden forks. Serve in hot soup bowls with the remaining sauce spooned atop. Serves 6.

SPAGHETTINI CON FINOCCHI E PICCOLE ARINGHE

Spaghettini with Fennel and Smelts

1 pound fennel
3 tablespoons butter
2 tablespoons olive oil
2 medium-size white onions, minced
1 pound smelts, cleaned and boned
1 tablespoon *pignoli*
1 tablespoon chopped raisins
1 teaspoon salt, or to taste
Milled black pepper
2 cups water
1 pound spaghettini
⅓ cup bread crumbs, toasted

Wash and trim the fennel, but do not remove the leaves. Cook it in a pot of boiling water for 25 minutes. Drain and mince. In a saucepan, over medium heat, heat the butter and oil and sauté the onions in it until soft. Add the smelts and brown them quickly on both sides. Stir in the minced fennel, pine nuts, raisins, salt, pepper, and water. Simmer, uncovered, for 15 minutes, stirring frequently, being careful to keep the fish intact. Cook spaghettini al dente, drain, and place in a warm bowl. With wooden forks toss pasta with half of the fennel and fish sauce. Add half of the bread crumbs and toss gently again. Serve in hot soup bowls with remainder of bread crumbs, sauce, and whole smelts spooned atop. Serves 4 to 6.

Note: In Milan the above sauce is given piquancy by adding 3 chopped drained anchovies and a chopped peeled ripe tomato.

TAGLIOLINI CON SOGLIOLA

Tagliolini with Sole

8 small sole fillets

Salt and freshly ground black pepper

Juice of ½ lemon

⅓ cup dry white wine

4 tablespoons butter

4 tablespoons flour

2 cups fish stock, or 1 cup chicken broth
  blended with 1 cup clam juice, or 1
  Knorr fish bouillon cube dissolved in
  2 cups water

12 ounces *tagliolini*, cooked in boiling
  salted water until al dente, drained

½ cup grated Asiago or Parmesan cheese

Arrange the sole in a single layer in a well-buttered shallow baking dish. Sprinkle lightly with salt and pepper and with the lemon juice and wine. Bake, uncovered, in a preheated 375° F. oven for 8 minutes, or until white and firm. Carefully transfer to an *au gratin* pan and set aside the dish in which the sole baked, with its liquid. Keep warm while you prepare the sauce.

In a saucepan, over medium heat, melt the butter. Stir in the flour and cook, stirring to a smooth golden paste. Gradually stir in the fish stock, stirring constantly to a smooth thickened sauce. Season with salt and pepper.

Mix the hot pasta with the liquid in the dish in which the fish baked. Arrange it in an even layer over the sole. Spoon on the hot sauce and sprinkle with the grated cheese. Place under a broiler for 5 minutes, or until bubbling and golden. Serves 4 to 6.

TRIANGOLI CON SOGLIOLA

"Triangles" with Sole

2 sole fillets
2 tablespoons butter
3 cups Marinara Sauce (page 81)
1 pound *triangoli*

In a saucepan, over medium heat, cook sole in the butter until almost half done, or about 5 minutes. Since this fish has most fragile connective tissues, *undercook*. Remove from the pan and make certain there are no bones in the fish. Carefully break it into small pieces with a wooden spoon and stir it into the hot marinara sauce. Remove from the heat immediately. Cook the *triangoli* al dente, drain, and place in a warm bowl. Pour in the fish and tomato sauce, toss, and serve in warm bowls. Serves 4 to 6.

FETTUCCELLE ALLA VENEZIANA

"Little Ribbons" Baked Venetian Style

2 medium-size white onions, sliced
1 cup white wine
1½ teaspoons salt
1½ pounds lemon-sole fillets, cut into ½-inch cubes
1 cup light cream
1 pound *fettuccelle* (narrow *fettuccine*)
½ pound shrimp, cooked and shelled
2 tablespoons grated Asiago cheese
2 tablespoons grated Romano cheese
1 tablespoon butter

In a saucepan simmer onions in the wine with 1 teaspoon of the salt. Stir in 1 pound of the sole pieces; cook for 10 minutes. Place the remaining raw fish in a blender with 2 tablespoons of broth from fish-and-onion mixture. Mix to a smooth paste. Remove from blender and fold in the cream, stirring well to a smooth mixture. Simmer this over very low heat, just until mixture thickens, then add remaining ½ teaspoon salt and stir until paste is smooth.

Cook *fettuccelle* al dente; drain. Butter a baking dish. Spread a layer of noodles in the bottom of the dish. Arrange a layer of fish cubes and shrimp atop, then a thin layer of fish paste. Repeat layers until all of noodles, fish, shrimp and fish paste have been used. Mix the two cheeses and sprinkle the mixture on top; dot with butter. Place under the broiler until sauce bubbles and top browns. Serves 6.

NAPLES—Campania

LINGUE DI PASSERI CON DUE PESCI

"Sparrows' Tongues" with Two Fishes

15 medium-size black olives, pitted
1 can (7 ounces) tuna
1 can (2 ounces) anchovy fillets, drained
3 cups Mushroom and Cheese Sauce
   (page 86)
1 pound *lingue di passeri*

Slice the olives. Drain tuna and break up with a fork. Blend olives, tuna, anchovies, and mushroom and cheese sauce in a saucepan. Simmer for 15 minutes. Cook *lingue di passeri* al dente; drain well. Place sauce in a warm bowl and toss in pasta. Serve quickly in warm bowls. Serves 4 to 6.

SPAGHETTI CON TONNO ALLA MARIA LIMONCELLI

Spaghetti with Tuna alla Maria Limoncelli

1 can (7 ounces) white tuna in olive oil
3 tablespoons butter
½ teaspoon chopped chives
1 tablespoon chopped Italian parsley
1 cup heavy cream, hot
½ teaspoon salt, or to taste
Liberal amount of milled black pepper
1 pound spaghetti

With a fork, break up the tuna in its oil. In a saucepan, melt butter, add tuna, chives, and parsley; simmer for 5 minutes. Blend in the cup of cream, add the salt, and mill in black pepper; simmer for 5 minutes. Cook spaghetti al dente; drain. Mix with tuna sauce, tossing gently with wooden forks. Serves 4 to 6.

SPAGHETTINI CON TONNO ED ACCIUGHE
Spaghettini with Tuna and Anchovies

Most Italians when thinking of pasta with seafood immediately reach for a can of tuna and one of anchovies. They team them in many ways and can whip up a tasty dish in minutes. This is one we had on a Friday in Naples after returning late from the opera. It was ready in 20 minutes.

    2 tablespoons butter
    1 can (7 ounces) white tuna in olive oil
    Liberal amout of milled black pepper
    1 can (2 ounces) anchovies, drained
    1 teaspoon capers
    1 pound spaghettini

Melt the butter in a saucepan and stir in the tuna with its oil, breaking it up into small pieces. Mill in pepper liberally, add anchovies and capers, and simmer for 15 minutes, stirring constantly. Cook spaghettini al dente, omitting salt from cooking water. Drain well and toss right in the saucepan with the tuna and anchovies, coating the strands of pasta well; toss gently with wooden forks. Serves 4 to 6.

VERMICELLI CON PISELLI E TONNO
Vermicelli with Peas and Tuna

    2 white onions, minced
    2 tablespoons butter
    1 can (7 ounces) white tuna in olive oil
    2 cups (one 1-pound can) tomatoes,
        pushed through food mill
    1 teaspoon salt, or to taste
    Milled black pepper
    ½ pound fresh peas, shelled and half cooked
    1 pound *vermicelli*

In a saucepan, over medium-low heat, sauté onions in the butter until soft. Stir in the tuna with its oil, breaking it into pieces; simmer for 10 minutes. Add the tomatoes, salt, and pepper; simmer, uncovered, for 10 minutes. Blend in the peas, stir well, and simmer for 10 minutes more. Cook *vermicelli* al dente; drain. Serve in hot soup bowls with 2 large spoonfuls of the sauce over each portion. Serves 4 to 6.

CAVIALE CORONATE PENNE RIGATE

Caviar-Topped Grooved "Feathers"

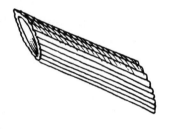

4 tablespoons olive oil

4 garlic cloves, coarsely chopped

12 ounces *penne rigate* (or other short heavy pasta), cooked in boiling, lightly salted water until al dente, drained

3 tablespoons butter

4 tablespoons lumpfish caviar

In a deep saucepan, over medium heat, heat the olive oil. Stir in the garlic and cook for 2 minutes, or until soft. Do not brown. Add the hot pasta and butter (in small pieces) and toss well. Add half of the caviar and toss well but carefully.

Serve on hot plates with the remaining caviar sprinkled on top. Serves 4 to 6 as a first course.

VERMICELLI AL CAVIALE

Vermicelli with Caviar

We are of the school that believes that the only way to eat the eggs of the Caspian sturgeon, the world's best caviar, is with a slender piece of toast and a spoon, or just with a spoon. We were somewhat shocked therefore when a friend in Rome who had just received a container of fresh caviar invited us to dinner, and served the caviar as first course—with pasta! Even though it is an ideal mating, we have it only once a year, for we still believe that the only thing that goes with caviar is a spoon.

    1 pound *vermicelli*
    ¼ pound butter, soft
    4 ounces Beluga caviar
    Juice of ½ lemon

Cook *vermicelli* al dente. Have a large hot bowl at hand with the soft butter in it. Lift the pasta directly from its boiling pot into the bowl, draining it over its pot before forking it into the bowl. It must be hot, and it must be al dente. Have 4 or 6 *hot* soup bowls ready. Now mix the caviar into the pasta in its bowl, tossing well with wooden forks. Add the lemon juice and toss again. Serve immediately in the hot soup bowls. Serves 4 to 6.

LINGUINE FINE CON VONGOLE ALLA MARIA

Maria's Fine Linguine with Clams

    18 cherrystone clams, in their shells
    6 tablespoons olive oil
    3 garlic cloves
    4 tablespoons chopped Italian parsley
    ¼ teaspoon crushed red pepper
    Much freshly milled black pepper
    Salt to taste
    Pinch of dried sweet basil
    1 pound *linguine fine*

Using a stiff brush, scrub the clams well, rinsing them carefully under cold running water. Heat the oil in a pan large enough to hold the 18 clams. Brown the garlic in it, then discard the garlic. Place the clams, parsley, red and black pepper, salt and basil in the pan. Cover and simmer for 10 minutes. Uncover, tip the clam shells to pour their juice into the pan, and simmer, uncovered, for 5 minutes longer. Cook *linguine fine* al dente, drain, and place in a hot bowl. Remove the clams in their shells from the saucepan; pour the liquid from that pan over the *linguine* and toss well, but gently with wooden forks. Serve in hot soup bowls with 3 clams in their shells atop each serving of pasta. Serves 6.

SPAGHETTINI CON SALSA BIANCA E VONGOLE
Thin Spaghetti with White Clam Sauce

Some recipes have stories. This one began in Nag's Head, North Carolina, five years ago, where we were visiting Maria Luisa's brother, Donald Limoncelli, and sister-in-law, Doris. As we were right on the Atlantic, in prime clam country, the Limoncellis asked us to prepare a dish of pasta with white clam sauce. Problem was, we couldn't find any decent cherrystone clams; they were all shipped else-where. There were plenty of the big ocean clams, tough, leathery, good for stews and chowders, but not for our purpose. So we bought a couple of cans of minced clams, a brand we knew was tender and sweet, and two bottles of clam juice.

Results were excellent. In fact, since that time, we have continued to experi-ment and believe now that our white clam sauce with canned minced clams is more likely to succeed than with the fresh, which can be rubbery because they are too easily overcooked. And, fresh clams are often unavailable. Also, we've discovered that the secret of a good clam sauce is in reducing the clam juice in the saucepan almost to an essence.

3 tablespoons olive oil

3 garlic cloves (crush 2, leave 1 intact)

Two 8-ounce bottles clam juice

Two 6½-ounce cans minced clams

⅓ cup dry white wine

⅛ teaspoon (or to taste) crushed red pepper

Salt to taste

12 ounces *spaghettini,* cooked al dente in
boiling salted water, drained

3 tablespoons butter

2 tablespoons minced Italian parsley

In a saucepan, over medium heat, heat the oil and cook the 2 crushed garlic cloves for 3 minutes, or until golden. Remove and discard the garlic. Push remaining garlic clove through a garlic press into the saucepan. Pour in the clam juice. Drain juice from the minced clams, add it to the saucepan. Pour in the wine and stir in the red pepper. Stir well, lower heat, and simmer, uncovered, for about 20 minutes, or until the liquid is reduced by one third. Taste before adding salt.

Place the hot pasta in a warm bowl. Add the butter (in small pieces) and toss well. Bring the clam sauce in the saucepan to a boil. Remove from heat and stir in the drained minced clams (reserve several spoonfuls to serve on top of pasta). Add the sauce with the clams by the tablespoonful to the pasta in the bowl and toss well. Add the parsley and toss.

Sprinkle the reserved clams on each serving. Serves 4 as a first course.

LINGUINE CON SALSA ROSSA E VONGOLE
Linguine with Red Clam Sauce

3 small white onions, chopped

1 garlic clove, minced

3 tablespoons olive oil

4 cups (one 2-pound can) Italian plum tomatoes

1 teaspoon salt

Milled black pepper

1 teaspoon crushed red pepper

1 teaspoon dried oregano

4 anchovies, chopped

1 large can (10½ ounces) minced clams

1 pound *linguine*

Sauté onions and garlic in oil until onions are soft. Put tomatoes through a food mill, and blend into onion-garlic mixture. Simmer for 10 minutes. Add salt, black and red pepper, oregano, and anchovies; cover and simmer for 20 minutes. Add the clams with their juice; stir well, mill in more black pepper, and simmer uncovered, until sauce thickens. Cook *linguine* al dente, drain, and place in a warm bowl. Pour in half the red clam sauce;

toss well, but gently, with wooden forks. Serve in hot rimmed soup bowls with the rest of the sauce spooned over. Serves 4 to 6.

SPAGHETTI CON VONGOLE ED ACCIUGHE
Spaghetti with Clams and Anchovies

2 white onions, chopped
2 tablespoons olive oil
30 shucked cherrystone clams and liquid
6 anchovy fillets, drained
10 ripe tomatoes, peeled and chopped
2 small green peppers, chopped
1 garlic clove, minced
1 pound spaghetti

In a saucepan, over medium heat, sauté onions in the oil until soft. Add clam liquid and the anchovies; simmer for 8 minutes. Stir in tomatoes, green peppers, and garlic; cook for 30 minutes until about half the moisture has evaporated. Add clams, cook 5 minutes. Cook spaghetti al dente, drain, and place in a warm bowl. Pour the clam sauce over the spaghetti and toss. Serve in hot bowls. Serves 4 to 6.

SPAGHETTI CON VONGOLE ED OSTRICHE
Spaghetti with Clams and Oysters

2 garlic cloves
3 tablespoons olive oil
¼ teaspoon crushed red pepper
Salt to taste
1 tablespoon minced fresh parsley
1 can (7½ ounces) clams, minced
1 can (11 ounces) oysters, minced
1 pound spaghetti

In a saucepan, over medium heat, sauté the garlic in the oil until brown. Discard garlic and stir in red pepper, salt, parsley, and the clams with their juice. Simmer, uncovered, for 5 minutes, stirring often. Add the oysters with one third of their juice; simmer for 5 minutes. Cook spaghetti al dente, drain, and place in a large hot bowl. Pour the clam-oyster sauce over pasta, toss well, and serve immediately. Serves 4 to 6.

CAPELLINI CON OSTRICHE

Baked Fine Vermicelli with Oysters

2 dozen fresh oysters, shucked, with
   their liquid
½ pound *capellini*
6 tablespoons butter, in all
½ cup dry bread crumbs
½ cup grated Parmesan cheese
¼ cup flour
2⅓ teaspoons salt, in all
⅜ teaspoon pepper, in all
1 tablespoon Worcestershire sauce
2 cups milk
⅓ cup Marsala
Dash of paprika

Drain oysters, reserving ½ cup of the liquid. Cook *capellini* less than al dente; watch closely, as they cook quickly. Drain and place in the bottom of a buttered casserole. Blend 4 tablespoons of the butter with the bread crumbs and cheese. In a saucepan melt remaining butter, add flour, 2 teaspoons of the salt, ¼ teaspoon of the pepper, and the Worcestershire, slowly stir in reserved oyster liquid and the milk. Simmer until sauce is smooth (about 8 minutes), stirring often, then blend in the Marsala. Now arrange the oysters on the *capellini*. Sprinkle in ⅓ teaspoon of salt, ⅛ teaspoon of pepper, and the paprika. Pour the sauce over all and spread the buttered bread crumbs and cheese on top. Bake, uncovered, in a preheated oven at 400° F. for 15 minutes. Serves 4.

FETTUCCINE CON COZZE ALLA CREMA

Fettuccine with Creamed Mussels

1 medium-size onion, thinly sliced

1 garlic clove, mashed

1 celery stalk, thinly sliced

1 bay leaf

1 cup dry white wine

48 fresh medium-size mussels, scrubbed, beards
    removed, and soaked for 1 hour in water

6 tablespoons butter

The liquid in which the mussels cooked
    (see below for amount)

1½ cups of heavy cream, lightly beaten
    with 2 egg yolks

1 cup small cooked peas

Salt to taste

1 pound *fettuccine*, cooked in boiling
    salted water until al dente, drained

Freshly ground black pepper to taste

3 tablespoons chopped Italian parsley

1 cup grated Asiago or Parmesan cheese (optional)

In a large heavy pot, over medium-high heat, combine the onion, garlic, celery, bay leaf, wine, and the mussels. Cover the pot, bring to a boil, and cook, shaking the pot, for 5 minutes, or until the shells open and the mussels are just firm. Do not overcook, as they will toughen. Discard any mussels that have not opened. Reserve the liquid in which they cooked. Remove the mussels from their shells and add any liquid in the shells to that in the pot. Set the mussels aside and keep warm. Strain the reserved liquid through layers of cheesecloth. Return to the pot and, over high heat, reduce to approximately ¾ cup.

In a saucepan, over medium heat, melt 2 tablespoons of the butter. Add the reduced liquid. Off heat, stir in the cream–egg-yolk mixture. Reduce heat to low and cook, stirring, until the sauce thickens. Do not allow to simmer or boil, as it will curdle. Stir in the peas and mussels and heat through without boiling. Taste, add salt.

Toss the hot pasta with the remaining butter (in small pieces), the black pepper, and two thirds of the sauce (without the mussels). Serve in hot soup bowls with mussels on each serving and parsley sprinkled atop the mussels. Serves 6.

Serve the remaining sauce at the table with the cheese on the side for those who want it.

SPAGHETTI CON COZZE
Spaghetti with Mussels

2 dozen mussels
1 garlic clove
3 tablespoons olive oil
4 cups (one 2-pound can) Italian plum to-
    matoes
½ teaspoon dried marjoram
1 teaspoon salt, or to taste
Milled black pepper
1 pound spaghetti

Scrub mussels well, rinsing several times under cold water. Place them in a large pot with 1 cup hot water, cover the pot, and steam over medium heat until the mussels are opened. Discard those that have not opened. Lift out the mussels and set aside. Strain their liquid into a bowl. Reserve 12 mussels in their shells. Remove the rest from the shells and add to the strained liquid.

In a saucepan, over medium heat, sauté garlic in the oil until soft. Add tomatoes, breaking them up with a wooden spoon as they cook. Add marjoram, salt, and pepper and simmer, covered, for 20 minutes. Add the shelled mussels and the strained liquid and simmer for another 5 minutes, stirring often, until sauce thickens. Cook spaghetti al dente, drain, and place in a warm bowl. Pour half of the mussel sauce over the spaghetti and toss. Serve in hot rimmed soup bowls, with another spoon of sauce over each serving and 2 open mussels in their shells atop. Serves 4 to 6.

VERMICELLI CON COZZE ED UOVA

Vermicelli with Mussels and Eggs

2 dozen mussels
1 tablespoon salt
2 tablespoons butter
2 tablespoons olive oil
2 small white onions, minced
1 tablespoon minced parsley
½ teaspoon salt, or to taste
Liberal amount of milled black pepper
Juice of 1 lemon
3 eggs, beaten
1 pound *vermicelli*

Scrub the mussels well; cover with cold water, add the tablespoon of salt, and soak for 4 hours. This will open the mussels and get rid of most of the sandy residue. In a saucepan heat butter and oil. Stir in onions, parsley, ½ teaspoon salt, and some pepper, and simmer until onions are soft. Add the opened mussels in their shells; cover pan and simmer for 7 minutes. Stir in the lemon juice and the beaten eggs, blending everything well. Simmer, uncovered, for 5 minutes. Cook *vermicelli* al dente; drain. Serve in hot soup bowls with the mussels in their sauce spooned atop. Serves 4 to 6.

LINGUINE CON ARAGOSTA ROSSA ALLA GIOVANNINO

Linguine with Red Lobster Sauce

1½ cups Red Lobster Sauce (page 89)
½ pound *linguine*
4 live lobsters (1 pound each)
Melted butter

PALERMO—Sicily

Make the red lobster sauce. Cook *linguine* al dente, drain, and place in hot soup bowls. Spoon liberal amounts of sauce over each portion and place a piece of lobster from the sauce atop the *linguine* in each bowl. Follow with an entrée of boiled or broiled lobsters served with melted butter. Serves 4.

SPAGHETTINI CON CARNE DI GRANCHIO
Spaghettini with Crabmeat

½ cup chopped onions
1 celery rib, scraped and chopped
1 garlic clove, minced
1 teaspoon chopped parsley
¼ cup olive oil
1 cup drained canned plum tomatoes
2 cups Basic Tomato Sauce (page 76)
1 cup water
Milled black pepper
1 teaspoon salt
½ teaspoon paprika
1 pound fresh or frozen crabmeat, fresh
    preferred
¼ cup sherry
1 pound spaghettini

In a saucepan, over medium heat, sauté onions, celery, garlic, and parsley in the oil until soft. Add tomatoes, tomato sauce, water, and seasonings; simmer, uncovered, for 1 hour. Add crabmeat and sherry, stir well, and cook over low heat for 10 minutes. Cook spaghettini al dente, drain, add to sauce, and toss. Serve in hot soup bowls. Serves 4 to 6.

CONCHIGLIE RIGATE CON ARAGOSTA
Grooved "Shells" with Lobster

2½-pound live lobster
7 tablespoons butter
1 garlic clove, minced
2 tablespoons fresh lemon juice
¼ cup dry white wine
½ cup heavy cream
½ cup grated Asiago or Parmesan cheese
Salt and freshly ground black pepper to
    taste
2 teaspoons salt
12 ounces *conchiglie rigate*

Bring a large pot of water to a boil. Drop in the lobster, head first, and cook for 12 minutes. Remove the lobster and reserve the water it cooked in. Cool the lobster, remove the meat from the tail and claws, and cut into small bite-size pieces. Add the lobster shells to the water in which the lobster cooked.

In a saucepan, over medium heat, melt 3 tablespoons of butter. Add the garlic and cook for 1 minute, or until soft. Do not brown. Add the lobster pieces and cook, stirring, for 2 minutes. Stir in the lemon juice and wine. Cook on high heat, stirring, for 2 minutes. Remove from heat. Do not overcook the lobster, as it will toughen. It should be just firm.

In another saucepan, over medium heat, melt the remaining butter, stir in the cream, cheese, salt, and pepper, blending well, stirring to melt the cheese. Do not boil.

Stir the cream-and-cheese sauce into the lobster saucepan and blend well over low heat. Remove from heat.

Add more water to the pot with the lobster shells in order to have approximately 7 quarts of water. Add the 2 teaspoons of salt, bring to a boil, and simmer 10 minutes. Remove shells, etc., with a slotted spoon or tongs, or strain through a sieve. Be sure to remove all bits of shell.

Add the pasta to the water and cook al dente. Drain well. Add to the lobster saucepan and toss well. Serves 4 as a first course.

LINGUINE ED ARAGOSTA BIANCA

Linguine and White Lobster

¼ pound butter
1 tablespoon olive oil
1 garlic clove, minced
2 small white onions, chopped
1 large carrot, scraped and chopped
1 tablespoon chopped parsley
¼ teaspoon crushed red pepper
2 live lobsters (1 pound each)
1 tablespoon salt
Milled black pepper
1 pound *linguine*

In a saucepan, over medium heat, heat the butter and oil and sauté garlic, onions, carrot, parsley, and red pepper until onions are soft. Cook the lobsters in boiling water with 1 tablespoon of salt in a 10-quart pot. Remove immediately when they turn red. When cool, remove the meat from the shells and dice. Return the shells to the pot and boil the liquid, uncovered, for 40 minutes. Strain this broth and set aside. Add the lobster meat to the vegetables and butter, stir in 1 cup of the strained lobster broth, and add pepper. Simmer for 20 minutes, uncovered.

Cook *linguine* al dente in the remaining strained lobster broth; drain. Place in a large hot bowl; pour half of the diced lobster and vegetable sauce over and toss gently. Serve in hot soup bowls with the remaining lobster and vegetable sauce spooned atop. Serves 4 to 6.

FUSILLI AL SALMONE

Short Pasta "Twists" with Smoked Salmon

4 tablespoons butter
½ teaspoon salt
2 tablespoons minced chives

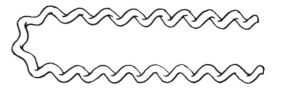

6 thin slices (about 4 ounces) of smoked
    salmon, cut into julienne strips

Juice of 1 lemon

2 ounces brandy

1 cup heavy cream

12 ounces *fusilli,* cooked in boiling salted
    water until al dente, drained

Milled black pepper

Blend together the butter, salt, and chives. In a deep saucepan, over medium heat, melt the seasoned butter. Stir in the salmon, lemon juice, and brandy. Cook about 2 minutes, over high heat, stirring, until most of the brandy has evaporated. Stir in the cream, lower heat, simmer for 3 minutes. Add the hot pasta, tossing well with the sauce until the pasta is coated. Serve in hot bowls with liberal millings of black pepper. Serves 4 to 6 as a first course.

TAGLIATELLE VERDI CON SALSA DI SALMONE
Green Tagliatelle with a Salmon Sauce

6 tablespoons butter

1 small onion, minced

2 cups heavy cream

2 tablespoons brandy

⅛ teaspoon nutmeg

¼ cup grated Asiago or Parmesan cheese

2 cups cooked flaked salmon, skin and
    bones discarded

1 tablespoon fresh lemon juice

Salt and freshly ground black pepper to
    taste

1 pound green *tagliatelle,* cooked in boiling salted water until al dente,
    drained

In a saucepan, over medium heat, melt 2 tablespoons of the butter. Add the onion and cook for 1 minute, or until soft. Do not brown. Pour in the cream and simmer for 5 minutes. Stir in the brandy, nutmeg, and cheese. Stir in the salmon and lemon juice. Season with salt and pepper.

Toss the hot pasta with the remaining butter (in small pieces). Serve on individual hot plates with the sauce evenly spooned on top. Serves 6 to 8 as a first course.

SPAGHETTINI CON SALSA BESCIAMELLA E GAMBERI

Spaghettini with Béchamel Sauce and Shrimp

    1 recipe Béchamel Sauce (page 85)
    4 ounces dried mushrooms
    2 dozen shrimp, shelled and chopped
    1 pound spaghettini

Prepare the Béchamel sauce and bring to a simmer in a saucepan. Soak the mushrooms in cold water for about 15 minutes; drain and chop. Add the shrimp and mushrooms to the sauce and simmer for 15 minutes, uncovered. Cook spaghettini al dente, drain, and place in a hot bowl. Pour half of the sauce mixture over the spaghettini and toss well with wooden forks. Serve in hot soup bowls with the remaining sauce spooned atop. Serves 4 to 6.

MARUZZELLE CON GAMBERI E CREMA ALLA ROMA

Small ''Shells'' with Shrimp and Cream

The reason so many exceptional dishes are discovered in Rome is that all the regional cooking of Italy can be found in that remarkable city. This recipe again exemplifies the classic simplicity of exceptional pasta sauces. The coupling of shells and shrimp sauce makes an appropriate and elegant presentation.

2 tablespoons butter

1 tablespoon olive oil

4 small white onions, finely chopped

1 cup heavy cream

Salt and freshly ground black pepper to
taste

½ pound fresh shrimp, shelled, deveined, and coarsely chopped

12 ounces *maruzzelle*, cooked al dente in
boiling salted water, drained and
mixed with 3 tablespoons butter

In a deep saucepan, over medium heat, heat butter and oil and sauté onions, stirring, for 3 minutes, or until soft. Do not brown. Stir in the cream;
turn heat to medium high and cook, stirring, until the cream has thickened. Add salt, pepper, and the shrimp. Cook, stirring, for 1 minute. Place
the hot buttered pasta in a warm serving bowl. Add the shrimp sauce and
toss with two wooden forks until well blended and shell crevices are filled
with sauce. Serves 4 as a first course.

LINGUINE FINE ALLA MARINARA

Fine Linguine with Fresh Tomato Sauce and Shrimp

3 white onions, chopped

2 garlic cloves, minced

3 tablespoons olive oil

8 large ripe tomatoes

3 teaspoons salt

1 teaspoon sugar

1 cup white wine

1 pound raw shrimp, shelled

2 tablespoons chopped parsley

1 pound *linguine fine*

In a saucepan, over medium heat, cook onions and garlic in oil until soft. Peel tomatoes, cut into pieces, and add to onions and garlic together with salt and sugar. Simmer for 25 minutes. Bring wine to a boil; drop in the shrimp and simmer for 3 minutes. Add wine and shrimp to the tomato sauce. Stir in parsley and cook for 5 minutes. Cook *linguine* al dente, drain, and place in a warm bowl. Pour half of the sauce over and toss lightly. Serve in individual bowls with some of remaining sauce and several shrimp atop each serving. Serves 4 to 6.

RICCIOLINI CON GAMBERI E PETTINI
"Little Curls" with Shrimp and Scallops

2 garlic cloves
2 tablespoons butter
2 tablespoons olive oil
½ pound shrimp, shelled and cleaned
½ pound bay scallops
1 tablespoon chopped parsley
3 fresh basil leaves, chopped
1 teaspoon salt, or to taste
Milled black pepper
4 cups (one 2-pound can) plum tomatoes,
    pushed through food mill
1 pound *ricciolini*

In a saucepan, over medium heat, sauté garlic in butter and oil until brown; discard garlic and add shrimp and scallops, parsley, basil, salt, and pepper. Simmer for 5 minutes. Add the tomatoes and stir in well; simmer, uncovered, until sauce thickens and shrimp and scallops are tender but not overdone. Cook *ricciolini* al dente; drain. Place in a hot bowl and toss well with half of the sauce; spoon remainder atop individual portions, and put equal shares of shrimp and scallops atop each serving. Serves 4 to 6.

PESARO, on the Adriatic—The Marches

SPAGHETTINI E CROSTACEI ALLO SPIEDINO
Spaghettini and Skewered Shellfish

This is a dish designed to give color and dash to a serving of pasta.

6 lobster tails
½ pound shrimp
½ pound scallops
¾ cup Marsala
2 tablespoons olive oil
½ teaspoon ground ginger
½ teaspoon salt
1 garlic clove, minced
¼ cup soy sauce
1 pound spaghettini
6 tablespoons butter

Boil lobster tails and shrimp until tender; be careful not to overcook. Take from shells. Put lobster, shrimp, and raw scallops in a bowl. Make a mixture of the wine, oil, ginger, salt, and garlic. Pour it over the seafood, tossing well to make sure seafood is well covered. Let the mixture marinate for 1 hour. Cut each lobster tail into 3 pieces. Divide the seafood into 6 portions and thread the pieces on 6 individual skewers. Brush with soy sauce and broil, turning skewers until seafood is browned on all sides and scallops are tender. Cook spaghettini al dente; drain and toss with the butter. Serve pasta in hot individual bowls, with 1 skewer of seafood atop each serving. Serves 6.

RAVIOLI QUARESIMALI CON SALSA DI MOLLUSCO

A Lenten Ravioli with Shellfish Sauce

Filling:

3 tablespoons butter

1 small onion, coarsely chopped

1 small carrot, coarsely chopped

1 celery stalk, coarsely chopped

1 teaspoon salt

½ teaspoon freshly ground black pepper

½ cup dry white wine

Water

1 pound fine-textured white fish, such as
    sole or flounder

1 tablespoon lemon juice

2 tablespoons heavy cream

2 tablespoons minced parsley

2 egg yolks

Salt and freshly ground black pepper to
    taste

In a large deep fry pan, melt the butter. Add the onion, carrot, celery, salt, and pepper and cook 5 minutes. Add the wine and ½ cup of water. Simmer for 3 minutes. Add the fish and enough water barely to cover it. Simmer for 8 minutes, or just until the fish flakes with a fork. Drain well, discarding the vegetables. Mash the fish with a fork or use a food processor.

In a bowl combine and blend well the fish, lemon juice, cream, parsley, egg yolks, salt, and pepper. Fill the ravioli as directed on page 355 for Ravioli with Five Cheeses.

Sauce:

3 tablespoons butter

1 tablespoon olive oil

1 small onion, finely chopped

1 garlic clove, minced

4 medium-size ripe tomatoes, peeled, seeded, and chopped

Salt and freshly ground black pepper to taste

8 small mushrooms, quartered, cooked in 2 tablespoons butter until tender-crisp (reserve liquid)

18 large mussels, removed from their shells

30 medium-size shrimp (about 1 pound), peeled and deveined, cut into halves lengthwise

2 tablespoons chopped Italian parsley

In a saucepan, over medium heat, heat the butter and oil. Add the onion and garlic and cook until soft, about 2 minutes. Do not brown. Add the tomatoes, salt, and pepper and simmer, uncovered, for 10 minutes, or until much of the liquid has evaporated and the sauce has thickened. Add the mushrooms with the liquid they cooked in and the mussels and cook 1 minute. Add the shrimp and cook until they just turn pink and the mussels are firm, about 2 minutes. Do not overcook the shellfish, as it will toughen. Taste for seasoning. Stir in the parsley.

Cook the ravioli as directed on page 354 for Ravioli with Five Cheeses. Drain thoroughly and serve with the mussel-and-shrimp sauce spooned atop. Serves 6.

LINGUINE TUTTO MARE

Linguine All Sea

8 tablespoons olive oil

2 garlic cloves

4 cups (one 2-pound can) plum tomatoes

1 tablespoon chopped Italian parsley

Pinch of dried rosemary

½ teaspoon capers

1 teaspoon salt

Milled black pepper

6 littleneck clams, scrubbed

6 mussels, scrubbed

12 shrimp, shelled and deveined

6 *calamari* (small squid), cleaned and
diced

1 pound *linguine*

Heat 6 tablespoons of the olive oil in a saucepan, add garlic, and sauté until light brown. Remove garlic and discard. Add the tomatoes, breaking them up with a wooden spoon as they simmer, the parsley, rosemary, capers, salt, and pepper. Simmer, uncovered, for 40 minutes. Place the remaining oil in another large pan; add the clams and mussels and cook over very low heat until shells open. Take meat from shells and add clams, mussels, and all their juices to the tomato sauce. Stir in the shrimp and the *calamari* and simmer, uncovered, for 10 minutes. Cook *linguine* al dente and drain. Toss with half of the seafood sauce and spoon the remainder over individual portions before they are served. Serves 6.

CONCHIGLIE (SCUNGILLI) ALLA MARINARA

Conch with Tomato Sauce

   1 small can (10 ounces) *conchiglie* (conch)
   2 tablespoons olive oil
   1 garlic clove
   2 cups (one 1-pound can) plum tomatoes
   1 teaspoon dried sweet basil
   ¼ teaspoon crushed red pepper
   1 pound *linguine*

Rinse the *conchiglie* three times, once in hot water, twice in cold, then drain and dice it. In a saucepan, over medium heat, heat the oil, add the garlic and diced conch, and sauté for 5 minutes. Remove and discard garlic. When conch bits are browned, stir in the tomatoes, breaking them up with a wooden spoon as they cook. When the sauce is smooth, stir in basil and red pepper. Simmer for 15 minutes, or until conch is tender and sauce is no longer watery, but be careful not to overcook. Cook *linguine* al dente; drain. Serve the pasta in hot soup bowls with the *conchiglie* sauce over each serving. Serves 4 to 6.

LINGUINE E CALAMARETTI AL BURRO

Linguine with Tiny Squid and Butter

This is a dish we have often had in restaurants along the Adriatic coast. Cala-maretti are tiny inkfish, a species of squid. About the size of a five-cent piece, they are nut-sweet and delicious.

   1 tablespoon olive oil
   ¼ pound butter
   2 dozen whole *calamaretti*

½ teaspoon salt
Milled black pepper
1 pound *linguine*

Heat the oil and butter in a saucepan. Add the *calamaretti,* sprinkle with the salt, and liberally mill pepper over them. Sauté, uncovered, for 15 minutes, or until the tiny squid are tender. Cook *linguine* al dente, drain, and place in a hot bowl. Pour squid with their liquid over the pasta; toss well but gently with wooden forks. Serve immediately in hot soup bowls. Serves 4 to 6.

Note: This is often varied with an addition of shrimp, and sometimes with a dozen tiny whole fish, too.

SPAGHETTINI CON CALAMARI

Spaghettini with Baby Squid

This dish is usually served before baked eel with bay leaf, on Christmas Eve. The small calamari *are used, and there is quite a difference between squid and octopus in the Italian culinary repertoire. The octopi, always larger and tougher, actually need a beating before they are cooked to make them tender.* Calamari *are naturally tender and sweet flavored.*

12 fresh *calamari*
3 tablespoons olive oil
1 garlic clove, cut into 3 pieces
4 cups (one 2-pound can) plum tomatoes
¼ teaspoon crushed red pepper
Salt to taste
1 pound spaghettini

Clean the *calamari*, removing the bones, which lift out like pieces of plastic. Split down the center, wash away the gelatinous matter, and rinse well. Then cut into pieces straight across, as you would slice a loaf of bread. In a saucepan, over medium heat, heat the oil and sauté the squid and garlic in it until the squid pieces curl into circles. Add the tomatoes, breaking them up with a wooden spoon as they simmer. Stir in red pepper and salt; simmer, uncovered, for 15 minutes until sauce thickens and pieces of *calamari* become fork-tender. Cook spaghettini al dente; drain well; serve in hot soup bowls with *calamari* sauce spooned liberally over each portion. Serves 4 to 6.

BARLETTA—Apulia

VII
Meats with Pasta

*T*he Italians have a high talent for combining a large variety of meats with pasta, which is demonstrated in this chapter (and in "Recipes from Friends, Romans, and Countrymen"). Their flexibility and versatility have inspired many of us to experiment. One such experiment resulted in perhaps the tastiest *carbonara* we've had. The pasta chef who contributed the recipe is David L. Minter, an American. Check it out on page 208.

Many of us find it odd that in Italy it is impossible to find that American favorite, spaghetti with meatballs, so popular here and served so often that it has become worse than a cliché. The Italians do use plenty of beef, beef ground in sauce, steak, fillets, beef stewed to produce a zesty sauce, even beef liver. But meatballs, no.

We did, however, find a meatball once. In Siena. A giant meatball that was not served with the pasta, but sliced afterward for the entrée. It is an exceptional dish. The recipe follows.

CHÂTEAU DE FENIS—Valle d'Aosta

SPAGHETTINI E POLPETTONE

Spaghettini and Meatball

2 white onions, chopped
4 tablespoons olive oil
3 pounds beef chuck, freshly ground
3 whole eggs, beaten
2 cups bread crumbs
2 tablespoons chopped fresh parsley
1 cup freshly grated Asiago cheese
1 tablespoon minced raisins
2 teaspoons salt
Liberal amount of milled black pepper
1 recipe Basic Tomato Sauce (page 76)
1½ pounds spaghettini

In a saucepan, over medium heat, sauté the onions in 1 tablespoon of the oil until they are soft and yellow but not brown or burned. Place another spoon of oil on a pastry board, put all of the meat on it, and work it with the hands until the meat is soft and malleable. Then add the beaten eggs, bread crumbs, parsley, and half of the cheese, working them all in well. Now add the cooked onions, the raisins, and salt, and mill in pepper liberally. Knead everything into the meat, forming it into a large solid ball and patting it into shape.

Pour the remaining 2 tablespoons of oil into a large pot, one that can go into the oven. On top of the stove over a low fire, brown the big ball of meat, turning it as it becomes crisp so that all areas of the surface are brown and firm. Heat the tomato sauce and pour over the meatball. Cover the pot and bake in a preheated 350° F. oven until the meat is cooked through; every 10 minutes spoon more sauce liberally over it, basting it as it cooks. Time should be about 1 hour.

Place meatball on a warm serving platter. Cook the spaghettini al dente, drain, and serve in individual hot soup bowls. Spoon some of the sauce that simmered with the meat over each serving. Serve remaining cheese at table with the pasta. Follow with the whole meatball on its platter and carve at the table. Serve remaining sauce in a sauceboat with the meat. Serves 6.

SPAGHETTI ALLA BOLOGNESE

A classic dish. This should be cooked for company at least every other month, to keep your hand in for making the sauce and keeping taste buds in trim. In our opinion, it is the best of all meat sauces and has been the means of converting many a gourmet who pooh-poohs pasta as an insignificant food. The last convert we made was a French chef, a duck-shooting companion who placed Italian cookery on the same plane with American—which can be pretty low. He ate so much of the pasta in this sauce, demanding second helpings, that the entrée of fillet of beef was left for another day.

   3 cups Bolognese Sauce (page 82)
   2 tablespoons soft butter
   ¼ pound Romano cheese, grated
   ¼ pound Parmesan cheese, grated
   1 pound spaghetti

Prepare the Bolognese sauce and simmer, uncovered. Mix the butter and half of the cheese and place in a large hot bowl. Cook spaghetti al dente, drain, and place in the bowl. Toss well but gently with butter and cheese, making certain each strand is coated. Serve in hot soup bowls with Bolognese sauce liberally spooned atop each serving. Pass remaining cheese at table. Serves 6.

RICCIOLINI GENOVESE

"Little Curls" with Beef-Vegetable Sauce

3 tablespoons olive oil

1 pound finely ground beef (lean chuck or round)

4 medium-size carrots, scraped, cut into
    1-inch pieces

2 celery stalks, scraped, cut into 1-inch pieces

1 medium-size onion, quartered

2 garlic cloves, halved

1 teaspoon salt

⅛ teaspoon (or to taste) crushed red pepper

1 pound *ricciolini*, cooked in boiling salted water
    until al dente, drained

4 tablespoons butter

1 cup grated Asiago or Parmesan cheese

In a deep saucepan, over medium heat, heat the olive oil and cook the beef, stirring, for 5 minutes. In a food processor, purée the carrots, celery, onion, and garlic. Add to the beef, blending well. Sprinkle with the salt and red pepper, and simmer, stirring, for 5 to 8 minutes. Taste for seasoning.

Place the hot pasta in a hot bowl. Add the butter to the sauce, stirring it in until melted and well blended. (Adding the butter at the last minute gives the sauce a burnished look.) Add the sauce to the pasta, several spoonfuls at a time, and toss after each addition. Serve in hot bowls. Pass the cheese at the table. Serves 6.

BUCATINI CON SALSA DI MANZO

Bucatini with Beef Sauce

We had this simple and classic dish in several homes in Rome and were lucky enough to get the recipe from one of our hostesses.

½ recipe Beef Sauce (page 82)

1 pound *bucatini* (small macaroni)

4 tablespoons butter, melted
½ cup grated Asiago cheese
Milled black pepper

Prepare the beef sauce. Cook the *bucatini* al dente, drain, and place in a hot bowl with the melted butter. Toss well with wooden forks. Mix the grated Asiago with liberal amounts of milled black pepper. Add to the pasta and toss again, gently. Serve in hot soup bowls with a large spoonful of the beef sauce atop each serving. Serves 4 to 6.

FETTUCCELLE CON BISTECCA ALLA PIZZAIOLA

"Little Ribbons" with Steak and Pizzaiola Sauce

4 tablespoons olive oil
2 garlic cloves
4 cups (one 2-pound can) plum tomatoes,
    pushed through food mill
1 teaspoon salt
Liberal amount of milled black pepper
1 tablespoon chopped Italian parsley
¼ teaspoon dried oregano
1 pound prime sirloin steak
1 pound *fettuccelle* (narrow *fettuccine*)

In a saucepan, over medium heat, heat 2 tablespoons of the oil; sauté garlic until brown; discard garlic. Stir in tomatoes, salt, pepper, parsley, and oregano; simmer, uncovered, stirring often, for 20 minutes, or until sauce has thickened. Slice the steak into thin bite-size pieces. In another saucepan heat the remaining olive oil and add the steak pieces. Sauté for 5 minutes, turning once. Pieces of steak should be pink and tender. When tomato sauce is sufficiently thickened, stir in the steak slices. Remove sauce from fire. Cook *fettuccelle* al dente; drain. Serve immediately in hot soup bowls with the sauce and steak slices generously spooned atop each portion. Serves 6.

Near ASCOLI PICENO—The Marches

LINGUINE CON BISTECCA TRITATA ALLA GIOVANNINO

Linguine and Chopped Beef alla Giovannino

2½ pounds beef sirloin, chopped
½ pound ripe Gorgonzola cheese
1 teaspoon salt
5 tablespoons butter, in all
½ pound *linguine*

Make 5 meat patties 2½ inches thick. In the center of each bury a 1½-inch cube of Gorgonzola cheese, centering it and molding the meat well around it so the cheese is completely covered. Sprinkle lightly with salt. Cook the patties in a frypan with 2 tablespoons of the butter, in the French style, sautéing, turning often, until they are browned outside but the meat inside is pink and the cheese melted. This takes about 15 minutes. Remove 4 of the patties to a warm plate; crumble the 1 remaining in the pan, stirring the meat well into the browned butter in the pan, adding another 2 tablespoons of butter as you stir.

Cook *linguine* in rapidly boiling salted water until al dente, drain, and toss with remaining tablespoon of butter. Then toss with half of the butter-meat mixture, spooning what is remaining over individual servings. Follow with the sirloin-cheese patties, with fresh broccoli and a romaine salad. Serves 4.

BAVETTINE ALLA CARNACINA GIOVANNINO

Giovannino's Bavettine with Meat

Since we sometimes like to cook on a chafing dish right in the dining room where we can talk with our guests, we dreamed up this recipe one night when we had a piece of fillet of beef and a few slices of prosciutto in the refrigerator. This is one of the pleasures of pasta—it blends happily with almost everything and gives free rein to the imagination.

1 beef fillet (¾ pound), uncooked

4 thin slices of prosciutto

5 tablespoons butter

4 shallots, chopped

1 garlic clove, minced

6 medium mushrooms, thinly sliced

1 pound *bavettine* (very narrow *linguine*)

1 cup dry white wine

⅓ cup grated Asiago cheese

2 tablespoons chopped Italian parsley

Between drinks and conversation, chop the beef and the prosciutto on a board until very fine. Melt the butter in a copper chafing dish over high flame. Sauté the shallots and garlic in the butter until they are soft. Stir in the mushrooms and the chopped beef and prosciutto. Cook for just under 10 minutes, stirring constantly. Cook *bavettine* only until chewy, just over half done; drain. Lower the flame under the chafing dish, stir in the wine, and blend well with the meat sauce. Add the underdone pasta, toss gently but well, and sprinkle in the cheese. Cook 3 minutes. Put out the flame, toss again, and sprinkle in the parsley. Serve immediately from the chafing dish. Serves 4 to 6.

LINGUE DI PASSERI ALLA MACELLAIO
"Sparrows' Tongues" Butcher's Style

4 tablespoons chopped prosciutto fat
   (only the fat)

2 garlic cloves, peeled and cut into quarters

2 tablespoons olive oil

½ pound beef chuck, ground

½ teaspoon salt, or to taste

Liberal amount of milled black pepper

2 cups (one 1-pound can) plum tomatoes

1 pound *lingue di passeri*

2 tablespoons butter

Cook prosciutto fat and garlic in the oil in a frypan until soft. Add the ground beef and salt and pepper, mixing well together. Cook until beef is done but not overdone, on the pink side. Put the tomatoes through food mill; stir the purée into the meat mixture, blending well. Mill in more black pepper, stir, and cook until most of the water has evaporated from the tomatoes. Cook *lingue di passeri* al dente; drain. Toss in the butter, then 2 spoonfuls of the meat combination. Serve in individual hot bowls, with another spoonful of meat sauce on top of each portion. If a guest bites into a garlic clove, it's a plus like finding a pearl in an oyster. Serves 4 to 6.

MOSTACCIOLI CON MANZO E MELANZANE

"Small Moustaches" with Beef and Eggplant

Here is an old-fashioned Italian "Sunday special" right out of Campobasso.

8 tablespoons olive oil, in all
4 slices of prosciutto, minced
2 white onions, chopped
2-pound piece of top round of beef
1 cup white wine
2½ pounds tomatoes, peeled and diced
1¼ teaspoons salt, in all
Milled black pepper
2 tablespoons butter
5 mushrooms, sliced
3 chicken livers, chopped
1 pound *mostaccioli*
1 eggplant (1½ pounds), cut in small strips
¼ cup grated Parmesan cheese

Heat 2 tablespoons of the oil in a large deep saucepan; stir in the prosciutto and onions and sauté until soft. Add the beef round and brown over high flame; lower heat, add the wine, and cook, uncovered, stirring and turning the meat until the wine has evaporated. Stir in the tomatoes and season with 1 teaspoon salt and some pepper. Cover the pan and simmer, stirring often and frequently basting the meat, for 2 hours, or until meat is tender. Remove and reserve beef.

In another large saucepan, over medium heat, sauté in the butter the mushrooms and livers for 5 minutes; sprinkle with ¼ teaspoon salt, stir, and keep warm. Push the sauce from the beef pot through a sieve; dice the beef; add beef and sauce to livers and mushrooms; blend well. Cook the *mostaccioli* al dente, drain, and place in a hot bowl. Sauté the eggplant strips in remaining olive oil until tender and lightly browned. Sprinkle Parmesan on the pasta; toss. Add half of the sauce and toss again well but gently. Serve in hot soup bowls, with strips of eggplant atop each serving. Pass extra sauce and grated cheese at table. Serves 6.

FUSILLI CON FEGATO DI MANZO

"Twists" with Beef Liver

In Rome beef liver may be used instead of calf's liver. Some believe that it has more flavor. We agree—if the liver is prepared their way; it must be sliced thin and cooked quickly.

5 tablespoons butter

1 tablespoon olive oil

10 mushrooms, chopped fine

1 white onion, minced

1 carrot, scraped and minced

1 celery rib, scraped and minced

½ cup Marsala

1 cup Beef Broth (page 96)

1 pound beef liver, cut into slices ¼ inch
    thick

1 teaspoon salt

Liberal amount of milled black pepper

1 pound *fusilli*

¾ cup grated Asiago cheese

In a saucepan, over medium heat, melt 4 tablespoons of the butter, add the oil, and sauté mushrooms, onion, carrot, and celery until onion is soft. Add wine and simmer until it has evaporated. Stir in beef broth and simmer. Dice liver, season with salt and pepper, and put in another saucepan with 1 tablespoon of butter. Cook for 1 minute, turn the pieces, and cook for another minute. Liver should be pink. Add to the vegetable sauce and blend well. Remove from heat. Cook *fusilli* al dente; drain. Place in a large hot bowl, pour the liver sauce over pasta, and toss well. Serve immediately in hot rimmed soup bowls. Pass cheese at table. Serves 6.

SPAGHETTINI CON DADINI DI VITELLO

Spaghettini with Little Veal Cubes

2 tablespoons olive oil
2 tablespoons butter
2 white onions, chopped
1 pound veal steak, cubed
1½ tablespoons flour
1 teaspoon salt, or to taste
Milled black pepper
¼ teaspoon dried oregano
1 cup Chicken Broth (page 96)
Juice of ½ lemon
¼ cup grated Parmesan cheese
1 pound spaghettini

In a saucepan, over medium heat, heat oil and butter and sauté onions until soft. Dredge the veal cubes in flour and season with salt, pepper, and oregano; brown in the oil and butter. Stir in the chicken broth and simmer, uncovered, for 10 minutes. Remove from fire and stir in the lemon juice. Place the mixture in a baking dish, sprinkle with a little of the cheese, and cover. Cook in a preheated 400° F. oven for 20 minutes, or until sauce is thickened and veal fork-tender. Cook spaghettini al dente, drain, and place in a hot bowl. Toss with the remaining cheese, then with half of the veal mixture. Spoon the rest of the veal sauce atop individual portions served in hot soup bowls. Serves 4 to 6.

PENNE CON VITELLO MILANESE

"Quills" with Veal Milanese Style

3 tablespoons chopped parsley

1 tablespoon grated lemon rind

1 garlic clove, minced

2 anchovy fillets, chopped

8 tablespoons (1 stick) butter

2 tablespoons olive oil

2 pounds veal from the leg, trimmed, cut into
    pieces ½ inch thick and 1 inch square

Flour for dredging

3 medium-size onions, chopped

Salt and freshly ground black pepper to taste

1 cup dry white wine

1 carrot, scraped, cut into ¼-inch cubes

1 celery stalk, scraped, cut into ¼-inch cubes

⅛ teaspoon dried rosemary

½ cup tomato purée

2 cups chicken broth

1 pound *penne* or other short pasta such as *fusilli* or *ziti*, cooked al
    dente in boiling salted water, drained

Combine parsley, lemon rind, garlic, and anchovies in a small bowl and blend well with a fork. Set aside.

In a heavy pot, over medium heat, heat 3 tablespoons of butter and the olive oil. Lightly dredge the veal with flour. Add it to the hot fat and brown evenly. Add the onions and cook until soft, about 5 minutes. Do not brown. Season with salt and pepper. Add the wine and cook off about half of it. Add the carrot, celery, rosemary, tomato purée, and the chicken broth. Bring to a boil, lower heat, and simmer, covered, for 30 minutes, or until the veal is fork-tender. If the sauce gets too thick before the veal is tender, add a few tablespoons of hot broth or water. If the veal is tender before the sauce thickens, remove cover. Taste for seasoning.

In a bowl toss the hot pasta with the remaining butter (in small pieces) and a liberal amount of black pepper. Spoon into hot individual plates. Spoon over it some of the veal and its sauce, and top that with a spoonful of the parsley/lemon rind/anchovy mixture. Serve any remaining veal at the table. Serves 6.

MACCHERONI ALLA BOLOGNESE

This recipe comes from a housewife in the Po Valley and is a specialty of her family, handed down from her grandmother. In that region they use macaroni a bit larger than medium, called "horse's teeth." Anything from ziti to elbow macaroni will do.

5 tablespoons butter
1 tablespoon olive oil
2 small white onions, chopped
2 small carrots, scraped and chopped
1 celery rib, scraped and chopped
½ pound veal rump, ground twice
2 ounces dried beef, minced
Pinch of flour
Milled black pepper
2 cups Beef Broth (page 96)
2 chicken livers, chopped
1 pound macaroni
¼ cup grated Parmesan cheese
1 white truffle, thinly sliced (optional)
½ cup heavy cream, warmed

In a saucepan, over medium heat, sauté in the butter and oil the onions, carrots, and celery until soft. Stir in the veal and beef and sauté until veal is brown; add the flour, pepper, and broth, blending well. Simmer, uncovered, stirring often, for 20 minutes. Add the chicken livers and simmer for 5 minutes, stirring in well. Cook macaroni al dente without salt, for dried beef is salty; drain, place in a large warm bowl, stir in the sauce, and toss well. Add the cheese, half of the truffle, and all of the cream; toss again. Taste for seasoning. Serve immediately in hot bowls with the remaining truffle atop; pass more grated cheese at table. Serves 4 to 6.

VERMICELLI CON GNOCCHI DI VITELLO

Vermicelli with Veal Dumplings

¾ pound finely ground veal

½ cup finely chopped prosciutto or other
  cooked ham

3 tablespoons minced Italian parsley

2 eggs, beaten

1 small onion, minced, cooked in 2 tablespoons butter until soft but
  not brown

½ teaspoon salt

¼ teaspoon freshly ground black pepper

1 cup grated Asiago or Parmesan cheese

Flour for dusting dumplings

6 tablespoons butter

2 tablespoons olive oil

3 tablespoons dry vermouth

4 medium-size ripe tomatoes, peeled, seeded, and chopped, or 2 cups
  canned tomatoes, drained and chopped

1 tablespoon chopped fresh basil or 1 teaspoon dried sweet basil

1 pound *vermicelli*, cooked in boiling salted water until al dente,
  drained

In a bowl combine and blend well the veal, prosciutto, parsley, eggs, onion, salt and pepper, and 3 tablespoons of cheese. Shape into ¾-inch-long, egg-shaped dumplings. Dust lightly with flour. In a saucepan, over medium heat, heat 3 tablespoons of butter and the oil and brown the dumplings evenly. Pour in the vermouth and simmer until it evaporates. Add the tomatoes and basil and simmer for 30 minutes, or until the sauce has thickened. Taste for seasoning.

Toss the hot pasta with the remaining butter (in small pieces) and serve on hot individual plates with the sauce and veal dumplings spooned on top. Pass the remaining cheese at table. Serves 4 to 6 as a main course.

SPAGHETTI CON ROGNONI DI VITELLO

Spaghetti with Veal Kidneys

2 garlic cloves, mashed
¼ pound butter
2 pounds veal kidneys, cleaned, cored,
    and sliced thin
2 tablespoons flour
1½ teaspoons salt
Liberal amount of milled black pepper
6 anchovy fillets, drained and minced
Juice of ½ lemon
½ teaspoon dried tarragon or 1½ tea-
    spoons chopped fresh tarragon
1 tablespoon chopped parsley
1 pound spaghetti

In a saucepan, over medium heat, sauté garlic in butter until brown; discard garlic. Dust kidneys lightly with flour, sprinkle with salt and pepper, and sauté in the butter for 30 seconds on each side. Stir in the anchovies; add the lemon juice, tarragon, and parsley; blend. Simmer for 5 minutes, breaking up the anchovies. Cook spaghetti al dente; drain. Place in a large hot bowl, pour the kidney sauce over, and toss well. Serve immediately in hot rimmed soup bowls. Serves 6.

ANIMELLE DI VITELLO CON TRENETTE
Veal Sweetbreads with Trenette

2 pairs of veal sweetbreads
2 tablespoons lemon juice
1 teaspoon salt
Flour for dredging
7 tablespoons butter
1 tablespoon olive oil
1 small onion, finely chopped
Salt and freshly ground black pepper to taste
¼ cup brandy
¼ cup dry white wine
¼ cup chicken broth
1 pound *trenette* (or other thin noodle), cooked in boiling salted water
    until al dente, drained
1 cup grated Asiago or Parmesan cheese
½ cup heated (not boiling) heavy cream
1 fresh white truffle or 25-gram can white truffle, chopped (or 4 or 5
    dried wild mushrooms, soaked in warm water for ½ hour,
    drained, chopped, and sautéed in 2 tablespoons butter)

Soak the sweetbreads in ice water with 1 tablespoon of the lemon juice for 1 hour. Drain, place in a saucepan, cover with boiling water. Add the teaspoon of salt and remaining lemon juice and simmer for 15 minutes. Drain and plunge into ice water to cool. Drain and carefully remove and discard all membranes and connecting tubes.

Dust the sweetbreads lightly with flour. In a deepfry pan, over medium heat, heat 3 tablespoons of the butter and the oil. Add the sweetbreads and cook until golden. Add the onion and cook until soft. Sprinkle with salt and pepper. Pour on the brandy, ignite, and burn it off. Pour in the wine and broth, cover, and simmer for 15 minutes, or until sweetbreads are just firm. Do not overcook, as they will toughen. Remove and cut into ¾-inch cubes, then return to the pan with the juices to keep moist.

In a bowl, toss the hot pasta with the remaining butter (in small pieces) and half of the cheese. Add the cream, sweetbreads, and the liquid in the pan and mix carefully. Serve on individual hot dishes with some chopped truffle (or mushrooms) sprinkled on top. Pass the remaining cheese at table. Serves 6.

PIACENZA, the Piazza Cavalli—Emilia-Romagna

RIGATONI CON FEGATO DI VITELLO

Rigatoni with Calf's Liver

½ pound calf's liver
12 medium mushrooms, cleaned and
   peeled
2 tablespoons butter
1 tablespoon olive oil
1 teaspoon salt, or to taste
Liberal amount of milled black pepper
½ cup white Chianti
1 pound *rigatoni* (grooved pasta tubes)
¼ cup grated Asiago cheese

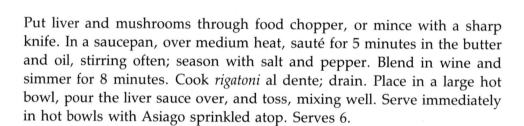

Put liver and mushrooms through food chopper, or mince with a sharp knife. In a saucepan, over medium heat, sauté for 5 minutes in the butter and oil, stirring often; season with salt and pepper. Blend in wine and simmer for 8 minutes. Cook *rigatoni* al dente; drain. Place in a large hot bowl, pour the liver sauce over, and toss, mixing well. Serve immediately in hot bowls with Asiago sprinkled atop. Serves 6.

SPAGHETTINI CON ANIMELLE DI VITELLO E PISELLI

Spaghettini with Veal Sweetbreads and Peas

4 small veal sweetbreads
2 tablespoons butter
2 tablespoons olive oil
1 teaspoon salt, or to taste
Liberal amount of milled black pepper
3 tablespoons fresh peas
1 pound spaghettini

Parboil sweetbreads in rapidly boiling water for 5 minutes; remove and plunge into cold water. When cool, remove the skins and membranes and cut sweetbreads into pieces the size of a fingernail. In a saucepan, over medium heat, sauté them in butter and oil, sprinkled with salt and pepper, for 15 minutes. Cook peas al dente, drain, and add to the sweetbreads; simmer for 5 minutes. Cook spaghettini al dente, drain, and place right in the saucepan with the sweetbreads and peas. Toss well and serve in hot bowls. Serves 4 to 6.

TAGLIATELLE CON TRIPPA ALLA ROMANA

Noodles with Tripe Roman Style

3 pounds fresh white veal honeycomb tripe

2 tablespoons chopped salt pork

3 tablespoons olive oil

1 lemon, cut into 1-inch slices

4 cups (one 2-pound can) plum tomatoes, mashed

⅓ teaspoon dried oregano

2 bay leaves

½ teaspoon salt

Liberal amount of milled black pepper

¼ teaspoon dried red pepper

3 tablespoons fresh peas, half cooked

1 pound *tagliatelle*

Wash tripe thoroughly in several waters; in a pot boil for about 3 hours in 4 quarts of salted water, covered, until tender, pouring off water twice during the boiling and replacing it with fresh hot water. When cooked, drain and cut into ½- by 2-inch pieces. In a saucepan, over medium heat, sauté salt pork in the oil, add lemon slices, tomatoes, oregano, bay leaves, salt, black pepper, red pepper, and drained tripe. Simmer, uncovered, for 30 minutes until sauce has thickened. Add the peas and simmer for 10 minutes longer. Remove and discard lemon slices and bay leaves. Cook *tagliatelle* al dente; drain. Serve in hot soup bowls with tripe sauce liberally spooned over each portion. Serves 4 to 6.

PERCIATELLI ALLA CARRETTIERE

"Pierced" Pasta Cart Driver's Style

3 tablespoons olive oil

1 garlic clove, minced

2 white onions, chopped

1 small piece of green *peperoncino* (hot pepper), diced finely

¼ pound pig's jaw, mostly lean, diced, or use thick-sliced lean bacon

½ teaspoon salt

3 large very ripe tomatoes, peeled and diced

1 can (3½ ounces) tuna in olive oil, broken into pieces

4 mushrooms, sliced

4½ tablespoons grated Romano cheese

1 pound *perciatelli*

In a saucepan, over medium heat, sauté in oil the garlic, onions, and green pepper; add the pig's jaw (or bacon) and sauté until soft. Sprinkle lightly with salt and stir in the tomatoes. Simmer, uncovered, for 25 minutes until pork is tender and sauce thickened. Add the tuna, mushrooms, and ½ tablespoon of the cheese; blend well; simmer for 10 minutes. Cook *perciatelli* al dente, drain, and place in a large hot bowl. Sprinkle in the cheese and half of the sauce; toss well with wooden forks. Serve immediately in hot soup bowls with generous spoonings of remaining sauce atop each portion. Pass more grated cheese at table. Serves 6.

MAGLIETTE SPACCATE CON DUE CARNI

"Split Links" with Two Meats

½ pound beef, chopped
½ pound lean pork, chopped
2 garlic cloves, minced
2 tablespoons olive oil
4 cups (one 2-pound can) plum tomatoes,
   pushed through a food mill
1 teaspoon salt, or to taste
Freshly milled black pepper
1 teaspoon sugar
1 teaspoon dried sweet basil
1 pound *magliette spaccate*
1 tablespoon soft butter
¼ cup grated ricotta siciliano cheese

In a saucepan, over medium heat, brown meats and garlic in the oil; stir in tomatoes, and add salt, pepper, sugar, and basil. Simmer sauce for 40 minutes, uncovered, stirring often with a wooden spoon. Cook *magliette spaccate* al dente, drain, and toss in a bowl with butter and cheese. Pour in half of the sauce and toss again. Serve in hot bowls with generous spoonful of remaining sauce atop each serving. Pass more grated cheese at table. Serves 4 to 6.

FARFALLONI ALLA FRANCESCO

"Big Butterflies" Francesco

This is a memorable dish cooked by a chef named Francesco in a little restaurant at San Remo. It overlooked a famous five-acre carnation garden that flowed like a red tide toward the sea, the perfume from the flowers so sweet and strong that we can never forget them—nor the dish.

6 tablespoons butter, in all

1 tablespoon olive oil

4 shallots, chopped

2 celery ribs, scraped and chopped

1 garlic clove, minced

6 mushrooms, sliced

¼ pound veal, ground twice

¼ pound pork, ground twice

¼ pound beef, ground twice

3 pounds fresh tomatoes, peeled, seeded,
    and diced

1 bay leaf

¼ teaspoon dried oregano

1 teaspoon salt, or to taste

Liberal amount of milled black pepper

1 pound *farfalloni*

1 tablespoon chopped Italian parsley

¼ pound Parmesan cheese, grated

Heat 4 tablespoons of the butter and the oil in a deep saucepan. Sauté shallots, celery, garlic, mushrooms, and the meats until meats are browned. Stir in the tomatoes, bay leaf, oregano, salt, and pepper. Simmer, uncovered, stirring often with a wooden spoon, for 35 minutes, or until sauce is thickened and smooth. Cook *farfalloni* al dente; drain. Place in a large hot bowl, add remaining butter, the parsley, and half of the cheese; toss well. Serve in large hot soup bowls with sauce liberally spooned atop each portion. Pass the remaining cheese at table. Serves 6.

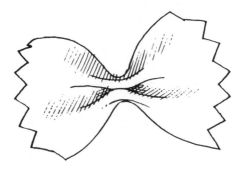

PAPPARDELLE ALLA TOSCANA

Broad Noodles with Pork, Anchovy Fillets, and Tomato Sauce

6 tablespoons butter
1 tablespoon olive oil
2 slices of *pancetta* (or bacon), chopped
1 medium-size onion, finely chopped
1 celery stalk, scraped, finely chopped
½ pound coarsely ground lean pork
½ cup dry vermouth
4 anchovy fillets, drained and chopped
2 cups Basic Tomato Sauce (page 76) or
    other mild tomato sauce
1 pound *pappardelle,* cooked al dente in
    boiling salted water, drained
Freshly ground black pepper to taste
1 cup grated Asiago or Parmesan cheese
Salt to taste

In a heavy saucepan, over medium heat, heat 2 tablespoons of the butter and the olive oil. Add the *pancetta* and cook 2 minutes. Add the onion and celery and cook until soft, about 5 minutes. Do not brown. Add the pork and cook, stirring, until browned. Pour in the vermouth and cook off about half of it. Stir in the anchovy fillets and tomato sauce, cover and simmer 20 minutes, stirring occasionally. The anchovies should be completely disintegrated by this time. If the sauce becomes too thick, add a few spoonfuls of hot water.

In a bowl toss the hot pasta with the remaining butter (in small pieces), pepper, and one third of the cheese. Taste before adding salt. Add one third of the sauce and toss. Spoon the remaining sauce over each serving. Pass the remaining cheese at table. Serves 6.

PASTA E FAGIOLI ALLA PASQUALE

Pasquale's Pasta and Beans

    1 pound dried pea beans
    3-pound loin of pork
    2 teaspoons salt
    Milled black pepper
    1 garlic clove
    3 tablespoons olive oil
    2 cups (one 1-pound can) plum tomatoes,
        pushed through a food mill
    2 cups *ditalini* ("little thimbles")

Soak beans in water for 5 hours; drain. Place pork in a large pot with 4 quarts water, cook for 1 hour, then pour off water. Add 4 quarts fresh water, 2 teaspoons salt, a liberal amount of pepper, the garlic, and oil. Add the drained beans and puréed tomatoes. Simmer for 40 minutes, or until beans and pork are tender, stirring often but carefully.

Cook *ditalini* al dente, drain, and add to the bean pot, stirring in well. Simmer, uncovered, for 10 minutes. Slice the pork. Serve beans and pasta in hot soup bowls, with pork slices on top and buttered hot Italian bread on the side. This is a main dish, not a first course. Serves 4 to 6.

LINGUE DI PASSERI CON SALSA D'UOVA

"Sparrows' Tongues" and Pork in Egg Sauce

    2 eggs
    3 tablespoons butter, in all
    1 tablespoon olive oil
    ½ pound lean pork, ground
    ¼ pound lean salt pork, cubed
    Pinch of cayenne pepper
    ¼ pound Parmesan cheese, grated

Rind of ½ lemon, grated

1 pound *lingue di passeri*

Take eggs from refrigerator to remove chill. Heat 1 tablespoon of the butter and the oil in a saucepan. Make little fingers of the ground pork, about half the size of your little finger, and sauté with the diced salt pork, turning often until browned. In a large warm bowl beat together the eggs, cayenne pepper, cheese, and lemon rind with a whisk until well blended and creamy. Stir in pork fingers and salt pork with their oil and butter. Cook *lingue di passeri* al dente. Fork directly from the boiling pot, draining water from each forkful back into the pot, into the bowl with the eggs and pork. Hot pasta should set eggs. Melt remaining butter and pour hot over the pasta in the egg bowl. Toss all quickly and serve immediately in hot soup bowls. Serves 4 to 6.

BUCATINI ALL'AMATRICIANA

This is a famous dish in Rome, where nearly every good restaurant offers it with pride. It is said to have originated in the Abruzzi region, known for its lusty but simple dishes, although we never found it there. It should be made with the cheek of a young pig, using all of the lean and half of the fat. Often it is made with a small hot red pepper chopped in, but as we had it in Rome, a sweet pepper was substituted, and bacon was used rather than pork cheek.

2 small white onions, chopped

1 sweet red pepper, cored and chopped

¼ pound salt pork, diced

3 tablespoons olive oil

8 slices of bacon, diced

4 cups (one 2-pound can) plum tomatoes, or
2 pounds fresh tomatoes, peeled, seeded, and diced

Liberal amount of milled black pepper

1 pound *bucatini* (thin macaroni)

2 tablespoons butter

½ cup grated Romano cheese

ROME, the Arch of Constantine

In a saucepan, over medium heat, sauté onions and pepper with salt pork in the oil until pork is nearly crisp but not too hard; stir, add bacon, and cook for 5 minutes. Blend in tomatoes, mill in pepper, and stir. Taste for seasoning. If salt is needed, add to taste, but salt pork and bacon should make it sufficiently salty. Stir well and simmer, uncovered, for 25 minutes. Cook *bucatini* al dente, drain. Place in a bowl with the butter, toss, add the cheese, mill in black pepper, and toss again. Serve pasta in individual hot bowls, with a liberal spooning of the sauce over each portion. Serves 4 to 6.

LINGUINE ALLA CARBONARA

Pasta alla carbonara is a favorite way of serving bacon and eggs in Rome. There are perhaps a dozen ways to prepare it: the bacon undercooked; the pasta tossed in the frypan with the bacon or with ham; mixed in a bowl, with wine and onion. The name is a difficult one to pin down. Carbonara *refers both to a secret society that at one time tried to overthrow the Italian government and to the men who work with coal. To us, however, it is one of the most unusual of the pasta dishes, and we read nothing else into its name except flavor.*

12 slices of bacon
2 eggs, beaten
1 cup grated Asiago cheese
3 tablespoons chopped Italian parsley
Much milled black pepper
1 pound *linguine*

Cut bacon into pieces the size of a fingernail; in a frypan, cook until crisp, pouring off the grease as it cooks. In a large bowl, combine the eggs, cheese, and parsley; mill in plenty of black pepper. Beat with a whisk, or an electric beater, until the mixture is creamy and very well blended. Add a tablespoon of the crisp bacon; mix again. Place the bowl on the back of the stove so that it warms, but doesn't get too hot and cook the eggs. Cook the *linguine* al dente. *Do not drain.* Fork directly from the pasta cooking pot into the warm bowl with the egg sauce, shaking off the water before you add each forkful of pasta to the bowl. The pasta *must* be very hot, so that it slightly sets the eggs as you toss it. Toss well, but gently, with forks. Serve in very hot soup bowls, with a large spoonful of the crisp hot bacon pieces atop each serving. Serves 4 to 6.

DAVID L. MINTER'S CARBONARA

One of the early fans of this book is our friend David Minter, who soon proved to be a master of pasta cookery. We suspect that's one of the appeals of pasta: It stirs the creative senses. Here, David Minter has taken a classic and converted it into a superclassic, better than any carbonara we've ever tasted.

½ pound thick-cut bacon, cut into 1-inch squares
4 tablespoons olive oil
3 medium-size onions, chopped
½ cup shredded prosciutto
1½ pounds *fedelini* (thin string pasta),
    cooked al dente after sauce is made
3 egg yolks, lightly beaten
⅛ teaspoon crushed red pepper
Much freshly milled black pepper
½ teaspoon dried oregano
1½ cups diced (¼-inch cubes) Fontina cheese
1½ cups grated Asiago cheese
1 cup chopped Italian parsley
1 cup chopped curly parsley

In a frypan, over medium heat, cook the bacon until crisp, but still somewhat on the chewy side. Remove and reserve the bacon, and drain the pan. Pour in the olive oil, add the onions, and cook over medium heat just until the onions are soft. Do not brown. Stir in the prosciutto and cook until hot.

Place the cooked, *very* hot *fedelini* in a large hot bowl. Add the bacon, onion, prosciutto (and the oil left in the pan), egg yolks, red pepper, a generous milling of black pepper, oregano, the diced Fontina, 1 cup of grated Asiago, and the parsley. Working fast, so everything remains warm, use wooden forks to toss all together well to blend. Serve immediately in hot bowls with the remaining Asiago sprinkled atop. Serves 6.

PASTICCIO DI PASTA E PROSCIUTTO
Fresh Pasta and Ham Pie

We note that in Chapter II we neglected to describe properly one of the oldest of pasta categories; pasticci—twice-cooked pasta. These are dishes in which the ingredients are cooked separately, then assembled, sometimes topped with a sauce, then baked. Technically, lasagne *is a* pasticcio, *which we have placed in the* pasta al forno *category. But* pasticci *is an older and more all-inclusive word.*

Sometimes, however, pasticci *are handled differently—placed in a thick pastry shell and then baked. Frequently, although some purists will disagree with the terminology, such* pasticci *are called* timballi *or* timpani. *We've made several and placed them in the chapters where they belong. Two follow.*

1 recipe Pasta Fresca for Ravioli (page 59)

5 tablespoons butter, softened

2 eggs, separated

6 slices of prosciutto, diced

1 cup yogurt

2 tablespoons bread crumbs

Prepare dough, cut into squares, and dry, according to recipe. Cook al dente; drain well. Place butter, egg yolks, prosciutto, and yogurt in a large bowl and beat with a whisk until well blended and creamy; stir in the pasta squares. Beat the 2 egg whites until stiff and stir them into the bowl, blending well. Butter a baking dish, dust it with the bread crumbs, and pour in the egg-ham-pasta mixture. Bake in a preheated 350° F. oven for 35 minutes. Serves 4 to 6.

PASTICCIO DI TAGLIATELLE ALLA PARMA

Baked Tagliatelle with Chicken Livers and Ham

9 tablespoons (1 stick plus 1 tablespoon) butter
1 tablespoon olive oil
1 medium-size onion, finely chopped
⅓ pound (about 6) chicken livers, trimmed and coarsely chopped
Salt and freshly ground black pepper to taste
2 ounces Marsala
¾ pound lean prosciutto (or other cooked ham), cut into julienne
    strips
8 small mushrooms, sliced and sautéed in 2 additional tablespoons
    butter with 1 tablespoon lemon juice until crisp-tender
1 pound *tagliatelle*, cooked in boiling salted water until quite al dente,
    drained
3 eggs
¾ cup medium cream (or half-and-half)
¾ cup grated Parmesan cheese
Fine dry bread crumbs

In a deep frypan, over medium heat, heat 3 tablespoons of butter and the
olive oil. Add the onion; cook for 2 minutes, or until soft. Do not brown.
Add the chicken livers, sprinkle lightly with salt and pepper, and cook
until brown on the outside but still slightly pink inside, about 3 minutes.
Add the Marsala, raise heat, and cook it off. Remove from heat and mix
in the prosciutto and mushrooms. Taste for seasoning.

In a bowl, toss the hot pasta with 4 tablespoons of butter (in small pieces)
until the butter has melted. Add the chicken-liver–ham mixture and toss
again carefully, blending well.

Butter a baking dish. Sprinkle the sides and bottom generously with
bread crumbs. Carefully spoon in the pasta.

In a bowl beat together the eggs, cream (or half-and-half), ½ cup of the
cheese, and a liberal amount of black pepper. Spoon this over the pasta.
Sprinkle with the remaining cheese and lightly with bread crumbs, and
dot with the remaining butter. Place in a preheated 350° F. oven for 30
minutes, or until the sauce has set and the top is golden. Serves 6.

TAGLIARINI FRESCHI ALLA GIUSEPPE

Homemade Noodles alla Joseph

1 pound *tagliarini,* fresh (pages 52 and 58)
¼ pound butter
¼ pound lean bacon, diced
1 pound fresh ricotta cheese
¼ pound Parmesan cheese, grated

Prepare the *tagliarini* and dry. While they are drying, melt butter in a saucepan, add the bacon, and cook until brown but not crisp. Cook the fresh pasta al dente; watch carefully, as fresh pasta cooks quickly; drain. Into hot soup bowls spoon a layer of ricotta cheese; place the drained *tagliarini* atop, spoon the bacon-and-butter sauce over it, and sprinkle with Parmesan. Serve immediately. Serves 6.

MAFALDA ALLA MARIA LIMONCELLI

Maria's Broad Noodles with Bacon, Veal, and Chicken Livers

10 slices of bacon, chopped
4 white onions, chopped
½ pound veal, chopped
2 tablespoons butter
1 very ripe large beefsteak tomato,
   peeled, seeded, and coarsely chopped
1 teaspoon salt, or to taste
Liberal amount of milled black pepper
1¼ cups Chicken Broth (page 96)
6 chicken livers, chopped
1 pound *mafalda* (a broad noodle, rippled
   on both edges)

Over medium heat, cook the bacon in a large frypan; when soft, add the onions and cook until golden. Add the chopped veal and cook, stirring bacon, veal, and onions together until veal is lightly browned. Simmer over low flame; add the butter, tomato, and salt, and mill in pepper. Add the chicken broth, cover, and simmer for 45 minutes. Blend in chicken livers and simmer, uncovered, for another 7 minutes. Cook *mafalda* al dente, drain, and serve in hot bowls. Spoon sauce over the pasta. Serves 4 to 6.

MAGLIETTE RIGATE ALLA GIOVANNINO

"Grooved Links" Giovannino

    12 slices of bacon
    2 medium-size white onions, chopped
    Tips of 2 celery ribs with leaves
    8 fresh basil leaves, chopped, or 1 table-
        spoon dried sweet basil
    4 cups (one 2-pound can) plum tomatoes,
        pushed through a food mill
    Liberal amount of milled black pepper
    Salt to taste
    1 pound *magliette rigate*
    2 tablespoons butter
    ½ cup grated Asiago cheese

Chop bacon and sauté over medium heat in a large frypan until half done. Add onions and celery; simmer until vegetables are soft. Add the basil and the tomatoes, mill in black pepper, stir well, and simmer for 15 minutes. Then cook for another 10 minutes over high flame to reduce the sauce and thicken it. Taste and add salt. Prepare *magliette rigate* al dente; be careful not to break the pasta tubes; drain. Toss in a hot bowl with the butter and cheese; pour half the sauce over the pasta and toss gently again. Serve in hot soup bowls with the remaining sauce spooned over individual portions. Serves 4 to 6.

QUADRETTINI AFFOGATI ALL'SAN MARINO
Smothered "Small Squares"

1 package (10 ounces) frozen chopped
    broccoli
½ pound prosciutto, chopped
3 tablespoons butter
½ cup grated Parmesan cheese
½ pound *quadrettini*

In a pot cook the broccoli in a small amount of salted water until crisp-tender; drain well. In a saucepan, over medium heat, sauté prosciutto in the butter for 10 minutes; stir in the broccoli, then the cheese. Remove from fire. Cook *quadrettini* al dente. Drain well and place in the pan with the other ingredients; blend well. Butter ramekins; divide the *quadrettini* mixture according to the number to be served. Brown under broiler for 5 minutes. Serves 4 to 6.

SPAGHETTINI CON PROSCIUTTO
Spaghettini with Italian Ham

This is a simple but classic dish often served in Parma, the region from which comes the best of that black-pepper-cured raw ham, prosciutto.

¼ pound unsalted butter
½ pound prosciutto, cut into long ju-
    lienne strips
1 pound spaghettini
Milled black pepper

Melt butter in a saucepan, add the ham and sauté until it begins to crisp. Cook spaghettini al dente; drain. Place in a hot bowl, pour in all of the butter and ham, mill in black pepper liberally, and toss well with wooden forks. Serve immediately in hot soup bowls. Serves 6.

GEMELLI GIOVANNINO

"Twins" Giovannino

1 pound hot Italian sausage
2 tablespoons butter
1 pound *gemelli*
¼ cup freshly grated Asiago cheese

Remove sausage casings and, in a saucepan, over medium heat, cook the loose meat in ½ tablespoon of the butter, stirring and breaking up the meat as it browns. If it is especially fatty sausage, pour off half the fat and discard. When sausage is brown, add the remaining butter and blend well with the meat. Cook *gemelli* al dente, drain, and add to the pan with the sausage meat. Toss meat and pasta together. Sprinkle on the cheese and toss again. Serve in individual hot dishes, with more grated cheese on the side. Serves 4 to 6.

VERMICELLI CON FILETTO DI POMODORO E SALSICCIA

Vermicelli with Tomato and Sausage

3 cups Filetto di Pomodoro (page 80)
1 pound sweet Italian sausage
1 tablespoon butter
1 teaspoon olive oil
1 pound *vermicelli*
1 cup grated Parmesan cheese

Make *filetto di pomodoro* and keep warm. Take casings from sausage. In a saucepan, over medium heat, sauté the meat in the butter and olive oil (oil keeps the butter from burning), breaking up the meat as it cooks. No other seasoning is necessary on the meat, as the sauce is rather spicy. When sausage is browned, add it to the warm sauce, stir well, and simmer for

10 minutes. Cook *vermicelli* in rapidly boiling water until al dente; drain. Toss gently with half of the cheese, top with the sausage and *filetto* sauce, and serve. Pass the rest of the cheese. Serves 4 to 6.

MACCHERONCELLI CON SALSICCIA
Baked Macaroni with Sausage Meat

1 pound loose sweet Italian sausage

½ cup chopped green pepper

½ cup chopped onion

4 cups (one 2-pound can) plum tomatoes

½ cup Chicken Broth (page 96)

½ teaspoon salt

¼ teaspoon dried oregano

¼ teaspoon freshly ground black pepper

1 pound *maccheroncelli* (small macaroni)

½ pound mozzarella cheese, sliced thin

⅓ cup grated Parmesan cheese

Preheat the oven to 400° F. Cook the sausage in a skillet until brown; set aside. Drain all but 2 tablespoons of the sausage fat, and sauté the green pepper and onion in what remains until soft. Add tomatoes put through a food mill, chicken broth, salt, oregano, and pepper to the skillet, and cook until most of moisture has evaporated, about 20 minutes. Cook *maccheroncelli* al dente; drain. Arrange alternating layers of the pasta, sausage and sauce, and mozzarella slices in a baking dish until everything is used. Sprinkle with Parmesan and bake until brown. Serves 4 to 6.

PERCIATELLI CON SALSA DI POMODORO E SALSICCIA

"Pierced" Pasta with Tomato Sauce and Sausage

  1 garlic clove, peeled and whole
  1 tablespoon olive oil
  1 pound sweet Italian sausage
  2 cups (one 1-pound can) plum tomatoes,
      put through food mill
  1 teaspoon salt, or to taste
  ½ tablespoon dried oregano
  Liberal amount of milled black pepper
  1 pound *perciatelli*
  ½ cup freshly grated Parmesan cheese

In a saucepan, over medium heat, sauté the garlic in the oil until golden, mash in the pan, then discard. Cut sausage in its casing into 1-inch pieces and sauté these until brown on both sides. Add tomatoes and salt, stir well, cover pan, and cook for 35 minutes. Remove cover, lower fire, add oregano and pepper, and stir well; cook 10 minutes, or until most of the watery liquid has evaporated from sauce. Cook *perciatelli* al dente; drain. Toss with cheese and serve in individual dishes topped with a generous spoonful of the sauce and sausages. Serves 6.

REGININI CON SALSICCE

Baked "Little Queens" with Sausages

  1½ pounds sweet Italian sausage, sliced thin
  2 garlic cloves, minced
  2 medium-size white onions, minced
  2 tablespoons olive oil
  4 cups (one 2-pound can) plum tomatoes
  ½ cup water

½ teaspoon dried sweet basil

1 pound *reginini* (small pasta tubes)

1 pound ricotta cheese

½ cup grated Parmesan cheese

In a saucepan, over medium heat, sauté sausage with garlic and onions in the oil until onions are soft. Stir in tomatoes, water, and basil. Bring to a boil, reduce heat, and simmer until liquid is absorbed, about 40 minutes. While sausage mixture simmers, cook *reginini* in boiling salted water until al dente; drain. Mix ricotta cheese in a bowl with 3 tablespoons water. Heat oven to 350° F.; butter a large casserole and arrange a layer of pasta on the bottom; top with a layer of meat sauce, a layer of ricotta, a sprinkle of Parmesan. Bake, uncovered, for 30 minutes. Serves 4 to 6.

PENNE ALLA GIOVANNINO

"Quill Pens" Giovannino

4 four-inch hot Italian sausages, casings
   removed

4 four-inch sweet Italian sausages, casings removed

1 tablespoon olive oil

8 slices of prosciutto, chopped

4 cups (one 2-pound can) plum tomatoes
   with basil leaf

1 pound *penne*

¼ cup grated Parmesan cheese

¼ cup grated Romano cheese

In a saucepan, over medium heat, cook the sausage meats in the oil until brown; if very fatty, pour off half of the fat. Add prosciutto and the to-matoes, which have been pushed through a food mill. Simmer, stirring, for 25 minutes. Cook *penne* al dente, drain, and toss with the cheeses. Serve in hot soup bowls with the sausage sauce spooned over right from the pan. Serves 4 to 6.

LASAGNE AL FORNO ALL'AMEDEO
Amedeo's Baked Lasagne

This is an unusual lasagne *recipe given to us by a chef who worked for an Italian industrialist; thus it bears the chef's name.*

- 1 recipe Pasta Fresca all'Uovo (page 57)
- 3 tablespoons olive oil, in all
- 2 small white onions, chopped
- 2 tablespoons chopped Italian parsley
- ½ pound top round of beef, ground twice
- ⅓ cup milk
- 1½ cups Basic Tomato Sauce (page 76)
- 1 recipe Béchamel Sauce (page 85)
- 1 cup grated Parmesan cheese

Roll out the pasta dough to ⅛-inch thickness and cut into strips 2½ by 5½ inches for *lasagne;* dry as recommended (page 18). Drop 2 at a time into boiling salted water to which 1 tablespoon of the oil has been added to keep the pasta from sticking. Cook for 4 minutes; remove with slotted spoon to dry on paper towels. Repeat until all pasta is cooked. In a saucepan, over medium heat, sauté onions, parsley, and beef in remaining oil until onion is soft but beef still pink. Stir in the milk; when it is well blended, add the tomato sauce and simmer for 20 minutes.

Meanwhile, prepare the Béchamel sauce. Butter a large heatproof glass baking dish. Carefully spread out in the dish a layer of the pasta strips, cover with meat sauce, and top with grated Parmesan. Repeat the layer of pasta, cover with Béchamel sauce, and sprinkle with cheese. Then again a layer of pasta, meat sauce, and cheese, then another covered with Béchamel and cheese. Bake in preheated 450° F. oven for 15 minutes until sauce bubbles and top is pale brown. Serves 4 to 6.

PASSO DI SELLA, in the Dolomites—Trentino-Alto Adige

AGNOLOTTI ALLA ROMANA

As we remarked earlier, agnolotti *are* ravioli, *but the name changes when the famous pasta squares are stuffed with meat (and sometimes made round instead of square). Properly,* ravioli *are filled only with eggs, cheeses, or vegetables.*

    2 cups ground beef
    6 slices of Genoa salami
    1 garlic clove
    Dash each of salt and pepper
    2 eggs, beaten
    4 tablespoons grated Parmesan cheese
    1 recipe Pasta Fresca for Ravioli (page 59)
    3 cups Mushroom and Cheese Sauce
        (page 86)

Finely mince (or put through food chopper) beef, salami, and garlic. Place in a large bowl, add salt and pepper, and beat in the eggs and cheese. Prepare the dough as suggested on page 59. Place a teaspoon of the filling in the center of each square, cover with the other sheet of dough, then firmly press between the mounds of filling. Cut into squares with a pastry cutter. Place on a dry white cloth, cover with another cloth, and dry for 40 minutes, or according to directions. Prepare mushroom and cheese sauce. Cook squares in gently simmering water until they float to the surface. Test for doneness by tasting one. Remove with slotted spoon; drain on paper towels. Place in hot soup bowls and serve with hot mushroom and cheese sauce spooned atop each square. Serves 4 to 6.

Note: Do not have water boiling violently or it will break up the *agnolotti* before they have cooked. They are usually, but not always, done when they float to the surface. Test often and return to the pot if not properly cooked.

AGNOLOTTI ALLA NIZZA

Agnolotti Nice Style

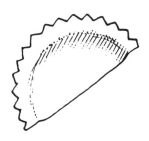

2-pound rump of beef
1 teaspoon salt
Milled black pepper
3 tablespoons butter
2 tablespoons olive oil
1 cup red wine
6 beets
1 egg
2 medium-size white onions, minced
½ cup grated Gruyère cheese
1 recipe Pasta Fresca for Ravioli (page 59)

Sprinkle the beef rump with salt and pepper and brown in a pot in 2 tablespoons of the butter and the oil. Lower heat, add the wine, stir in well, cover pot, and cook for 1 to 1½ hours, until meat is tender. Remove meat and cool. Simmer the liquid in the pot, stirring often, until it is thickened; set aside. Cook beets and peel. Finely mince beef and beets (or put through grinder) and place in a large bowl. Blend in the egg. In a saucepan, over medium heat, sauté the onions until soft in the remaining tablespoon of butter; blend this into the mixture along with 2 tablespoons of the cheese and salt and pepper to taste.

Prepare dough for *ravioli*. Fill one sheet with the beet-and-beef mixture, cover with the second sheet of dough, press, and dry according to directions. Cook in simmering water until the filled *agnolotti* float to the top. Test. Remove with slotted spoon, drain, and serve in hot bowls. Spoon the sauce from the meat pot atop, sprinkle with remaining cheese, and serve immediately. Serves 4 to 6.

AGNOLOTTI ALL'ANTONIO

1 recipe Pasta Fresca for Ravioli (page 59)

6 slices of prosciutto

4 slices of mortadella

1 veal sweetbread, blanched and cleaned,
    membranes removed

1 egg, beaten

¼ teaspoon salt, or to taste

Milled black pepper

Pinch of grated nutmeg

6 mushrooms, sliced

4 tablespoons butter

6 tablespoons peas

4 quarts Chicken Broth (page 96)

4 tablespoons grated Parmesan cheese

Prepare pasta dough according to directions. Finely mince (or put through food chopper) prosciutto, mortadella, and sweetbread. Place in a large bowl, stir in the beaten egg, salt, pepper, and nutmeg, blending well. Fill and cut the *agnolotti* according to directions. In a saucepan, over medium heat, sauté mushrooms in butter for 10 minutes. Lightly cook peas in a small amount of salted water, drain, and add to mushrooms and butter. Bring chicken broth to a gentle boil, drop in the *agnolotti*, and cook until they float to top. Test. Do not drain. Butter an ovenware serving dish; take *agnolotti* directly from the broth and arrange in the buttered dish. Spoon mushrooms and peas over them and sprinkle with Parmesan; place under broiler for 5 minutes. Serves 4 to 6.

CAPPELLETTI ALLA ROMANA
"Little Hats" Roman Style

Roman cappelletti *differ from others, being larger and having a raw rather than cooked filling. Also, they are usually cooked in broth.*

1 recipe Pasta Fresca for Ravioli (page 59)
1 small calf's brain
½ boned chicken breast, minced
2 slices of prosciutto, chopped
2 slices of mortadella, chopped
¼ pound lean pork, ground
1½ teaspoons salt
Liberal amount of milled black pepper
2 eggs, beaten
2 tablespoons Marsala
2 quarts Chicken Broth (page 96)
¼ cup grated Asiago cheese
Melted butter

Prepare dough, but do not yet roll out into sheets. Parboil the calf's brain, remove skin and membrane, and mince. In a bowl mix all meats together, season with salt and pepper, and blend in eggs and Marsala. Mix well. Roll out pasta dough into sheets; cut into 2½-inch circles. Place a teaspoon of the raw-meat filling in each, fold across into half-moons, then pull edges together into "little hat" shapes. Dry for 20 minutes. Bring the broth to a simmer and drop in the *cappelletti*, a few at a time. Remove them when they are tender, usually in less than 15 minutes, with a slotted spoon; drain. Serve as a first course with a light sprinkling of Asiago and hot melted butter. Serves 4 to 6.

FIDENZA, the west porch of the Cathedral—Emilia-Romagna

TORTELLINI ALLA BOLOGNESE

Here are the "little twisted ones," the copy of Venus's navel, the favorite pasta of Bologna.

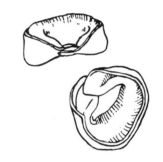

½ small turkey breast, boned

4 small slices of prosciutto

1 medium-size veal sweetbread, blanched
  and cleaned, membranes removed

¼ pound lean pork

¼ pound lean beef

7 tablespoons butter, in all

¼ pound Parmesan cheese, in all, grated

2 egg yolks, beaten

Salt

Pinch of grated nutmeg

Light pinch of ground cinnamon

Liberal amount of milled black pepper

1 recipe Pasta Fresca for Tortellini (page
  59)

4 quarts Chicken Broth (page 96)

1 cup heavy cream

Cut the turkey breast, prosciutto, sweetbread, pork, and beef into pieces. Melt 4 tablespoons of the butter in a large saucepan, and in it sauté the meats until pieces of sweetbread are cooked. Remove from stove; cool. Put mixture through a meat grinder twice so that all is very finely ground. Place in large bowl and stir in half the cheese, the beaten egg yolks, a little salt, the nutmeg, cinnamon, and some pepper; blend well.

Prepare the pasta dough and cut it into circles for *tortellini* (page 59); fill with the stuffing mixture and dry. Bring the chicken broth to a gentle simmer, not violent or it will break up the pasta. Heat remaining butter in a large saucepan or flameproof serving dish over low heat. Now carefully drop filled *tortellini,* a few at a time, into the gently simmering broth, and simmer until they are cooked through but al dente, about 12 minutes. Remove with a slotted spoon, drain, and place in the saucepan with the melted butter. Pour in the cream and sprinkle remaining cheese over the *tortellini,* gently stirring with a wooden spoon until butter, cream, and cheese have blended into a smooth sauce. Serve immediately in hot bowls and pass additional grated Parmesan at table. Serves 8 as a first course.

CANNELLONI VERDI

Baked Green Cannelloni

1 recipe Pasta Verde (page 60)

1 cup Béchamel Sauce (page 85)

2 cups Bolognese Sauce (page 82)

1 tablespoon olive oil

1 pound ricotta cheese

10 slices of lean prosciutto, finely chopped

½ cup grated Parmesan cheese

½ cup grated Romano cheese

1 garlic clove, minced

2 tablespoons chopped Italian parsley

2 egg yolks, beaten

1 teaspoon salt

Milled black pepper

3 tablespoons melted butter

Prepare the green pasta dough, cut it into 4-inch squares, and dry for 1 hour. Prepare the sauces. Cook 2 squares of pasta at a time in boiling salted water with the olive oil added to keep pasta from sticking. As each 2 squares are cooked al dente, remove, drain well, and dry on paper towels. Continue until all pasta has been cooked. Drain the ricotta in a strainer, place in a bowl, and blend in the prosciutto, Parmesan and Romano, garlic, parsley, beaten egg yolks, salt, and pepper. Mix well. In the center of each pasta square place a heaping tablespoon of this filling; then roll carefully into a tube. Place filled tubes, without touching, side by side in a buttered heatproof glass baking dish; brush them with melted butter. Lightly cover them with Béchamel sauce, then with Bolognese sauce, pouring the remainder of the sauce on either side. Brown in a preheated 400° F. oven for 15 minutes. Serves 4 to 6.

MANICOTTI ALLA TOSCANA
Baked Manicotti Tuscan Style

1 recipe Pasta Fresca all'Uovo (page 57)
4 cups Basic Tomato Sauce (page 76)
4 tablespoons butter
1 tablespoon olive oil
1 garlic clove, minced
6 mushrooms, minced
1 pound beef round, ground twice
1 teaspoon salt
Liberal amount of milled black pepper
½ pound ricotta cheese
¼ pound Asiago cheese, grated

Prepare pasta dough, cut into 3-inch squares, and dry for ½ hour. Prepare tomato sauce, simmer. Heat 3 tablespoons of the butter and the oil in a saucepan; sauté garlic until soft. Add mushrooms, beef, salt, and pepper and sauté until brown, stirring often. Stir in the ricotta and half of the Asiago, blending well. When *manicotti* are dry, spread a liberal tablespoon of beef mixture on each square and roll up tightly, carefully pressing edges together and sealing; if necessary, moisten the edges with water to make sealing more effective; filling has to be completely sealed in or it will be lost during boiling of the pasta. Cook *manicotti* al dente in gently boiling salted water, remove with skimmer, and drain. Arrange a layer in a buttered baking dish. Cover with tomato sauce and sprinkle with Asiago; arrange another layer crosswise, cover with sauce, and sprinkle with Parmesan. Bake in a preheated 350° F. oven for 25 minutes, until cheese browns and sauce bubbles. Serves 6.

TUFOLI IMBOTTITI CON CARNE

Baked Meat-Stuffed Tufoli

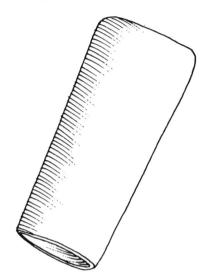

1 pound veal, ground
1 pound pork, ground
2 shallots, chopped
1 egg, beaten
½ cup bread crumbs
1 tablespoon raisins, minced
½ tablespoon salt, or to taste
2 tablespoons olive oil, in all
½ cup grated *Pepato* cheese
1 pound *tufoli* (very large tubes)
3 cups Basic Tomato Sauce (page 76)

In a large bowl, mix together meats, shallots, beaten egg, bread crumbs, raisins, salt, ½ tablespoon of the oil, and the grated cheese; mix well. Sauté mixture in another ½ tablespoon of oil in a frypan for 15 minutes, stirring and blending well. Remove from heat and let cool. Cook *tufoli* in boiling salted water with remaining tablespoon of olive oil added to keep this large pasta from sticking. Cook for 6 minutes, or until half done; drain. When cool enough to handle, spoon the meat mixture into the tubes, filling them. Oil a baking dish or casserole, place *tufoli* in it, side by side but not touching, and cover each with a liberal spoonful of tomato sauce. Bake, uncovered, in a preheated 400° F. oven for 15 minutes. Serve remaining sauce from a sauceboat. Serves 4 to 6.

SPIEDINI ALLA ROMANA

"Little Skewers" Roman Style

We had this specialty of the ancient city on a bed of noodles, and recommend it highly as an unusual way to serve that American favorite, spaghetti and meatballs.

1½ pounds good beef, preferably sirloin,
    ground twice

2 tablespoons grated Romano cheese

2 tablespoons grated Parmesan cheese

½ cup bread crumbs

4 eggs, in all, beaten

1 tablespoon chopped Italian parsley

1 garlic clove, finely minced

½ teaspoon salt

Milled black pepper

½ pound mozzarella cheese

½ pound Genoa salami, unsliced

12 small skewers

½ cup flour

½ cup very dry bread crumbs

6 tablespoons butter, in all

4 tablespoons olive oil

1 pound *fettucce* (wide *fettuccine*)

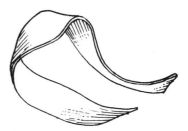

In a large bowl place beef, both cheeses, bread crumbs, 2 of the eggs, the parsley, garlic, salt, and pepper. Blend thoroughly, then form oblong rolls 1 inch thick, 3 inches long. Cut mozzarella and salami into 1-inch cubes. Place a meat roll on a skewer, crosswise, then a piece of mozzarella, then one of salami, another beef roll, another cube of cheese, and one of salami. Thread all skewers this way. Dip the skewers into the flour, then into remaining beaten eggs, then into the dry bread crumbs. Sauté in 4 tablespoons of the butter and the oil in a deep saucepan, turning the skewers until meat, cheese, and salami are golden. Cook *fettucce* al dente, drain, and toss with remaining butter. Serve on individual plates, with 2 skewers to each person atop the *fettucce*. Serve 6.

BAVETTINE CON BRACIOLINE DI MANZO
Bavettine with Stuffed Beef Rolls

This is a popular Italian dish which can be made in a number of ways, with beef, pork, veal, even with breast of chicken.

2 pounds round steak
5 cups Basic Tomato Sauce (page 76)
½ pound salt pork
4 slices of prosciutto
2 tablespoons chopped Italian parsley
Pinch each of salt and pepper, or to taste
2 tablespoons grated Asiago cheese
2 tablespoons olive oil
1 pound *bavettine* (very narrow *linguine*)

Have butcher cut the beef into pieces 8 by 9 inches, ½ inch thick, and pound the pieces to flatten them as for veal *scaloppine*. Prepare the tomato sauce and bring to a simmer. Mince the salt pork, prosciutto, and parsley. Sprinkle lightly with salt and pepper, mix in the cheese, and mince everything again until it is a fine paste. Spread this liberally over the flat pieces of beef. Roll from short end into compact rolls and tie with string. In a saucepan, over medium heat, sauté the *bracioline* (beef rolls) in the oil, turning often, until brown. Add them, with the oil they have cooked in, to the tomato sauce and stir well. Simmer, uncovered, until meat is tender and sauce thickened. Cook *bavettine* al dente; drain. Serve in hot soup bowls with tomato sauce liberally spooned atop. Cut one of the *bracioline* into ½-inch rounds and center 2 slices on each dish of pasta. Serve remaining beef rolls, with more sauce, as entrée, with a salad. Serves 6.

SAN MARINO—The Marches

GRAVEDONNA, Baptistery of Santa Maria del Tiglio—Lombardy

RIGATONI CON FETTA DI MANZO
Rigatoni with Pot Roast

Here is an all-time Italian favorite that we have had in Rome, in Florence, Naples, and Genoa, each time on a Sunday, correcting the misconception that tomato and beef cooked this way is confined to the south.

2 tablespoons olive oil
2 garlic cloves, mashed
1 teaspoon salt
Liberal amount of milled black pepper
3-pound beef chuck roast
4 cups (one 2-pound can) plum tomatoes
1 bay leaf
Pinch of dried rosemary

1 cup red wine

6 mushrooms, sliced

1 pound *rigatoni* (grooved pasta tubes)

Heat the oil in a large pot; sauté garlic, moving it around in the oil until it is brown; discard garlic. Sprinkle salt and pepper on meat and sear it in the oil on all sides over high flame. Lower flame and stir in tomatoes, bay leaf, rosemary, and wine; cover pot and simmer for 2 hours, stirring often and basting meat, until it is fork-tender. Lift meat to a warm platter. Add the mushrooms to the pot and simmer for 10 minutes, stirring with a wooden spoon as they cook. Cook *rigatoni* al dente, drain, and place in a hot bowl. Spoon one third of the sauce over and toss well. Serve in hot soup bowls with liberal spoonings of sauce. The pot roast, sliced, serves as entrée with salad and vegetables. Serves 6.

Another great meat dish should be mentioned here. It is Italian through and through, but we have eaten it only in New England. See Catherine Spadaccino's Foggia Beef Roll on page 78.

OSSI BUCHI ED ORZO ALLA MILANESE

Veal Shanks and Orzo Milanese

6 veal shanks, cut into 2-inch pieces

¼ cup flour

4 tablespoons olive oil

2 tablespoons butter

1 teaspoon salt

Milled black pepper

Pinch of dried rosemary

1 garlic clove, chopped

2 large white onions, chopped

1 large carrot, scraped and chopped

1 large celery rib, scraped and chopped

2 cups dry white wine

1 cup Basic Tomato Sauce (page 76)

1½ cups Chicken Broth (page 96)

Dredge the pieces of veal with flour and place them in a pan with 2 table-spoons of the olive oil and the butter; sprinkle with salt and mill in pepper. Cook over medium heat, turning the veal until all sides are brown. Add more oil if needed. Place the veal shanks upright, so marrow doesn't drop out, in a large deep pot. Add remaining oil and sprinkle lightly with rosemary, then with the garlic, onions, carrot, and celery. Cover the pot and simmer for 15 minutes.

Add wine, tomato sauce, and chicken broth. Stir well, cover pot again, and simmer on top of stove for 1½ hours, or until veal is fork-tender and sauce thickened. Stir often. This can also be placed in a preheated 300° F. oven, eliminating stirring. Meanwhile, prepare the pasta.

Orzo Milanese:

2 tablespoons butter

2 small white onions, chopped

1 garlic clove, minced

2 cups *orzo* (pasta that looks like barley or rice)

5 cups Chicken Broth (page 96), warm

⅓ cup grated Asiago cheese

¼ teaspoon ground saffron

Melt the butter in a deep pan, add onions, and simmer until soft; stir in garlic. Add the *orzo* and stir well into butter and onion and garlic until the pasta kernels are coated. Blend in 1 cup of broth and stir gently as the *orzo* absorbs the liquid, adding more broth as it is needed; 10 minutes should see the pasta cooked. Now stir in the cheese and saffron; add more chicken broth, stir, and simmer until broth is absorbed and pasta is still al dente.

Serve *orzo* in the center of a large platter surrounded with the *ossi buchi*, the veal sauce on the side. Each serving should have a veal shank and a large spoonful of *orzo* with sauce spooned over it. Provide marrow spoons, so that each guest can pry out that tasty tidbit from the veal bone. Serves 6.

Note: To give the veal added piquancy, mix together 1 tablespoon chopped parsley, 1 minced garlic clove, and 1 tablespoon grated lemon rind. Lightly sprinkle over each veal shank before serving. This is called *gremolata* in Milan.

SPAGHETTINI E COSCIOTTI D'AGNELLO
Spaghettini with Lamb Shanks

4 carrots, chopped
2 celery ribs, chopped
4 tablespoons butter
3 pounds lamb shanks, cut into 2-inch
   pieces
Salt
Milled black pepper
1 tablespoon flour
1 cup canned plum tomatoes
1 cup dry white wine
1 cup water, approximately
1 teaspoon chopped fresh thyme
1 bay leaf
1 pound spaghettini
2 strips of lemon rind, chopped
1 tablespoon chopped parsley

In a deep saucepan, over medium heat, sauté carrots and celery in 2 tablespoons of the butter. Add the meat and season generously with salt and pepper. When the vegetables are soft and the meat brown, add remaining butter blended with the flour; stir and cook until the flour browns. Add the tomatoes, wine, and water to cover meat; add the herbs; simmer for 1 hour, or until lamb is tender. Fifteen minutes before serving remove meat from pot and strain the sauce. Cook spaghettini al dente, drain, and toss with sauce. Serve in individual bowls. Before serving lamb as an entrée, sprinkle with chopped lemon rind and parsley. Serves 4.

SPAGHETTI CON CAPRETTO IN UMIDO

Spaghetti with Kid Stew

This is a peasant dish we had in a farmhouse just outside Foggia several years ago when caught there in a snowstorm, the first in years; it was just the dish for the day.

3 tablespoons butter

3 tablespoons olive oil

2 garlic cloves

3 small white onions, chopped

2 pounds of lean kid (or lamb), cubed

1 cup Chianti or other dry red wine

4 cups (one 2-pound can) plum tomatoes
    with basil leaf

1½ teaspoons salt

Liberal amount of milled black pepper

2 tablespoons chopped parsley

2 celery ribs, scraped and chopped

1 large potato, peeled and diced

1 pound spaghetti

Heat butter and oil in a large deep saucepan. Add garlic and onions and sauté until garlic is brown; discard garlic. Stir in the meat cubes; brown. Stir in the wine slowly, mixing well with the meat with a wooden spoon. Add the tomatoes, salt, pepper, parsley, and celery; simmer for 40 minutes. Add the potato and cook, uncovered, until sauce is thickened and potato and meat tender. Cook spaghetti al dente, drain, and toss with half of the meat stew. Serve in hot soup bowls with a liberal amount of sauce atop each portion. Serves 4 to 6.

TAGLIATELLE VERDI CON MAIALE USO PIEMONTESE

Green Noodles with Pork Piedmont Style

1 fresh pork shoulder
2 white truffles, sliced thin (optional)
Milled black pepper
3 tablespoons butter
1 teaspoon salt, or to taste
4 slices of prosciutto, chopped
2 small white onions, chopped
2 celery ribs, scraped and chopped
2 small carrots, scraped and chopped
1 tablespoon chopped parsley
Pinch of dried sweet basil
2 cups (one 1-pound can) plum tomatoes,
    pushed through food mill
1 cup white wine
2 cups Chicken Broth (page 96)
1 recipe Pasta Verde (page 60) or 1
    pound commercial green noodles

Have butcher skin, bone, and split the pork shoulder so it will lie flat. Trim off most of the outside white pork fat, leaving a thin layer. Place truffle slices over entire meat surface and liberally mill black pepper over meat. Roll up tightly and tie with soft white string into a compact roll. Heat butter in a large pot and brown pork roll in it on all sides. Sprinkle with salt and pepper, add the prosciutto, onions, celery, carrots, parsley, and basil, and stir in the tomatoes, wine, and broth. Cook, covered, on top of stove over low flame for 2 hours. Remove cover and cook for 1 hour longer, stirring often until meat is fork-tender and sauce thickened.

Meanwhile, prepare green pasta dough and cut into *tagliatelle* (page 58); dry. Cook al dente and drain. Serve noodles in hot soup bowls with liberal amounts of the pork sauce spooned atop each portion. Cut wafer-thin slices from the pork shoulder; place 3 atop each dish of pasta. Meat roll, untied and sliced, serves as entrée with a fresh vegetable and salad. Serves 6.

PORCELLINO RIPIENO ARROSTITO
Roast Stuffed Suckling Pig

This is a dish we saw prepared at a wedding in Florence; it is an impressive one that everyone should have at least once. Six piglets were cooked there, but we have reduced the recipe so that only one piglet is required.

1 suckling pig (8 to 10 pounds)
2 teaspoons salt
3 garlic cloves, peeled and halved
1 pound *mezzani* (medium-size macaroni)
Pinch of grated nutmeg
¼ cup grated Parmesan cheese
1 cup light cream
1 teaspoon crushed red pepper

Wash the piglet well; scrape its skin with a sharp knife, and sprinkle it inside and out with salt. Insert the tip of a pointed knife in the skin in 6 places, preparing slits large enough to insert ½ garlic clove in each. Cook *mezzani* one third done, very, very chewy, and drain well. Sprinkle lightly with nutmeg, add cheese and cream, and toss. Stuff the piglet with the pasta and sew the opening so it is completely sealed. Dust piglet with the crushed red pepper and place in an uncovered roasting pan. Roast in a preheated 500° F. oven until the meat is brown. Then lower heat to 350° F., cover the pan, and cook the piglet for 3 hours, basting with pan juices frequently, until it is tender inside and crisp outside. Serve whole, on a large hot platter, and carve at the table, giving each person a portion of piglet and a spoonful of *mezzani*. At the wedding, a crisp cold salad of hearts of romaine and orange slices accompanied it. Serves 6.

TORINO—Piedmont

COURMAYEUR and the Mont Blanc—Valle d'Aosta

VIII
Poultry & Game with Pasta

*T*he Italians love game. One of the interesting sights of Rome in the fall is the game hanging outside restaurants and markets—pheasant, partridge, and quail in feather, rabbits, hare, deer, sometimes even wild boar. Poultry in feather also is displayed—fat chickens, turkeys, ducks, geese, guinea hens. The displays are dramatic. The food chain in Italy often starts at the bottom, even with live poultry, which the customer selects, then waits to have delivered, plucked and eviscerated, warm and fresh.

Game in the United States used to be difficult to obtain unless one was a hunter. Today we've become sophisticated, so much so that even a supermarket chain does carry some game, quail and pheasant especially. The gun isn't necessary anymore, just money.

We consider that some of the very best pasta sauces start with poultry and game, particularly because the main course is quite often lifted from the pasta sauce itself. We've also discovered that poultry, chicken, ducks, Cornish hens, can be substituted in some game recipes. Poultry is the most versatile of foods.

The Italians realized that versatility, especially of turkey, long ago, and they ingeniously pair all kinds of poultry with pasta.

POLLO ALLA MILANESE CON RIGATONI

Chicken Milan Style with Rigatoni

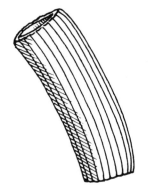

⅛ teaspoon powdered saffron

2 tablespoons brandy

5 tablespoons olive oil

Salt and freshly ground black pepper to
    taste

3-pound chicken, cut into small serving
    pieces (do not use the wing tips or
    back; use those for making stock); re-
    serve the liver

8 tablespoons (1 stick) butter

2 medium-size onions, finely chopped

3 garlic cloves, minced

6 fresh ripe tomatoes, peeled, seeded,
    and chopped, or 1-pound, 12-ounce
    can plum tomatoes, drained and
    chopped

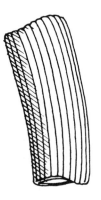

1 head of finocchio, trimmed and
    chopped, white part only

2 tablespoons chopped fresh basil, or 2
    teaspoons dried sweet basil

⅛ teaspoon (or to taste) crushed red pep-
    per

12 ounces *rigatoni* (grooved pasta tubes),
    cooked in boiling salted water until al
    dente, drained

½ cup grated Asiago cheese

3 tablespoons chopped fresh Italian pars-
    ley

In a large bowl, combine and blend well the saffron, brandy, 3 tablespoons of the olive oil, salt, and pepper. Add the chicken (not the liver),
turning the pieces to coat evenly. Marinate for 2 hours, turning 2 or 3 times.

In a heavy-bottomed pot, over medium heat, heat 2 tablespoons of the
olive oil and 1 tablespoon of the butter. Cook the onions and two thirds
of the garlic until soft, about 5 minutes. Do not brown. Add the tomatoes

and cook, uncovered, for 5 minutes, stirring occasionally. Add the chicken, its marinade, finocchio, and basil. Cover, lower heat, and simmer for 45 minutes, or until the chicken is almost tender. Remove top and cook until the sauce thickens. Taste for seasoning.

In a small saucepan, over medium heat, heat 3 tablespoons of butter and cook the remaining garlic until soft. Do not brown. Add red pepper and the liver and cook for 1 minute. Stir in ⅓ cup of the sauce the chicken cooked in, blending well.

Toss the hot pasta with the remaining butter (in small pieces) and the cheese. Serve on individual hot plates with the chicken and its sauce over the pasta and a spoonful of the hot chicken-liver sauce on top. Sprinkle with parsley. Serves 4.

FUSILLI E POLLO ALLA ROMANA

"Twists" and Chicken Roman Style

We've had this for dinner at trattorie *in Rome several times with a green salad and a bottle of Frascati. It's a favorite there and also in our home.*

2 tablespoons olive oil
3 tablespoons butter
1 stewing chicken (5 pounds), trussed
1 teaspoon salt
Liberal amount of milled black pepper
1 leek, sliced thin
Pinch of dried rosemary
2 cloves
1½ tablespoons chopped parsley
1 large ripe tomato, peeled, seeded, and
    diced
2 cups Chicken Broth (page 96)
1 pound *fusilli*

Heat the oil and 2 tablespoons of the butter in a large pot. Add the chicken, season with salt and pepper, and brown on all sides over medium-high flame. Add the leek, rosemary, cloves, and 1 tablespoon of the parsley.

Continue to brown chicken with the herbs, turning bird often. Don't rush this stage, as slow cooking is the way to achieve final flavoring. Stir in the tomato, mixing well. Add half of the broth, cover pot, and simmer for 1 hour. Remove cover, stir, turn chicken on its side, and pour in remaining broth. Cover pot, simmer for 30 minutes, and turn chicken on its other side. Simmer for 30 minutes longer. Remove chicken from pot and simmer the sauce, uncovered, stirring often, until sauce is smooth and thick. Rub remaining butter over chicken, sprinkle with remaining parsley, and place in a low oven. Cook *fusilli* al dente, drain, and stir directly into the chicken sauce, mixing well. Serve *fusilli* on a large hot platter with the whole chicken, untrussed, in the center. Serves 6.

PASTA E POLLO ALLA CONTADINA

Chicken and Spaghetti Farmer's Style

    2 tablespoons butter
    4 slices of prosciutto, finely minced
    1 teaspoon salt, or to taste
    Milled black pepper
    1 chicken (3 pounds)
    1 garlic clove, quartered
    ½ teaspoon dried rosemary
    12 plum tomatoes, peeled, seeded, and
        diced
    1 cup Chicken Broth (page 96)
    1 pound spaghetti

Heat butter in a large pot, stir in minced prosciutto, and sauté until soft. Sprinkle salt and pepper over chicken. Make 8 slits in the bird; insert the garlic pieces in 4, rosemary in 4. Brown on all sides. Add the tomatoes and simmer, covered, for 1½ hours until tender, basting with warm chicken broth every 20 minutes. Remove chicken for serving as entrée. Simmer sauce, uncovered, until it is smooth and thickened, stirring often. Cook spaghetti al dente; drain. Serve in hot soup bowls with hot chicken-tomato sauce liberally spooned atop each portion. Serves 6.

PERCIATELLI E POLLO ALLA PIZZAIOLA

"Pierced" Pasta and Chicken with Tomato Sauce

2 garlic cloves, minced

4 tablespoons olive oil

1 young fryer chicken, cut up

1 teaspoon salt

Liberal amount of milled black pepper

12 plum tomatoes, peeled, seeded, and
   diced

½ teaspoon dried oregano

3 basil leaves, chopped, or ½ teaspoon
   dried sweet basil

1 pound *perciatelli*

In a saucepan, over medium heat, sauté garlic in the oil until soft. Toss chicken pieces in garlic and oil in the pan, sprinkle with salt and pepper, and cook over medium-high heat until chicken is well browned on both sides. Add tomatoes, oregano, and basil, cover pan, and cook for 40 minutes, stirring often, until chicken is tender but not falling apart. Remove chicken to a warm platter for second course. Cook remaining sauce, uncovered, for 5 minutes, until it thickens, stirring often. Cook *perciatelli* al dente, drain, and toss with half the sauce. Spoon the remainder of sauce over each serving. Serves 4.

RIGATONI CON POLLO ALLA ZINGARA

Rigatoni with Chicken Gypsy Style

2 tablespoons butter

2 tablespoons olive oil

1 chicken (3 pounds), cut into serving
   pieces

½ cup dry white wine

2 garlic cloves

Pinch of ground sage

Pinch of dried rosemary

1 teaspoon salt

Liberal amount of milled black pepper

2 cups Chicken Broth (page 96)

3 anchovy fillets

½ tablespoon wine vinegar

6 plum tomatoes, peeled, seeded, and
   diced

½ pound *rigatoni* (grooved pasta tubes)

Grated Asiago cheese

In a deep saucepan, over medium heat, heat butter and oil; sauté the chicken pieces in it, browning them evenly. Pour in the wine and continue cooking, uncovered, until wine evaporates. Add the garlic, sage, rosemary, salt, pepper, and broth. Cover pan and simmer for 1 hour, or until chicken is fork-tender. Transfer chicken to a warm platter in a low oven. Meanwhile soak the anchovies in cold water to desalt them; drain. Chop the anchovies, then crush into a paste with the vinegar. Stir this into the sauce; add the tomatoes. Simmer over a low fire, uncovered, stirring often, for 20 minutes, or until sauce is smooth and thickened. Cook *rigatoni* al dente, drain, and place in a large hot bowl. Pour in two thirds of the sauce; toss well. Serve immediately in hot soup bowls. Pass the cheese at table. Chicken, topped with the remaining sauce, comes as second course. Serves 4.

FETTUCCINE ALLA TEDESCA

Fettuccine German Style

6 tablespoons butter, in all
1 tablespoon olive oil
1 chicken (4 pounds)
1 teaspoon salt
Liberal amount of milled black pepper
4 tablespoons brandy
1 recipe Pasta Fresca all'Uovo (page 57)
½ cup grated Parmesan cheese
½ cup heavy cream, warmed
1 white truffle, grated

In a large pot, over medium heat, heat 4 tablespoons of the butter and the oil. Brown the chicken, seasoning it with salt and pepper. Bake the chicken in a covered pan in a preheated 350° F. oven for 2 hours, or until fork-tender, basting the bird often with its own juices and with the brandy. Remove and cool. Skin and bone chicken, cutting meat into small strips. Return strips to the brandy-flavored drippings in the roasting pan, blend, and simmer, uncovered, for 10 minutes.

Meanwhile prepare pasta dough, cut into *fettuccine* (page 00), and let them dry for 1 hour. Cook them al dente; drain. Place in a large hot bowl and toss with the remaining butter and the cheese. Add the warm cream and the chicken strips in their sauce; toss again with wooden forks. Serve immediately in hot bowls. Sprinkle some grated truffle atop each portion, and pass more grated cheese at table. Serves 4 to 6.

CANNELLONI ALLA GIORGIO
George's "Large Reeds"

1 recipe Pasta Fresca all'Uovo (page 57)
1 chicken (3 pounds)
4 teaspoons salt
½ recipe Mornay Sauce (page 86)
2 egg yolks, beaten
Liberal amount of milled black pepper
⅓ cup grated Pecorino cheese
⅓ cup grated Parmesan cheese
½ cup bread crumbs
2 tablespoons olive oil
2 tablespoons butter

Prepare the fresh pasta dough, cut into squares, and dry (page 58). In a pot cover chicken with water and add 3 teaspoons salt; cook covered over medium heat for 1½ hours, or until fork-tender. Remove; cool. Discard skin and bones and dice the chicken meat. In a saucepan prepare Mornay sauce. Blend in chicken, egg yolks, remaining salt, pepper, and cheeses. Simmer, uncovered, stirring often with a wooden spoon, until sauce is extremely thick. Chill. Cook the dried pasta squares and drain. Spoon chicken filling on each pasta square, roll up, and sprinkle with bread crumbs. Sauté carefully in olive oil and butter until golden. Serves 6.

CAPELLINI E POLLO
Baked Fine Vermicelli and Chicken

1 chicken (4 pounds), roasted
½ pound mushrooms, sliced
10 tablespoons butter, in all
½ cup flour
4 cups Chicken Broth (page 96)
1½ cups milk

½ cup heavy cream
Salt and pepper
½ pound *capellini*
½ cup bread crumbs
½ cup grated Asiago cheese

Cut meat from chicken into cubes. In a saucepan, over medium heat, sauté mushrooms in 2 tablespoons of the butter for 5 minutes. Melt remaining butter and blend in flour, broth, and milk. Cook over low heat until sauce begins to thicken, stirring frequently. Add cream and season well with salt and pepper. Cook *capellini* al dente (for no more than 4 minutes); drain. Place in a greased casserole; arrange chicken and mushrooms over it and pour sauce over all. Sprinkle bread crumbs and cheese on top and bake in preheated 450° F. oven until sauce bubbles and crumbs brown. Serves 4 to 6.

FETTUCCELLE CON FILETTI DI POLLO E PEPE NERO
"Little Ribbons" with Fillets of Chicken and Black Pepper

2 whole chicken breasts, boned
8 tablespoons butter, in all
1 teaspoon olive oil
1½ teaspoons salt, or to taste
Liberal amount of milled black pepper
1 pound *fettuccelle* (narrow *fettuccine*)

Cut chicken into pieces the size of your thumbnail. Sauté in 6 tablespoons of the butter and the oil (to keep butter from burning) in a frypan for 15 minutes. When chicken is done, but still juicy—don't overcook—add salt and mill in much black pepper. Stir well, adding more butter if needed; chicken should be moist. Remove from fire, but keep warm. Cook *fettuccelle* al dente; drain. Toss with remaining butter, then with half of the chicken mixture. Serve in individual dishes with the remaining chicken sauce spooned atop. Serves 4 to 6.

BERGAMO, the Colleoni Chapel—Lombardy

RIGATONI E PETTO DI POLLO

Rigatoni and Chicken Breast

1 pound *rigatoni* (grooved pasta tubes)
½ chicken breast, boned
¼ pound butter
¼ pound Parmesan cheese, grated
2 egg yolks, beaten
1 cup heavy cream
1 teaspoon salt
Liberal amount of milled black pepper

Cook *rigatoni* for 10 minutes in boiling salted water; drain. Grind raw chicken twice. Blend butter, half of the cheese, the egg yolks, cream, salt, pepper, and chicken. Place pasta in a large pot and stir in the chicken mixture, blending well. Simmer for 15 minutes, stirring often, until *rigatoni* is al dente. Serve immediately in hot rimmed soup bowls. Pass the remaining cheese at table. Serves 4 to 6.

SPAGHETTINI CON PETTO DI POLLO E PISELLI

Spaghettini with Chicken Breast and Peas

1 boned chicken breast, cubed
2 tablespoons olive oil
½ teaspoon salt, or to taste
Milled black pepper
1 cup (one 8-ounce can) baby peas
1 pound spaghettini
3 tablespoons grated Asiago cheese
1 egg, beaten

In a saucepan, over medium heat, sauté chicken cubes in the oil until golden; season with salt and pepper. Heat peas in their liquid; pour liquid into saucepan with chicken and simmer, uncovered, for 5 minutes. Add peas and more black pepper, stir, and simmer for 5 minutes. Cook spaghettini al dente, drain, and place in a large hot bowl. Just before serving blend cheese and beaten egg and stir into the chicken and peas. Add half of this to the hot spaghettini and toss well with wooden forks. Serve in hot bowls with the remainder of the sauce spooned atop individual portions. Serves 4 to 6.

CANNELLE CON PURÉ DI POLLO
"Small Reeds" with Puréed Chicken

    2 slices of bread
    1 cup milk
    1 whole chicken breast
    1 cup Beef Broth (page 96)
    Pinch of grated nutmeg
    ½ teaspoon salt, or to taste
    Milled black pepper
    2 tablespoons butter
    3 tablespoons Marsala
    ½ pound *cannelle*
    1 egg yolk, beaten
    ½ lemon

Soak the bread in the milk and squeeze almost dry. Mince the raw chicken breast and pound in a mortar with 1 tablespoon of the broth and the bread. Put chicken and bread through a food mill. Season with nutmeg, salt, and pepper and stir into the butter in a saucepan. Sauté for 5 minutes. Add Marsala and remainder of broth; simmer, uncovered, stirring often, for 15 minutes. Cook *cannelle* al dente; drain. Take chicken sauce from stove and stir in beaten egg yolk and the juice from the lemon half, blending well. Place over low flame for 2 minutes while you blend. Divide pasta among 4 hot rimmed soup bowls; liberally spoon chicken sauce atop each portion. Serves 4.

BAVETTE CON BRACIOLINE DI POLLO ALLA GIOVANNINO

Chicken Rolls with Bavette

2 whole chicken breasts, boned

8 slices of prosciutto

6 walnuts, ground

12 *pignoli* (pine nuts), ground

¼ cup grated Parmesan cheese

1½ teaspoons salt, or to taste

Liberal amount of milled black pepper

1 tablespoon minced parsley

1 garlic clove

2 tablespoons butter

1 tablespoon olive oil

4 cups (one 2-pound can) Italian plum to-
    matoes, pushed through food mill

1 teaspoon dried sweet basil

1 pound *bavette* (narrow *linguine*)

Cut each chicken breast into quarters. Between sheets of wax paper pound the pieces with a wooden mallet or flat side of a cleaver into thin, but intact, scallops. Place 1 slice of prosciutto on each scallop; sprinkle lightly with all the ground walnuts and *pignoli*, a little Parmesan, some salt and pepper, and the parsley. Tie with string into compact rolls. In a saucepan sauté the 8 chicken rolls with the garlic in the butter and oil over medium-high flame, turning often, until they are brown; remove garlic. Lower heat; stir in tomatoes, basil, remaining salt, and more pepper. Simmer, uncovered, stirring often, until chicken rolls are tender and sauce smooth and thickened. Cook *bavette* al dente; drain. Place in a large hot bowl and toss with remaining cheese and half of the tomato sauce. Serve in hot bowls with 2 chicken *bracioline* and a liberal amount of remaining sauce atop each portion. Serves 4.

LINGUINE CON FEGATINI DI POLLO

Linguine with Chicken Livers

   2 medium-size white onions, chopped
   2 slices of bacon, diced
   2 tablespoons olive oil
   1 teaspoon salt, or to taste
   Milled black pepper
   2 cups (one 1-pound can) plum tomatoes
   ⅛ teaspoon crushed red pepper
   ½ pound chicken livers, quartered
   1 tablespoon butter
   1 pound *linguine*

In a saucepan, over medium heat, sauté the onions and bacon in the oil until soft. Add the salt, pepper, and tomatoes, breaking up the tomatoes with a wooden spoon as they simmer for 20 minutes. Stir in the red pepper. Continue cooking until sauce is thickened and has body and flavor; taste for flavor. In another saucepan, over medium heat, sauté quartered livers in the butter for 5 minutes, turning so livers are well buttered. Add to the sauce, stir in well, and simmer for 5 minutes. Cook *linguine* al dente; drain. Serve in ramekins or soup bowls with sauce and livers spooned atop. Serves 4 to 6.

TAGLIARINI BENEVENTO

   2 tablespoons butter
   1 tablespoon olive oil
   1 medium-size onion, finely chopped
   1 garlic clove, minced
   ½ cup dried mushrooms, well rinsed, soaked in warm
      water for 30 minutes, squeezed dry, and coarsely chopped
   8 chicken livers, trimmed and quartered

Salt and freshly ground black pepper to taste

½ cup Marsala

1 pound *tagliarini*, cooked slightly firmer than
    al dente in boiling salted water, drained

2 cups Bolognese Sauce (page 82), omitting chicken
    livers recommended in the recipe

1 cup grated Asiago or Parmesan cheese

In a frypan, over medium heat, heat the butter and oil. Add the onion and garlic and cook for 2 minutes, or until soft. Do not brown. Add the mushrooms and cook for 3 minutes. Add the livers and cook, turning, for 1 minute, or until just brown outside and still very pink inside. Season with salt and pepper. Pour in the Marsala, raise heat, and cook off half of it.

Arrange half of the pasta in a shallow baking dish. Distribute half of the chicken-liver mixture over it. Coat with the Bolognese sauce and sprinkle 3 or 4 tablespoons of cheese over the sauce. Repeat, ending with cheese sprinkled over the top. Place in a preheated 425° F. oven for 15 minutes, or until the cheese is golden and the sauce bubbling. Serve any remaining sauce and cheese at the table. Serves 6.

ORTA—Piedmont

BUCATINI CON VENTRIGLI DI POLLO ALLA NAPOLETANA

Bucatini with Chicken Gizzards Neapolitan Style

Most of us consider chicken gizzards cat food. We did too until we had the following dish in Naples. Now it is one we make often.

    12 chicken gizzards
    1 large onion
    1 large carrot
    4 teaspoons salt, in all
    3 tablespoons butter
    1 garlic clove
    2 basil leaves, chopped
    1 tablespoon chopped parsley
    4 cups (one 2-pound can) tomatoes,
        pushed through food mill
    ¼ teaspoon crushed red pepper
    1 pound *bucatini* (thin macaroni)

Boil chicken gizzards with onion, carrot, and 3 teaspoons of the salt in water to cover in a stewpot for 1 hour. Remove gizzards, cool; remove skins and membranes. Dice the lean dark meat and place it in a saucepan with the butter and garlic. Sauté until garlic is soft, then discard garlic. To meat and butter add basil, parsley, tomatoes, 1 teaspoon salt, and the red pepper. Simmer, uncovered, stirring often, for 20 minutes, or until sauce is smooth and thickened and diced meat tender. Cook *bucatini* al dente, drain, and toss with half of the tomato-meat sauce. Serve in hot bowls with remaining sauce liberally spooned atop each portion. Serves 6.

FARFALLETTE CON RIGAGLIE DI POLLO

"Little Butterflies" with Chicken Giblets

    ¾ pound chicken giblets (half livers)
    1 small white onion, minced

4 tablespoons butter

3 tablespoons olive oil

½ cup white wine

1 cup canned tomatoes, mashed

1 bouillon cube

Salt

1 cup heavy cream

1 pound *farfallette*

4 tablespoons grated Asiago cheese

Wash the giblets; cut them into pieces the size of a fingernail; set livers aside. In a saucepan, over medium heat, sauté the onion in 2 tablespoons of the butter and the oil. When onion is soft, stir in the gizzards and hearts; simmer for 15 minutes while adding the wine, a spoonful at a time. When the wine is used up, stir in the tomatoes and add the bouillon cube and salt to taste. Blend well, cover pan, and simmer for 1½ hours, stirring in, over this period, half of the cup of cream.

At the end of 1½ hours, stir in the livers; taste and adjust the seasoning; simmer for 10 minutes longer. Cook the *farfallette* al dente; drain. Place in a hot bowl, pour in the sauce, the rest of the cream, warmed, the cheese, and remaining butter. Toss well with wooden forks. Serve immediately in hot bowls. Serves 4 to 6.

CAPPONE ALL'ARISTOCRATICA

Stuffed Baked Capon

1 recipe Mornay Sauce (page 86)

1 capon (6 pounds), trussed

1 large carrot

1 large white onion

1 teaspoon salt

½ pound elbow macaroni

2 tablespoons grated Parmesan cheese

Prepare Mornay sauce. In a pot, simmer capon with carrot, onion, and salt in plenty of water until tender, 1½ to 2 hours. Remove intact and cool and untruss. Cook macaroni less than al dente, drain well, and toss with half of the Mornay sauce. Stuff capon with the pasta, sewing or skewering cavity. Place capon in a buttered baking dish, spoon remaining Mornay sauce over it, and sprinkle with cheese. Bake, uncovered, in a preheated 375° F. oven until brown. Serves 6.

GAMBA DISOSSATA DI CAPPONE ALLA TOSCANA
Boned Leg of Capon Tuscan Style

We tried this recipe in the home of a writer friend in Florence, and liked it so much that we have prepared it often since. He used the tasty wild mushrooms, porcini, *which impart a special flavor, but ordinary mushrooms do too.*

    2 capon legs (or plump chicken legs)
    2 eggs, beaten
    4 tablespoons butter, in all
    2 tablespoons olive oil
    1 teaspoon salt, or to taste
    Liberal amount of milled black pepper
    1 garlic clove, mashed
    6 large mushrooms, quartered
    ½ lemon
    1 white truffle, sliced thin
    1 pound *fettuccelle* (narrow *fettuccine*)
    2 tablespoons grated Parmesan cheese
    3 tablespoons heavy cream

Skin and bone capon legs and pound the meat as for *scaloppine*. Dip into beaten eggs. Sauté in a saucepan in 2 tablespoons of the butter and the oil over medium-high flame until golden. Sprinkle with salt and pepper; add the garlic and mushrooms. Turn the capon legs once and simmer for 5 minutes. Discard garlic. Take capon from saucepan and cut into julienne strips. Replace in saucepan, squeeze lemon juice over all, and stir in the sliced truffle; blend. Simmer for 5 minutes, uncovered, stirring constantly. Cook *fettuccelle* al dente; drain. Place in a large hot bowl and toss with the cheese, remaining butter, melted, and the cream. Add half of the sauce and toss again. Serve immediately in hot bowls with the remaining capon sauce spooned atop individual portions. Pass more grated Parmesan at table. Serves 4 to 6.

LINGUINE FINE CON FILETTI DI TACCHINO
Fine Linguine with Turkey Fillets

This we had in Alberto Wirth's fine Victoria Hotel in Rome. Knowing that we were tifosi di pasta, *our friend Alberto had one of the turkey fillets cut into thin strips and tossed with a dish of* linguine fine *as first course. We finished with that classic Bolognese dish of turkey breast so popular in Rome.*

    4 cups Basic Tomato Sauce (page 76)
    1 breast from an 8-pound turkey
    2 eggs, beaten
    1 cup seasoned bread crumbs
    3 tablespoons olive oil
    3 tablespoons butter
    ½ pound lean prosciutto, sliced thin
    2 tablespoons grated Parmesan cheese
    1 small ball of mozzarella cheese
    1 pound *linguine fine*

Prepare the tomato sauce; simmer. Cut the turkey breast into slices ⅓-inch thick. Dip each slice first into beaten eggs, then into bread crumbs; do this lightly; use not too much of either so that neither egg or bread dominates the flavor. In a saucepan, over medium heat, sauté the slices in oil and butter until golden brown, turning once. Butter a casserole or baking dish and arrange the sautéed slices in it. Place a slice of prosciutto on each slice of turkey, sprinkle lightly with Parmesan, and then lay a slice of mozzarella on each. Bake in a preheated 375° F. oven for 15 minutes, or until cheese melts and turkey is tender. Cook pasta al dente, drain, and place in a large hot bowl; toss with half of the tomato sauce. Slice one turkey

fillet into very thin strips; toss with the pasta. Serve immediately in hot rimmed soup bowls. Follow with the turkey slices, each topped with a small spoonful of tomato sauce, as a main course, accompanied with a green salad and a glass of very cold Soave Bertani, a classic Italian white wine. Serves 6.

ZITI CON PETTO DI TACCHINO ALLA MODENESE

Baked "Bridegrooms" with Turkey Breast Modena Style

½ small turkey breast, cubed

2 tablespoons flour

½ teaspoon salt, or to taste

Milled black pepper

Light pinch of grated nutmeg

3 tablespoons butter

1 white onion, minced

1 celery rib, scraped and minced

1½ cups Chicken Broth (page 96)

4 mushrooms, sliced

1 pound *ziti*

1 cup sour cream, warm

¼ cup buttered bread crumbs

Lightly dredge the turkey cubes with flour and season with salt, pepper, and nutmeg. In a saucepan, over medium heat, sauté in the butter until golden. Blend in onion and celery and sauté until vegetables are soft. Add broth, cover the pan, and simmer until meat is tender, about 25 minutes. Remove cover, stir in mushrooms, and simmer for 10 minutes, stirring often. Cook *ziti* al dente, drain, and place in a large hot bowl. Pour turkey-mushroom sauce over *ziti*, stir in the sour cream, and toss well. Place in a 2-quart casserole and sprinkle bread crumbs atop. Bake in preheated 400° F. oven for 15 minutes, until top is browned. Serves 4 to 6.

MODENA, the Piazza Grande—Emilia-Romagna

TAGLIOLINI CON PICCIONCELLI

Baked Narrow Egg Noodles with Squabs

In our opinion, squabs are the best of poultry and game, being 26-day-old pigeons that have become butterball-fat from being force-fed by their parents. At this age they have never left the nest, so they are tender, succulent fare, prized by those who know fine food. Here's one way the Italians team them with pasta.

1 recipe Béchamel Sauce (page 85)
2 tablespoons butter
2 tablespoons olive oil
4 slices of prosciuttini (lean ham), diced
2 shallots, chopped
1 carrot, scraped and chopped
½ cup chopped celery leaves
3 plump squabs
1 teaspoon salt, or to taste
Liberal amount of milled black pepper
½ cup rosé wine
2 cups Chicken Broth (page 96)
Squabs' livers, hearts, gizzards, minced
1 pound *tagliolini*
¼ cup grated Asiago cheese

Make the Béchamel sauce. In a deep saucepan, over medium heat, sauté in the butter and oil the ham, shallots, carrot, and celery leaves until soft. Add the squabs and brown, turning on all sides; season with the salt and plenty of black pepper. When birds are well browned, pour in the wine and cook over medium-high flame until it has evaporated. Add the broth, cover the pan, and simmer for 30 minutes until birds are fork-tender. Remove squabs; cool. Take meat from bones and cube; add with minced giblets to saucepan and simmer, uncovered, for 10 minutes, stirring often. Cook *tagliolini* al dente, drain, and place in a casserole. Pour the squab sauce, half the Béchamel sauce, and all the cheese over the pasta; blend. Cover with remaining Béchamel and brown in a preheated 400° F. oven for 10 minutes. Serves 6.

PAPPARDELLE CON PICCIONCELLI
Broad Egg Noodles with Squab

2 squabs (about 1 pound each)
½ teaspoon salt
Liberal amount of milled black pepper
2 tablespoons soft butter
½ cup dry white wine
1 cup sour cream
1 pound *pappardelle*

Clean squabs well, rub with salt and pepper, and spread with soft butter. Place in a baking pan, add the wine, and cook, covered, in a preheated 400° F. oven for 40 minutes. Remove. Take breasts from squabs and cut into strips ½ inch long, ¼ inch wide. Replace in baking pan, cover with sour cream, and cook, uncovered, in 350° F. oven for 15 minutes until cream has browned. Stir often during this last cooking stage. Cook *pappardelle* al dente, drain well, and toss with squab and sour cream. Serve in warm bowls. Serves 4 to 6.

TORTELLINI DI PICCIONCELLO
Tortellini of Squab

Italians use squab often, in many ways. Here is one of the simplest and tastiest in a dish we sampled first in Piacenza.

1 recipe Pasta Fresca for Tortellini (page 59)
1 squab
4 teaspoons salt, in all
6 slices of prosciutto
¼ teaspoon grated nutmeg
Milled black pepper
¼ cup grated Parmesan cheese
4 quarts Chicken Broth (page 96)
3 tablespoons butter, melted

Prepare the fresh pasta dough. In a small pot, boil squab in water with 3 teaspoons salt for 35 minutes. Remove, cool, skin; take meat from bones. Mince finely (or put through grinder) squab meat and prosciutto; work meats into a paste, mixing in nutmeg, 1 teaspoon salt, pepper, and half of the cheese. Cut dough and fill with this mixture, to make *tortellini* (page 59); shape as suggested and dry. Cook a few at a time in just simmering chicken broth (do not let the broth boil vigorously or it will break open the *tortellini*) until done. Remove with a slotted spoon to a warm platter, cover with hot butter, and sprinkle with remaining cheese. Serve immediately. Serves 4 to 6.

MAFALDA E FARAONA

Broad Noodles and Guinea Fowl

The route of the guinea fowl is an adventurous one—from Africa's dark jungles and plains to ancient Carthage, to epicurean Rome, where we first had it, naturally, with pasta.

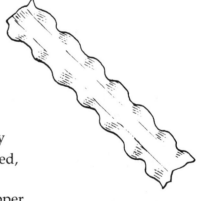

    4 tablespoons butter, in all
    2 tablespoons olive oil
    2 guinea hens, halved
    2 guinea hen livers, minced
    2 ounces dried beef, minced
    1 onion, minced
    1 carrot, scraped and minced
    1 celery rib, scraped and minced
    1 tablespoon minced Italian parsley
    2 very ripe tomatoes, peeled, seeded,
        and diced
    Liberal amount of milled black pepper
    2 cups Chicken Broth (page 96)
    ½ pound *mafalda* (a broad noodle, rippled on both edges)
    ¼ cup grated Asiago cheese

In a deep saucepan, over medium heat, heat 3 tablespoons of the butter and the oil, and in it sauté the guinea hens until brown. Stir in the minced livers, beef, onion, carrot, celery, parsley, tomatoes, plenty of pepper, and the broth. Simmer for 1½ hours, covered, or until guinea hens are tender. Remove birds to a warm platter for second course, spooning one third of the sauce over them to keep them moist. Simmer rest of sauce 15 minutes. uncovered, until smooth and thickened. Cook *mafalda* al dente, drain well. Place in a large hot bowl, toss with 1 tablespoon butter and the cheese. Serve immediately in hot bowls with more sauce spooned atop each portion. Pass more grated cheese at table. Serves 4.

LINGUINE ALLA CACCIATORA TOSCANA
Linguine Tuscan Hunter Style

    1 5-pound duckling
1½ tablespoons salt
Milled black pepper
3 tablespoons chopped parsley
2 small carrots
1 onion
1 celery rib
Duckling's liver
6 tablespoons butter
1 pound *linguine*
½ cup grated Parmesan cheese

Place the duckling in a large pot, cover with water, and add salt, pepper, 2 tablespoons of the parsley, the carrots, onion, and celery. Cover, bring to a boil, lower heat, and simmer for 1½ hours, or until duckling is tender. Remove duckling, save the water, and cool. Take meat from bones and put through grinder with the remaining tablespoon of parsley, mincing finely. Mince the liver and sauté in a small saucepan, over medium heat, for 5 minutes in the butter. Cook *linguine* al dente in the water in which duckling simmered; drain. On a hot serving platter arrange one layer of *linguine*, cover with minced duckling, sprinkle with Parmesan, then cover with minced liver and butter; repeat with at least another layer of all ingredients. Serves 4 to 6.

ANITRA STUFATA CON UN CONTORNO DI FARFALLE

Stewed Duck with a Surround of Pasta "Butterflies"

5-pound duckling, cut into small pieces,
    all excess fat removed, with heart,
    gizzard, and liver

3 cups Chicken Broth (page 96), or use
    Knorr chicken bouillon cubes dis-
    solved in 3 cups water

1 onion, coarsely chopped

1 carrot, coarsely chopped

1 celery stalk, coarsely chopped

¼ teaspoon dried thyme

¼ teaspoon dried rosemary

3 whole cloves

Flour for dredging

Salt and freshly ground black pepper to
    taste

4 tablespoons olive oil

½ cup dry red wine

Water

6 tablespoons butter

1 pound *farfalle*, cooked in boiling salted
    water until al dente, drained

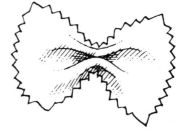

In a heavy-bottomed pot, over medium heat, place the neck, wings, heart, gizzard, and back of the duck, the broth, onion, carrot, celery, thyme, rosemary, and cloves, and simmer, covered, for 45 minutes. Strain the liquid, discarding the vegetables and duck parts. Set broth aside.

Lightly dredge the duck pieces with flour. Sprinkle lightly with salt and pepper. In a heavy deep pot, over medium-high heat, heat the oil and brown the duck pieces evenly. Remove from pan and pour off all fat. Pour in the wine and ½ cup of the strained broth and deglaze the pan, scraping up the browned bits on the bottom. Return the duck to the pot. Pour in the remaining broth and enough water to just cover the duck. Cover pot and simmer for 1 hour, or until the duck is fork-tender and the sauce has thickened. If the duck is tender and the sauce has not thickened enough, remove the duck and allow the sauce to cook down. Siphon off any fat that appears on the surface.

Chop the liver and cook for 1 minute in 2 tablespoons of butter. Stir into the duck pot.

Toss the hot pasta with the remaining butter (in small pieces) until the butter has melted. Serve the duck and its sauce in a hot rimmed serving dish, surrounded by the pasta. Serves 4 to 6 for a first course.

LASAGNE RICCE CON ANITRA

"Curly" Lasagne with Duck

This is one of those rare pasta dishes that is used in Italy as the main course. But lasagne *with sauce and meat often is considered a meal in itself, although we have also had it many times in a small first serving before the entrée. Here is a recipe we enjoyed after a duck shoot in Italy's northern lakes region. Only the duck breasts were used; there is little meat on the legs and wild duck wings are tough.*

1 duck liver
2 duck breasts
4 tablespoons butter
1 tablespoon olive oil
4 small white onions, chopped
4 cups (one 2-pound can) plum tomatoes
1 cup red wine
Pinch of dried rosemary
Pinch of dried oregano
1½ teaspoons salt, or to taste
Milled black pepper
1 pound *lasagne ricce*

Chop and put aside the duck liver; cut each half breast into quarters. In a large saucepan, over medium heat, brown duck pieces in the butter and oil; remove. Add the onions and sauté until soft. Stir in the tomatoes; simmer for 20 minutes. Return the duck to the pan and blend in the wine, rosemary, oregano, salt, and pepper. Now simmer, uncovered, for 1 hour, or until duck is tender, stirring often. Cook *lasagne ricce* al dente; drain with slotted spoon. Place the pasta on a large warm serving dish. Stir the chopped duck liver into the sauce; simmer for 5 minutes. Spoon the hot sauce and duck pieces over the noodles. Serves 4 to 6.

ARZAVOLA E SALSA COI FUNGHI
Wild Duck and Mushroom and Cheese Sauce

  2 tablespoons butter
  2 tablespoons olive oil
  1 white onion, chopped
  2 whole mallard duck breasts, boned
  Milled black pepper
  8 slices of prosciutto
  4 cups Mushroom and Cheese Sauce
      (page 86)
  ½ pound spaghettini
  4 tablespoons grated Parmesan cheese

Heat butter and oil in a pot; sauté onion in it until soft. Add the duck breasts, liberally mill in pepper, and sauté over medium-high flame until brown, turning often. Remove breasts, wrap 4 slices of prosciutto around each, and skewer in place with toothpicks. Return to pot and sauté, turning often, for 15 minutes. Prepare mushroom and cheese sauce. Pour sauce over duck breasts and simmer, uncovered, for 30 minutes, or until breasts are fork-tender. Remove breasts; cut 2 wafer-thin slices from each breast and add the slices to the pot with the mushroom and cheese sauce. Place remaining breasts on a warm platter, to be sliced and served as entrée with vegetable and salad. Cook spaghettini al dente, drain, and place in a warm bowl. Toss with the cheese and serve immediately in hot soup bowls with liberal spoonings of the mushroom sauce atop, and 1 slice of duck centering each portion. Serves 4.

FOLAGHE STUFATE CON LINGUINE

Stewed Coots with Linguine

This is a dish we had in Pisa after waterfowling on nearby Lake Massaciuccoli. Coots are waterfowl with a penchant for fish; consequently it is difficult to tell whether you are eating fish or fowl, so much so, that many Italians believe it is proper to eat them on meatless Fridays. We offer this as we saw it prepared, but earnestly suggest that you use a duckling instead of the coots.

4 tablespoons butter

1 tablespoon olive oil

1 white onion, chopped

1 carrot, chopped

1 celery rib, chopped

1 tablespoon chopped parsley

2 coots (or 1 duckling)

1 teaspoon salt, or to taste

Liberal amount of milled black pepper

½ teaspoon dried oregano

6 cups Basic Tomato Sauce (page 76)

1 pound *linguine*

Grated Asiago cheese

Melt butter and oil in a large pot; sauté onion, carrot, celery, and parsley until soft. Add the coots (or duckling), season with salt, pepper, and oregano, and brown over high flame on all sides. Reduce flame; add tomato sauce, cover pot, and simmer for 1½ to 2 hours until birds are fork-tender. Remove birds from pot; cool; take meat from bones and mince. Strain tomato sauce from the cooking pot into a saucepan, stir in the minced poultry; simmer, uncovered, stirring often, for 10 minutes. Cook *linguine* al dente; drain. Serve in hot soup bowls with sauce liberally spooned atop. Pass grated cheese at table. Serves 4 to 6.

AGNOLOTTI BERGAMO CON PERNICI ALLA GIOVANNINO

Giovannino's Agnolotti Bergamo with Partridges

1 recipe Pasta Fresca for Ravioli (page 59)
5 red-legged partridges or grouse
5 garlic cloves
8 tablespoons butter
4 tablespoons olive oil
1 tablespoon salt, or to taste
Much freshly milled black pepper
2 white onions, chopped
2 tablespoons chopped raisins
1 egg, beaten
5 tablespoons grated Parmesan cheese
4 tablespoons dry bread crumbs
1 tablespoon flour
3 tablespoons warm water
4 tablespoons red currant jelly

Prepare *ravioli* dough and set aside. Rub the partridges with 3 of the garlic cloves, mashed. Then spread 1 tablespoon soft butter over each bird. Place remaining garlic and the oil in a roasting pan and brown garlic on top of stove; remove garlic. Place partridges in the pan, sprinkle with salt and pepper, and brown the birds well. Cover the roasting pan and cook the birds in a preheated 400° F. oven for 1 hour, or until they are tender to the fork. Remove 4 birds to a warm platter for main course. Cool the remaining bird and remove meat from bones; discard skin and bones. Grind the partridge meat or mince finely, and sauté in a saucepan, over medium heat, with the onions in 3 tablespoons of the butter until the onions are soft. Take from the fire and stir in the raisins, beaten egg, cheese, and bread crumbs. Sprinkle with salt and pepper and blend well.

Roll out pasta dough into thin sheets. Spoon teaspoons of the partridge mixture on one sheet of dough, placing the mounds 2 inches apart; place the other sheet of dough on top and carefully press around each mound of filling. Cut around the mounds with a pastry cutter or sharp knife, making 2-inch circles. Press the edges of each one again, sealing;

dry for 20 minutes. Cook al dente in simmering salted water, about 8 minutes. Lift out the *agnolotti* with a slotted spoon.

Now place the partridge roasting pan on top of the stove over a low fire. Stir in the flour with a wooden spoon; scrape the brown particles from sides of pan, and stir into a smooth paste with the juices remaining in the pan. Add the warm water and currant jelly, stirring and blending everything well. Spoon 1 teaspoon of this sauce over each hot dumpling and serve immediately. Split the remaining partridges, and serve half of a bird per person for the main course. Serves 6 to 8.

LUMACHE CON PERNICIOTTE

"Snails" with Young Partridge

2 tablespoons olive oil
4 tablespoons butter
2 partridges
Pinch of dried rosemary
2 shallots, minced
Partridge livers and hearts, minced
10 black olives, pitted and sliced
1 teaspoon salt, or to taste
Liberal amount of milled black pepper
4 cups Chicken Broth (page 96)
1 pound *lumache*
¼ cup grated Asiago cheese

Heat oil and 2 tablespoons of butter in a large pot and sauté the partridges in it, browning evenly. Stir in the rosemary, shallots, minced livers and hearts, olives, salt, pepper, and broth. Cover pot and bake in a preheated 350° F. oven for 1 hour, basting often, until the partridges are fork-tender. Remove the birds; cool. Skin the birds and take meat from bones; cut into 1-inch strips. Place them in the sauce and simmer all on top of the stove, uncovered, for 15 minutes, stirring often, until sauce is smooth and thickened. Cook *lumache* al dente; drain. Place in a large hot bowl, toss with the remaining butter, then with the cheese. Serve immediately in hot rimmed soup bowls, with partridge strips in sauce liberally spooned atop each portion. Pass more cheese at table. Serves 6.

SPAGHETTI CON SALSA DI FAGIANO ALLA "POOR SHOT"

Spaghetti with Pheasant Sauce

Shooting on the estate of a friend of a friend in the north, near Bologna, one of us shot too quickly as the big pheasant rose, cackling hoarsely, the sun flaming on his iridescent ruff. "That one is for the pot and pasta," our host said to the embarrassed gunner. That night, using just the breast meat of the shot-riddled bird, which he had soaked in heavily salted water then drained, he prepared a sauce to remember.

1 pheasant breast, boned
1 small white onion, chopped
4 tablespoons butter
1 tablespoon olive oil
1 teaspoon salt, or to taste
¼ teaspoon crushed red pepper
2 basil leaves, chopped
6 very ripe tomatoes, peeled, seeded,
    and diced
Giblets of the bird, including liver
1 pound spaghetti

Cut the pheasant meat into pieces the size of your thumbnail. In a saucepan sauté the onion in the butter and oil over medium flame until soft. Stir in the diced pheasant and the salt. Simmer until the meat is brown, stirring constantly with a wooden spoon. Blend in the red pepper, basil leaves, and tomatoes, breaking up the tomatoes with a wooden spoon as they cook. Simmer, uncovered, for 25 minutes until sauce is satiny and the meat tender. Chop the giblets and stir in; simmer for 15 minutes. Cook the spaghetti al dente, drain, and place in a warm bowl. Spoon in half of the pheasant sauce and toss gently with wooden forks. Serve in hot soup bowls, with a heaping spoon of the remaining sauce over each serving. Serves 4 to 6.

SPAGHETTI E FAGIANO ALLA GRECO

Spaghetti and Pheasant Greek Style

We call this unusual dish Greek because when we had it, on an Italian shooting preserve, it was cooked by a chef from Athens, proving that pasta has no nationality, its appeal is truly international.

½ cup flour
½ tablespoon salt
Generous amount of milled black pepper
1 pheasant, cut into pieces
3 tablespoons olive oil
8 medium-size white onions, chopped
2 garlic cloves, minced
2 cups Chicken Broth (page 96), warmed
½ pound spaghetti

Place the flour, salt, and much pepper in a paper bag. Shake the pheasant pieces in the bag until they are evenly floured. In a saucepan, over medium heat, sauté in the oil until the meat is brown; remove the pheasant pieces to a heatproof casserole or roaster. Stir the onions and garlic into the oil, scraping the sides and bottom of the pan with a wooden spoon to dislodge browned particles. When onions are soft, stir in the warm broth; simmer until you have a smooth brown gravy. Pour the gravy over the pheasant, cover, and cook in a preheated 350° F. oven for about 25 minutes until meat is fork-tender. Cook spaghetti al dente, drain, and place in a warm bowl. Remove pheasant to a warm platter for second course. Spoon half of the sauce that remains over the spaghetti and toss gently with forks. Serve remaining sauce atop individual bowls of spaghetti. Serves 4.

FETTUCCE RICCE E FAGIANO ALLA PASQUALE

Pasquale's "Curly Ribbons" with Pheasant

1 large pheasant, cut into serving pieces
3 tablespoons olive oil
2 tablespoons chopped parsley
2 garlic cloves, minced
¼ teaspoon minced fresh rosemary
10 medium mushrooms, sliced
4 tablespoons butter
1 large beefsteak tomato, peeled, seeded, and diced
½ cup white wine
1½ cups Chicken Broth (page 96)
1 teaspoon salt, or to taste
Milled black pepper
½ pound *fettucce ricce*

In a pot, over medium heat, brown pheasant in the sizzling oil, stirring in parsley, garlic, and rosemary. When completely browned, pour off oil, add mushrooms, butter, and tomato; simmer for 8 minutes. Blend in wine and chicken broth and sprinkle in salt and pepper; stir well. Simmer, covered, until pheasant is tender, about 40 minutes. Cook *fettucce ricce* al dente; drain. Serve in hot soup bowls with the pheasant sauce spooned over. Serve pheasant for second course with a salad and vegetable. Serves 4.

TAGLIOLETTE CON QUAGLIE

Noodles with Quail

Italians eat just about anything that flies except crows, vultures, hawks, and owls, and they are considered Europe's most avid bird watchers. Warblers, buntings, thrushes, larks, finches, most birds that we fill our bird feeders for, are fair game. And we must admit the birds come to table as superb fare. In the larger cities there are even vendors (somewhat like our hot-dog stands) that sell tiny birds, broiled on a spit, and glasses of wine. But in deference to the Audubon Society and bird

MATERA—Basilicata

lovers, *we will omit the many recipes for the birds of the field, and concentrate on game birds. One of the best, the most delicate, is the quail. The following we had in Turin on a nest of noodles and it is a superlative dish.*

> ½ pound salted butter
> 8 quail, dressed
> 1 cup heavy cream
> 1 pound *tagliolette*
> Salt and black pepper to taste

Melt butter in a deep saucepan, add the quail, and sauté over medium-high flame, continually basting the little birds, inside and out, until they are fork-tender and golden-crisp; probably 25 minutes will do it. Remove to a warm platter. Stir the cream into the melted butter. Simmer, stirring constantly, until mixture forms a smooth and thick sauce. Add salt and pepper. Cook *tagliolette* al dente; drain. Place on a large hot serving platter; arrange the quail on the noodles and pour the butter-cream sauce over all. Serve 2 quail on a nest of noodles to each guest. Serves 4.

LINGUE DI PASSERI E BECCACCE CON SALSA ALLA MILANESE

"Sparrows' Tongues" and Woodcock with Milanese Sauce

Woodcock are long-billed, darting game birds with breasts of delicately flavored dark meat. Here's the way we had them in Milan.

> 7 tablespoons butter, in all
> 4 woodcock
> 6 mushrooms, minced
> 2 anchovies, minced
> ½ tablespoon flour
> 1 cup Chicken Broth (page 96)
> ½ cup white wine
> ¼ cup caper vinegar
> ½ teaspoon Dijon mustard
> ½ teaspoon salt

Pinch of cayenne pepper

1 pound *lingue di passeri*

1 teaspoon capers

In a deep saucepan, over medium heat, melt 4 tablespoons of the butter and braise woodcock until evenly browned. Add minced mushrooms and anchovies; simmer. Make a *roux* by blending remaining butter and the flour in a saucepan; stir in broth, wine, caper vinegar, mustard, salt, and cayenne, blending well. Pour this over woodcock; cover pan and simmer, stirring often, for 45 minutes, or until birds are tender. Remove woodcock, retaining only the breasts; keep warm. Simmer sauce, uncovered, stirring, until it is smooth and thickened. Cook *lingue di passeri* al dente, drain, and place in a large hot bowl. Strain sauce; add the capers. Pour half of the sauce over the pasta and toss well. Serve immediately in hot rimmed soup bowls, with 1 woodcock breast, covered with sauce, atop each portion. Serves 4.

CONCHIGLIE CON CONIGLIO IN UMIDO
"Shells" with Rabbit Stew

Rabbit is a dish often served in Rome, usually on Saturday, the same day the Romans serve their famous tripe (see page 199). Here's a rabbit and pasta stew we had there.

1 young rabbit, boned (save bones)

4 tablespoons butter

12 small onions, peeled

10 small carrots, scraped

4 tablespoons flour

1 tablespoon salt

Liberal amount of milled black pepper

1 teaspoon prepared mustard

1 bay leaf

2 cups Chicken Broth (page 96)

1 cup tomato juice

1 pound *conchiglie*

Cut rabbit into cubes. In a saucepan, over medium heat, brown the bones in the butter. Add the rabbit meat; brown. Place rabbit cubes in a casserole; add onions and carrots. Blend flour, salt, pepper, mustard, bay leaf, broth, and tomato juice. Pour into the saucepan with the butter and rabbit bones; simmer, uncovered, stirring often, for 15 minutes. Discard bones. Pour sauce over the rabbit and vegetables in casserole; cover. Bake in preheated 325° F. oven for 1 hour, or until tender. Cook *conchiglie* al dente; drain. Remove cover from casserole and spoon pasta around the border, pushing it into the sauce. Increase heat to 400° F.; bake for 10 minutes until sauce is bubbling. Serves 6.

LINGUINE CON CONIGLIO E FUNGHI

Linguine with Rabbit and Mushrooms

4 small white onions, chopped

1 garlic clove, minced

4 tablespoons olive oil

1 young rabbit, cut up

1 teaspoon salt, or to taste

Liberal amount of milled black pepper

12 small plum tomatoes, peeled, seeded,
    and diced

Pinch of grated nutmeg

1 clove

⅓ teaspoon dried red pepper

1 pound mushrooms, sliced

1 pound *linguine*

In a saucepan, over medium heat, sauté onions and garlic in the oil until soft. Place rabbit pieces in the pan and sprinkle with salt and pepper; toss rabbit in the oil and onions, coating it, and brown over medium-high heat. Blend in tomatoes and stir in nutmeg, clove, and red pepper. Cover, but stir often, and cook for 35 minutes until rabbit is fork-tender. Remove to a warm platter for a second course.

Stir sliced mushrooms into the sauce and cook, uncovered, for 8 minutes. Cook *linguine* al dente, drain, and toss with half of the sauce. Spoon the remainder over individual portions of pasta. Serves 4 to 6.

MOSTACCIOLINI CON CONIGLIO

"Tiny Moustaches" with Rabbit

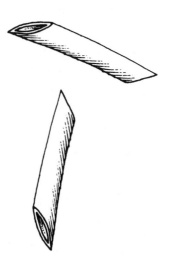

1 young rabbit
2 tablespoons butter
2 tablespoons chopped ham fat
1 medium-size white onion, chopped
1 celery rib, scraped and chopped
1 bay leaf, broken up
1 teaspoon salt
1 teaspoon flour
2 cups Chicken Broth (page 96)
1 pound *mostacciolini*
¼ cup grated Parmesan cheese

Remove meat from rabbit and dice. In a saucepan, over medium heat, sauté in the butter, stirring in ham fat, onion, celery, and bay leaf. Sprinkle in salt and simmer until ham fat is crisp and onion soft. Add the flour, sprinkling in evenly, then the broth. Cover the pan and simmer until rabbit is tender, about 25 minutes. Remove cover, increase heat, and stir sauce, cooking until it is thickened. Cook *mostacciolini* al dente, drain, and toss in a bowl with the cheese, using forks. Add half of the rabbit sauce and toss again. Serve in hot rimmed soup bowls with a spoon of the sauce over each serving. Serves 4 to 6.

TAGLIATELLE CON CONIGLIO

Broad Egg Noodles with Rabbit

6 slices of prosciutto
1 small onion
1 carrot, scraped
1 tablespoon chopped parsley
5 tablespoons butter, in all
1 tablespoon olive oil
1 young rabbit, cut into serving pieces
1 teaspoon salt, or to taste
Liberal amount of milled black pepper
4 ripe tomatoes, peeled, seeded, and
    diced
2 cups Chicken Broth (page 96)
½ tablespoon flour
1 pound *tagliatelle*
½ cup grated Asiago cheese

Finely mince prosciutto, onion, carrot, and parsley. In a saucepan, over
medium heat, sauté in 3 tablespoons of the butter and the oil until onion
is soft and ham beginning to crisp. Add the rabbit, season with salt and
pepper, and brown evenly on all sides over medium-high flame. Reduce
heat, add tomatoes and broth, and simmer, covered, for 1½ hours, or until meat is fork-tender. Remove rabbit pieces and cool; take meat from bones
and chop coarsely. Make a *roux*, or smooth golden butter paste, by melting remaining 2 tablespoons butter and stirring in the flour. Stir this and
the coarsely chopped rabbit meat into the tomato-vegetable sauce; simmer, uncovered, for 10 minutes until the sauce is smooth and thickened.
Cook *tagliatelle* al dente; drain. Place in a large hot bowl, toss with half of
the cheese, then with half of the sauce. Serve immediately in hot bowls,
passing extra sauce and extra cheese at table. Serves 4 to 6.

PAPPARDELLE CON SALSA DI LEPRE
Wide Egg Noodles with Hare Sauce

Pasta with hare sauce is a favorite of ours. We've had it in many places in Italy, but the memorable ones come from Chianti and La Fontanella in Rome, both specializing in game cookery as practiced in Tuscany. This, we believe, is the classic hare sauce.

1 small hare, boned (save the bones)
3 tablespoons butter
2 tablespoons olive oil
2 carrots, scraped
3 shallots
1 garlic clove
1½ teaspoons salt
Liberal amount of milled black pepper
1 teaspoon dried tarragon
2 large very ripe tomatoes, peeled and
    diced
1½ cups red wine
Liver of the hare, chopped
2 chicken livers, chopped
1 pound *pappardelle*
¼ cup grated Romano cheese

Brown the hare bones in 2 tablespoons of the butter and the oil in a deep saucepan. Finely mince carrots, shallots, and garlic; stir in; simmer, uncovered, for 15 minutes. Mince hare meat, or put through grinder. Remove hare bones from saucepan, add minced hare to remaining vegetables, stirring well, and season with salt, pepper, and tarragon; brown. Add the tomatoes and wine, cover the pot, and simmer for 2 hours, stirring often. Remove cover and simmer for 15 minutes until sauce is smooth and thickened. Add the livers; simmer 4 minutes. Cook *pappardelle* al dente, drain, and toss with remaining butter and half of the cheese. Serve in hot bowls with hare sauce liberally spooned atop; pass more cheese at table. Serves 4 to 6.

FETTUCCE CON LEPRE

Wide Fettuccine with Hare

Hare, especially if it isn't young, is a rather dry meat; the Germans offset this by larding. The Italians have several ways of moistening the meat. Here's one method we learned in Ravenna.

    1 recipe Mornay Sauce (page 86)
    2 ounces dried beef
    1 small white onion
    1 carrot, scraped
    1 celery rib, scraped
    3 tablespoons butter
    1 tablespoon olive oil
    1 small hare, boned
    Pinch of grated nutmeg
    Milled black pepper
    Liver and kidney of hare, diced
    1 pound *fettucce* (wide *fettuccine*)

Make the Mornay sauce. Finely mince the dried beef, onion, carrot, and celery; in a saucepan, over medium heat, sauté in butter and oil until onion is soft. Cube the hare meat and sauté in the same pan until brown. Sprinkle in nutmeg and pepper, blending well. Add the liver and kidney and sauté for 5 minutes. Blend in the Mornay sauce and simmer, uncovered, until sauce is smooth and thickened and ingredients well blended. Cook *fettucce* al dente; drain. Place in a large hot bowl, pour in half of the hare sauce, and toss well. Serve immediately in hot bowls with the remaining sauce liberally spooned atop the portions. Serves 4 to 6.

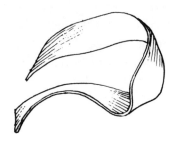

LEPRE ALLA FIORENTINA

Hare in the Florence Style

1 loin of hare
4 tablespoons olive oil
3 carrots, chopped
3 celery ribs, chopped
3 medium-size white onions, chopped
½ teaspoon salt, or to taste
Milled black pepper
1½ cups red Chianti
4 very ripe tomatoes, peeled, seeded,
    and diced
2 garlic cloves
4 rosemary leaves
2 sage leaves
3 slices of bacon, chopped
2 anchovies, chopped
1 pound *fettucce* (wide *fettuccine*)
2 tablespoons butter
¼ cup grated Parmesan cheese

In a saucepan, over medium heat, brown the hare in the oil, turning often. Lower flame and add the carrots, celery, and onions; season with salt and pepper and simmer, stirring often, for 15 minutes. Add the wine, tomatoes, garlic, rosemary, sage, bacon, and anchovies; blend well. Simmer, uncovered, basting often, for 1½ hours, or until meat is tender and sauce is dark brown and thickened. Remove hare, cube the meat, and return it to the sauce; simmer. Cook *fettucce* al dente, drain, and place in a hot bowl with the butter; toss. Add the cheese; toss again. Serve in hot soup bowls with the hare sauce liberally spooned atop each portion. Serves 4 to 6.

TAGLIATELLE VERDI CON CAPRIOLO

Green Noodles with Venison

1 recipe Pasta Verde (page 60)
2 garlic cloves, chopped
2 tablespoons chopped parsley
14 very thin slices of prosciutto with fat
3-pound loin of venison, well hung
2 tablespoons olive oil
8 mushrooms, sliced
1 cup red wine
2 white onions, chopped
2 carrots, chopped
2 celery ribs, chopped
12 small very ripe plum tomatoes, peeled
1 clove
2 cups boiling water
1 teaspoon salt
½ cup grated Asiago cheese

Prepare the green pasta dough, cut into *tagliatelle* (page 58), and dry. Mix half of the garlic and half of the parsley and mince together. Roll 10 slices of prosciutto in the mixture until they are well coated. Lard the venison; make deep incisions in the meat; push the prosciutto into the slits. Chop remaining prosciutto. Sauté remaining garlic and parsley and the chopped prosciutto in the oil in a heavy pot. When ham fat is crisp, add the venison and brown on all sides over a medium flame. Add the mushrooms and wine, cover the pot, place over low flame, and simmer for 10 minutes. Stir in the chopped onions, carrots, and celery, blending in well. Cook for 15 minutes, lifting the meat and stirring with a wooden spoon to dislodge browned particles that have stuck to the bottom of the pan. Now add the whole plum tomatoes and the clove, stirring them in well. Simmer for 20 minutes, covered, stirring often. Pour in the boiling water and add the salt, stirring in well. When venison is fork-tender remove to a warm platter for the second course.

Stir sauce in pan well and strain through a fine strainer. Replace in pan and simmer for 15 minutes, uncovered. Cook *tagliatelle* al dente; watch carefully, as fresh pasta cooks more rapidly than dry. Drain, place in a warm bowl, and toss with the cheese, using wooden forks. Serve in hot rimmed soup bowls with strained venison sauce lavishly spooned over each serving. Serves 4 to 6.

ROME, the colonnade, Piazza San Pietro

Near GRIMALDI—Calabria

IX
Vegetables with Pasta

*T*he versatility of pasta was never more clearly pointed out to us than one evening when we arrived at Maria Luisa's mother's home, hungry for a dish of her spaghetti. She wasn't planning pasta for dinner that night, but it took her only thirty seconds to make her decision. She went into her garden and picked a head of snowy cauliflower. She quickly boiled it, and when it was just tender she separated it into little "flowers." These she placed in a frypan over low heat with one quarter pound of butter and generously milled black pepper over it. (Cauliflower is very partial to black pepper.) Then she gently stirred until cauliflower and butter were blended and steaming hot. Covering the pan, she lowered the fire to a bare simmer and in another pot cooked the spaghetti less than al dente. Drained, it was then placed in the pan with the butter and cauliflower and tossed. It was a unique, delicious, fresh-tasting meal right from the garden.

Although pasta is popular everywhere now, many of us still do not realize what superb sauces are growing in the garden for dishes that can come to table as fresh as springtime and as savory as summer.

LINGUINE CON ASPARAGI
Linguine with Asparagus

18 tips of fresh young asparagus
1 teaspoon salt
¼ pound butter
Milled black pepper
1 pound *linguine*
½ cup grated Parmesan cheese

Carefully cook the asparagus tips in salted water to cover until they are almost done; do not let them break up, just over 5 minutes should do it; drain. Replace asparagus in the pot with half of the butter; mill in black pepper and shake the pan well so asparagus is butter coated. Cook *linguine* al dente; drain. Toss in a warm bowl with remaining butter and the cheese; mill in black pepper and toss gently again. Serve in hot soup bowls with the asparagus tips atop, evenly divided among the servings. Serves 4 to 6.

BUCATINI CON BROCCOLI ALLA CALABRESE
Bucatini with Broccoli Calabrian Style

This is a specialty of Calabria that we always have at least twice when we go there.

1 large bunch of broccoli, separated into
    flowerets
2 garlic cloves, minced
4 tablespoons olive oil
2 pounds ripe tomatoes, peeled, seeded,
    and cut into strips
4 tablespoons mixed raisins and pine
    nuts, minced
1 pound *bucatini* (thin macaroni)
2 tablespoons minced parsley

Clean broccoli and rinse well; boil in salted water until tender; drain. Remove flowerets and place on a warm platter. In a saucepan, over medium heat, sauté garlic in the oil until brown; add tomatoes and simmer for 15 minutes, uncovered. Add raisins and pine nuts, stir in well, and simmer for 5 minutes. Cook *bucatini* al dente, drain, and place in a large hot bowl. Add the broccoli flowerets, pour the sauce over, and toss well but carefully with wooden forks. Serve immediately in hot soup bowls, sprinkled with parsley. Serves 6.

CAPPELLI DI PRETE CON BROCCOLI

Baked "Priests' Hats" with Broccoli

1 large bunch of broccoli
7 quarts water
2 tablespoons salt
2 garlic cloves
5 tablespoons olive oil, in all
4 tablespoons butter
1 pound *cappelli di prete*
1 cup grated Asiago cheese

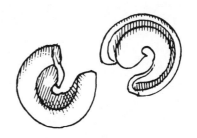

Remove all leaves from the broccoli and separate heads from stalks. Separate the heads into flowerets or buds. In a large pot, over medium heat, cook the leaves and stalks in the water with the salt for 10 minutes. Add the broccoli flowerets and cook them for 5 minutes. Remove the broccoli stems and leaves, discard; save the water. Put the drained flowerets in a pan with the garlic, 3 tablespoons of the oil, and the butter; cook over medium heat for 5 minutes. Cook the *cappelli di prete* in the broccoli water until less than al dente; drain. Oil a casserole with the remaining olive oil and arrange a layer of pasta in it. Place a layer of broccoli flowerets over the pasta and sprinkle with cheese; repeat until broccoli and pasta have been used; end with a heavy sprinkling of cheese atop. Bake for 10 minutes in a preheated 375° F. oven. Serves 4 to 6.

Near BRIENNO, on Lake Como—Lombardy

TAGLIATELLE CON CAVOLO
Noodles with Cabbage

1 pound hot Italian sausage
1 medium head of cabbage, cored and
    shredded
Much freshly milled black pepper
Salt
1 pound *tagliatelle*

Remove casings from sausage and break meat into pieces. In a saucepan, over medium heat, sauté sausage until well cooked; drain, saving 3 tablespoons of the fat. Place the fat, the cooked sausage, and ½ cup water in the saucepan. Add the shredded cabbage, plenty of black pepper, and 1 teaspoon of salt, or to taste. Cover the pan tightly and cook over low fire for 20 minutes. Cook the *tagliatelle* al dente, drain, and add to the cabbage and sausage. Toss lightly until well mixed. Serves 4 to 6.

SPAGHETTI CON VERZA ALLA LOMBARDA
Spaghetti with Savory Cabbage Lombard Style

2 tablespoons butter
2 tablespoons olive oil
¼ pound bacon, minced
4 ripe tomatoes, peeled, seeded, and
    diced
1 large white onion, minced
½ garlic clove, minced
1 tablespoon minced Italian parsley
1½ teaspoons salt
Liberal amount of milled black pepper
1 small head of Savoy cabbage, washed,
    cored, and diced
1 quart Beef Broth (page 96)
½ pound spaghetti
6 tablespoons grated Parmesan cheese

In a large pot, over medium heat, melt butter, add oil, and sauté minced bacon in it until nearly brown. Stir in tomatoes, onion, garlic, and parsley and season with salt and pepper. Simmer, uncovered, for 15 minutes. Add cabbage and broth, cover, and simmer for 45 minutes. Add spaghetti and cook, uncovered, stirring gently with a wooden fork, for 15 minutes, or until pasta is al dente. Serve immediately in hot rimmed soup bowls with Parmesan sprinkled atop. Serves 4.

TAGLIOLINI FRESCHI CON CAROTE
Fresh Noodles with Carrots

1 recipe Pasta Fresca all'Uovo (page 57)

3 tablespoons butter

3 tablespoons olive oil

6 mushrooms, sliced

4 large carrots, scraped, diced, and
cooked al dente

8 thin slices of prosciutto, cut into julienne strips

Grated Asiago cheese

Prepare fresh pasta dough and cut it into noodles ¼ inch wide. Dry for 1 hour. While they are drying, prepare the sauce. In a saucepan, over medium heat, heat butter and oil and in it sauté the mushrooms, carrots, and prosciutto for just 5 minutes; remove from heat. Cook noodles al dente; drain, saving 4 tablespoons of the boiling pasta water. Reheat sauce and stir in reserved pasta cooking water; blend well. Serve noodles immediately in hot bowls with the sauce spooned atop. Pass cheese at table. Serves 6.

AGRIGENTO, the Temple of Hercules—Sicily

CONCHIGLIE CON CAVOLFIORE

"Shells" with Cauliflower

    1 small cauliflower, leaves still attached
    1 teaspoon salt
    ½ pound *conchiglie*
    4 tablespoons butter
    Liberal amount of milled black pepper
    ½ cup grated Parmesan cheese

Place cauliflower in a 4-quart pot, cover with water, and add the salt. Simmer, covered, for 15 to 20 minutes, or until cauliflower is just tender. Lift it from the water and cool; take flowerets from cauliflower and put them aside on a warm platter. Return base of cauliflower to pot. Add *conchiglie;* cook al dente. Remove cauliflower, then drain pasta. Place in a large hot bowl, stir in butter, mill in black pepper, and mix well. Add the cauliflowerets and toss. Serve immediately in hot rimmed soup bowls with Parmesan liberally sprinkled atop. Serves 4.

TAGLIATELLE CON CAPONATA

Tagliatelle with a Tangy Eggplant "Sauce"

Many of us are familiar with the zesty cold antipasto caponata, *but few of us have enjoyed it hot tossed with pasta. We were introduced to this in Naples a couple of years ago.*

    2 medium-size eggplant, peeled, cut into
        ½-inch-thick slices, salted, arranged in
        several stacks with a weight placed
        atop, and allowed to stand for 1 hour
    4 tablespoons olive oil
    3 garlic cloves, minced
    2 medium-size white onions, chopped

2 medium-size red peppers, cored,
  seeded, and diced

6 medium-size ripe tomatoes, peeled,
  seeded, and chopped, or 3 cups
  drained canned tomatoes, chopped

12 black olives (the plump purplish
  ones), coarsely chopped

1½ teaspoons fresh basil chopped, or ½
  teaspoon dried sweet basil

⅛ teaspoon (or to taste) crushed red pepper

½ teaspoon dried oregano

½ cup dry red wine

Salt and freshly ground black pepper to
  taste

2-ounce can rolled anchovies with capers,
  drained and coarsely chopped

1 pound *tagliatelle,* cooked in boiling
  salted water until al dente, drained

Rinse, dry, and cube the eggplant slices.

In a deep pot, over medium heat, heat the olive oil and cook the garlic and onion for 4 minutes, or until soft. Do not brown. Add the eggplant, peppers, and tomatoes and cook, uncovered, for 15 minutes, stirring occasionally. Stir in the olives, basil, red pepper, oregano, and wine, Season with pepper and lightly salt (keeping in mind that the anchovies added later will supply salt), stirring well to blend. Reduce heat and simmer, stirring occasionally, for 20 minutes, or until the *caponata* sauce has thickened and most of the liquid has evaporated. Stir in the anchovies. Taste for seasoning.

Serve the pasta in heated individual plates, generously topped with *caponata,* which each guest will toss or stir into the pasta as he desires. Serves 6.

MEZZANI CON MELANZANE

Baked Macaroni with Eggplant

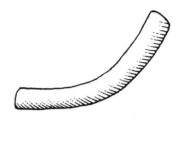

½ pound broken *mezzani* (medium-size macaroni)
1 large eggplant, peeled and diced
5 cups Basic Tomato Sauce (page 76)
1 small mozzarella cheese, sliced thin

Cook the *mezzani* al dente; drain. Arrange a layer of pasta in bottom of a baking dish, top with a layer of eggplant, then tomato sauce, then slices of cheese to cover; repeat until all the eggplant, sauce, cheese, and pasta are used. Bake in a preheated 325° F. oven for 30 minutes. Serves 4 to 6.

PERCIATELLI CON MELANZANE ALLA SICILIANA

"Pierced" Pasta with Eggplant Sicilian Style

3 tablespoons olive oil
2 garlic cloves, mashed
1 eggplant, peeled and cubed
½ small chili pepper, diced
1 sweet red pepper, diced
2 tablespoons minced parsley
½ teaspoon salt
Liberal amount of milled black pepper
8 cups (two 2-pound cans) plum tomatoes, put through food mill
6 anchovy fillets, drained and minced
1 pound *perciatelli*

In a saucepan, over medium heat, heat oil; sauté garlic until brown, then discard garlic. Add eggplant cubes, peppers, parsley, salt, and pepper; simmer for 10 minutes, uncovered, stirring often. Blend in tomatoes; simmer, uncovered, stirring often, for 30 minutes, or until sauce is smooth and thickened. Stir in the anchovies and simmer for another 10 minutes. Cook *perciatelli* al dente; place in a large hot bowl, pour in half of the sauce, and toss well with wooden forks. Serve immediately in hot rimmed soup bowls with the remaining sauce lavishly spooned atop. Serves 6.

RIPIENO DI MELANZANE CON CHICCHI DI RISO
Baked Eggplant Stuffed with "Grains of Rice"

½ cup *chicchi di riso*

2 small eggplant

3 tablespoons olive oil

1 large white onion, minced

3 large ripe tomatoes, peeled, seeded,
    and diced

¼ pound beef round, ground twice

1½ teaspoons salt, or to taste

Liberal amount of milled black pepper

4 tablespoons grated Asiago cheese

Cook the grains of pasta firmer than al dente; drain. Halve the eggplant, remove pulp and chop, keeping shells intact. In a deep saucepan, over medium heat, sauté together in the oil the eggplant pulp, onion, tomatoes, and beef; season with salt and pepper and simmer for 10 minutes, blending the mixture well. Remove from heat and stir in the pasta. Fill the eggplant shells with the mixture and top with grated cheese. Place 1 cup hot water in a casserole and arrange the eggplant halves in it. Bake in a preheated 400° F. oven for 20 minutes or until eggplant is tender. Serves 4.

BUCATINI CON LATTUGA ARRICCIATA

Bucatini with Escarole

1 large head of escarole, washed and
    chopped
2 tablespoons olive oil
2 tablespoons butter
1 teaspoon salt, or to taste
Liberal amount of milled black pepper
1 pound *bucatini* (small macaroni)
6 tablespoons grated Asiago cheese

Cook the escarole, covered with water, until tender; drain well. In a small saucepan, over medium heat, heat olive oil and butter until butter is melted. Place escarole in a large hot bowl, add hot olive oil and butter, salt and pepper; blend. Cook *bucatini* al dente, drain, and place in bowl with hot escarole; toss well, using wooden forks. Serve immediately in hot bowls with cheese sprinkled atop. Serves 6.

FARFALLETTE CON FAVE GRANDI

"Little Butterflies" with Beans

2 cups fresh shelled lima beans
1 teaspoon salt
4 slices of lean bacon
1 pound *farfallette*
3 tablespoons butter

In a pot half cover beans with water and add the salt; cook, covered, until nearly done, but firm, not soft; drain. Cut bacon into small pieces and sauté in a saucepan, over medium heat, until crisp. Pour off half of the grease; combine drained lima beans with the bacon and mix. Cook *farfallette* until al dente; drain well. Toss in a warm bowl with the butter, add lima beans and bacon, and toss again. Serve individually in hot bowls. Serves 4 to 6.

SPAGHETTI CON FAVE PICCOLE

Spaghetti with Lima Beans

½ pound spaghetti, broken into 1-inch
  pieces
3 cups baby limas, cooked al dente
1 large white onion, sliced thin
1 large celery rib, scraped and chopped
2 cups Basic Tomato Sauce (page 76)
1 tablespoon minced fresh basil
¼ cup grated Parmesan cheese
Two 4-inch sweet Italian sausages, sliced

Cook the spaghetti pieces al dente; drain. Blend limas, onion, celery, tomato sauce, and basil; stir in spaghetti. Butter a baking dish and pour in
the mixture. Sprinkle the cheese on top and arrange the sausage slices;
bake, uncovered, in a preheated 375° F. oven, for 15 minutes until sausage
browns and mixture bubbles. Test a piece of sausage and a piece of onion;
when they are done, it is time to remove from oven. Serves 6.

CAPELLINI CON FUNGHINI

Fine Vermicelli with Small Mushrooms

24 whole button mushrooms, washed
¼ pound butter
Liberal amount of milled black pepper
1 pound *capellini*
3 tablespoons grated Parmesan cheese

In a saucepan, over medium heat, sauté the mushrooms in the butter for
10 minutes, or until soft, milling in much black pepper. Cook *capellini* al
dente; be careful, as this is a fragile pasta and probably will be ready in
less than 5 minutes; drain. In a large hot bowl, place half of the mush-

room and butter sauce, add the *capellini* and toss; sprinkle in the grated cheese and toss again. Serve immediately in hot rimmed soup bowls, with the remaining mushroom-butter sauce spooned atop. Pass more grated cheese at table. Serves 4.

FARFALLONI CON FUNGHI ALLA MARIA LIMONCELLI
"Big Butterflies" with Mushrooms

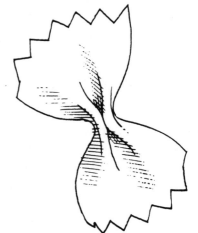

1½ pounds fresh mushrooms
5 shallots, chopped
½ cup butter
½ cup Chicken Broth (page 96)
½ tablespoon salt, or to taste
¼ teaspoon crushed red pepper
1 pound *farfalloni*
½ cup grated Romano cheese

Wash mushrooms and chop them, stems and all, without peeling. In a deep saucepan, over medium heat, simmer shallots in butter until soft. Add mushrooms and chicken broth and simmer, stirring often, for 20 minutes. Add salt and red pepper, stir in well, and cook for a further 5 minutes. Cook *farfalloni* al dente, drain, and place in a large hot bowl. Add cheese and toss. Pour mushroom sauce over the pasta and toss well but gently. Serves 4 to 6.

FEDELINI CON FUNGHI DEL TERRENO BOSCOSO
Fedelini with Wild Mushrooms

In Italy this is a specialty of those brave souls who wander the meadows and woodlands gathering mushrooms. These can be found here in the United States, of course, but if you do not know your wild mushrooms, buy fresh ones from your grocer.

4 tablespoons olive oil

4 medium-size white onions, chopped

4 tablespoons butter

6 large firm wild mushrooms (or use the
cultivated ones from the grocer)

1 cup rich Chicken Broth (page 96)

1 cup small cubes of provolone

½ cup grated Asiago or Parmesan cheese

12 ounces *fedelini,* cooked in boiling
salted water until al dente, drained

2 tablespoons chopped fresh basil mixed
with 3 tablespoons chopped Italian
parsley

In a saucepan, over medium heat, heat the oil and cook the onions for 5
minutes, or until soft and slightly golden. Do not brown. Add the butter
and mushrooms, raise heat, and cook for 2 minutes. Lower heat, stir in
the broth and cheese cubes, and cook, stirring, for 3 minutes. Add the
grated cheese and cook, stirring, for 4 minutes.

Toss the hot pasta with the chopped basil and parsley, then with the
hot cheese-mushroom sauce. Serves 4 as a first course.

BUCATINI ALLA DOMENICANA

Bucatini with Anchovies and Mushrooms

4 ounces dried mushrooms

12 anchovies

3 tablespoons olive oil

2 tablespoons water

¼ teaspoon salt

1 garlic clove

1 pound *bucatini* (thin macaroni), broken
into 3-inch lengths

1 tablespoon minced parsley

⅓ cup bread crumbs

Soak the dried mushrooms in warm water until they are flexible and somewhat puffed into shape; drain, rinse in cold water, drain again; mince. Rinse the anchovies well in cold water, drain, and mash. In a saucepan, simmer the mushrooms in 1 tablespoon of the olive oil, the water, and the salt for 10 minutes. Push through a sieve with half of the cooking liquid and put aside. In the saucepan sauté the garlic in 1 tablespoon of the oil until brown; discard the garlic. Add the mushrooms and liquid and the anchovies; simmer for 5 minutes and remove from fire. Cook *bucatini* in lightly salted water until al dente, drain, and place in a casserole. Cover the *bucatini* with the mushroom-anchovy sauce; sprinkle with parsley. Brown the bread crumbs in the remaining olive oil and sprinkle over casserole. Bake in a preheated 400° F. oven for 10 minutes. Serves 4 to 6.

CAPELLINI CON CIPOLLE PICCANTI

"Fine Hairs" with a Piquant Onion Sauce

¼ pound (1 stick) butter

6 medium-size onions, finely chopped

2-ounce can anchovy fillets, drained,
    each anchovy cut into 4 pieces

12 ounces *capellini,* cooked in boiling
    salted water until al dente (this won't
    take long, as this very thin pasta
    cooks quickly, so start testing soon
    after it is submerged), drained

In a deep saucepan, over medium heat, melt the butter. Lower heat and simmer, stirring, until the butter is light brown. Add the onions and cook, stirring, until they attain a caramel glaze. Stir in the anchovy pieces and simmer, stirring, for 5 minutes. Anchovies should disintegrate and be well blended with the onions. Add the hot pasta to the sauce in the saucepan, tossing well, but gently, with wooden forks until the pasta is well coated with the onion sauce. Serve immediately in hot bowls. Serves 4 to 6.

SPAGHETTINI CON PISELLI ED UOVA

Spaghettini with Peas and Eggs

1 pound spaghettini
6 tablespoons grated Parmesan cheese
1½ teaspoons salt, or to taste
Liberal amount of milled black pepper
2 cups fresh shelled peas, cooked al
    dente and drained
3 eggs, beaten

Cook spaghettini al dente; drain, saving ⅓ cup of the cooking water. Return spaghettini and water to the pot and, over low flame, quickly blend in 2 tablespoons of the cheese, the salt, pepper, peas, and eggs; toss well; remove from fire. Serve immediately in hot rimmed soup bowls with remaining cheese sprinkled atop. Serves 6.

STELLE E PISELLI

"Stars" and Peas

4 tablespoons butter
2 tablespoons olive oil
4 slices of prosciutto, diced
2 tablespoons minced Italian parsley
2 small white onions, minced
6 cups Beef Broth (page 96)
1½ cups fresh shelled peas
1 teaspoon salt, or to taste
Liberal amount of milled black pepper
½ pound *stelle*
6 tablespoons grated Asiago cheese

In a deep saucepan, over medium heat, melt butter, add oil, and sauté the prosciutto, parsley, and onions until onions are soft and ham is almost crisp. Stir in 4 cups of the broth and the peas, and season with salt and pepper. Simmer, covered, for 20 minutes, stirring often. Now add the *stelle* and more broth and simmer until pasta is al dente. Serve immediately in hot rimmed soup bowls. Dot with remaining butter and sprinkle with Asiago. Serves 6.

TAGLIATELLE CON PISELLI

Noodles with Peas

3 large white onions
2 celery ribs, scraped
6 slices of bacon
2 tablespoons butter
2 tablespoons olive oil
1 pound fresh peas, shelled
6 very thin slices of prosciutto, cut into
    julienne strips
1 tablespoon minced parsley
1 teaspoon salt
Liberal amount of milled black pepper
1 cup Chicken Broth (page 96)
1 pound *tagliatelle*
¼ cup grated Parmesan cheese

Mince finely onions, celery, and bacon. In a deep saucepan, over medium heat, sauté in butter and oil until onions are soft. Add the peas, prosciutto strips, and parsley; season with salt and pepper. Simmer for 5 minutes; add broth, cover pan, and simmer for 20 minutes, or until peas are tender. Cook *tagliatelle* al dente, drain, and place in a large hot bowl. Sprinkle cheese on the pasta and toss well. Add half of the sauce and toss again. Serve immediately in hot soup bowls with remaining sauce spooned atop. Serves 6.

FEDELINI CON PISELLI E TARTUFI BIANCHI

Fedelini with Peas and White Truffles

Vernon Jarrett, owner of George's Restaurant in Rome, once told us, "If your recipe calls for fresh white truffles and you do not have them, change your menu." However, not being spoiled by having white truffles readily available, we find that the canned ones work out pretty well. At times we have also substituted dried wild mushrooms for the truffles, tripling the amount.

6 tablespoons butter

2 cups frozen tiny green peas, cooked
slightly less than package directs

25-gram can (which will contain 1 truffle
about 1 inch in diameter) white truffles, thinly sliced (use a *tagliatartufi*—a
special truffle slicer—if you have one);
reserve the liquid in the can

½ teaspoon freshly ground black pepper

Salt to taste

12 ounces *fedelini*, cooked in boiling
salted water until al dente, drained

½ cup grated Asiago or Parmesan cheese

In a saucepan, over low heat, melt 2 tablespoons of the butter. Add the peas and truffle and cook for 2 or 3 minutes to heat through. Stir in the pepper, salt, and liquid from the can.

Toss the hot pasta with 4 tablespoons of butter (in small pieces), then toss lightly with the peas-truffle mixture and the cheese. Serves 4 to 6.

VERMICELLI CON PEPERONI VERDI

Vermicelli with Green Peppers

1 large white onion, minced
1 garlic clove, minced
2 tablespoons olive oil
3 tablespoons butter
4 small sweet green peppers, cored, de-
   seeded, and diced
1 cup Chicken Broth (page 96)
1 teaspoon salt, or to taste
Liberal amount of milled black pepper
1 pound *vermicelli*
4 tablespoons grated Asiago cheese

In a saucepan, over medium heat, sauté onion and garlic in oil and butter until onion is soft; add peppers and simmer for 10 minutes. Add the broth, salt, and pepper; stir well and simmer, uncovered, for 15 minutes. Cook *vermicelli* al dente; drain. Add the pepper sauce and toss well, using wooden forks. Serve immediately in hot rimmed soup bowls with cheese sprinkled atop. Serves 6.

TAGLIOLETTE CON PEPERONI ED ACCIUGHE

Noodles with Peppers and Anchovies

As this is written, peppers seem to be a fad food in the United States. "Jump-aboard" faddists who write about food and "teach" cooking use them in just about everything except ice cream. This turns us off, as peppers, not just the hot variety either, dominate food, overwhelming delicate nuances. For example, the pepper people even use them with sole and swordfish!

Once, however, not long ago when we were touring Italy's Abruzzi, where Maria Luisa's family originated, and where the best pasta is made, a pastaio *(pasta manufacturer), to prove the point that Abruzzi pasta retains its personality, no matter the sauce, introduced us to a zingy pepper-anchovy sauce.*

4 tablespoons olive oil

3 small red sweet peppers, cored,
    seeded, and cut into julienne strips

2 tablespoons hot water

2 garlic cloves, put through a garlic press

½ a 2-ounce can (about 5 fillets) of an-
    chovies, drained and finely chopped

6 medium-size ripe tomatoes, peeled,
    seeded, and finely chopped

½ teaspoon sugar

Freshly ground black pepper to taste

Salt to taste

1 pound *tagliolette*, cooked in boiling
    salted water until al dente, drained

In a deep saucepan, over medium heat, heat the olive oil. Add the peppers and cook for 5 minutes. Add the hot water, lower heat, cover pan, and simmer for 10 minutes. Add the garlic, anchovies, tomatoes, sugar, and black pepper, stirring to blend well. Simmer, uncovered, stirring occasionally, for 20 minutes, or until the sauce has thickened. Taste before adding salt, as the anchovies may have supplied enough.

Toss the hot noodles with the sauce. Our Abruzzi host was not lavish with the sauce, and the flavor of the pasta itself certainly was evident. Serves 6.

PASTA POLPETTE CON SALSA DI PEPERONI ARROSTITI E POMODORI

Pasta Croquettes with a Roasted Pepper and Tomato Sauce

2 egg yolks
2 tablespoons water
2 tablespoons olive oil
½ teaspoon salt
3 tablespoons butter
2 tablespoons flour
1½ cups milk
½ cup heavy cream
½ teaspoon nutmeg
¼ teaspoon cayenne
½ cup grated Fontina cheese
Salt and freshly ground black pepper to
    taste
2 cups broken-up *tagliolini* (a very thin
    noodle), cooked in boiling salted
    water until cooked firmer than al
    dente, well drained
1 egg, beaten
Fine dry bread crumbs for dredging
Hot oil for deep frying
Sweet Pepper and Tomato Sauce (see be-
    low)

In a shallow bowl, beat together the egg yolks, water, olive oil, and salt. Set aside. In a saucepan, over medium heat, melt the butter. Stir in the flour and cook, stirring, to a smooth paste. Gradually add the milk and cook, stirring, to make a smooth sauce. Stir in the cream, nutmeg, cayenne, and cheese. Simmer until the cheese has melted and the sauce thickened. Season with salt and pepper.

In a saucepan, combine the pasta and sauce and cook over very low heat, stirring, until the mixture is very thick. Remove from the heat and stir in the egg. Cool thoroughly. Shape into tablespoonful-size cylinders and dip into the egg yolk-water-oil mixture. Dredge with bread crumbs. With a slotted spoon or skimmer, lower, a few at a time, into the hot oil and cook until golden. Do not crowd. Drain on paper towels and keep warm in a preheated 200° F. oven while you cook the others. Serve with the Sweet Pepper and Tomato Sauce. Serves 4 to 6.

Sweet Pepper and Tomato Sauce:

2 tablespoons butter

2 tablespoons olive oil

4 small onions, thinly sliced

1 cup chopped prosciutto or other cooked ham

4 medium-size ripe tomatoes, peeled,
    seeded, and chopped

½ teaspoon dried oregano

2 tablespoons fresh chopped basil, or 2
    teaspoons dried sweet basil

Salt and freshly ground black pepper to taste

3 large roasted sweet bell peppers,
    skinned, seeded, and cut into ½-inch
    strips (prepare them yourself, or use a
    good commercial brand such as Pro-
    gresso or Goya)

In a heavy saucepan, over medium heat, heat the butter and oil. Add the onions and cook until soft, about 4 minutes. Do not brown. Add the prosciutto and cook for 1 minute. Add the tomatoes, oregano, and basil, and simmer for 15 minutes, or until the liquid has evaporated and the sauce is thickened. Season with salt and pepper. Add the roasted peppers and cook for 2 or 3 minutes, just to heat through. Serve alongside the pasta *polpette.*

To Roast Peppers:

Place the peppers on a baking sheet and broil them under a low flame, turning often until they blister and all surfaces are charred. Cool slightly and peel under cold running water. Discard the seeds and white membranes. Do not roast too long, as they'll get too soft.

The peppers can also be held on a fork directly over a gas flame, turning them often, until they are evenly charred.

FETTUCCINE FRESCHE CON SPINACI

Baked Fresh Fettuccine with Spinach

1 recipe Pasta Fresca all'Uovo (page 57)
2 pounds fresh spinach
1 large white onion, minced
1 garlic clove, minced
8 slices of prosciutto, diced
2 tablespoons butter
2 tablespoons olive oil
2 tablespoons flour
1½ cups light cream
Juice of 1 lemon
1 teaspoon salt, or to taste
Liberal amount of milled black pepper
4 tablespoons grated Parmesan cheese

Prepare the fresh pasta dough, cut it into *fettuccine* (page 58), and dry. While it is drying, cook spinach without water in a covered pan until soft. Drain spinach and press out all liquid from it; put through a food chopper. In a saucepan, over medium heat, sauté onion, garlic, and prosciutto in butter and oil until onion is soft. Add the flour and blend it in; stir in the cream slowly until the sauce is smooth. Blend in spinach and lemon juice and season with salt and pepper. Cook noodles much less than al dente (for they will be cooked further); be careful, as fresh pasta cooks quickly. Drain, place in a large hot bowl, pour the spinach sauce over, and toss. Place in a buttered baking dish or casserole and sprinkle with cheese. Bake in a preheated 375° F. oven for 10 minutes, until cheese browns and sauce bubbles. Serves 6.

FUSILLI CON GORGONZOLA VERDE

Pasta "Twists" with Gorgonzola and Spinach

Here's a new one (at least to us) that we discovered in Milan, a simple combination that produces a delicious pasta dish.

1 pound fresh spinach, trimmed,
    stemmed, and washed
4 tablespoons butter
6 ounces Gorgonzola, crumbled
2 tablespoons Chicken Broth (page 96)
⅓ cup dry Marsala
1 cup heavy cream
1 garlic clove, minced
Freshly ground black pepper
Salt to taste
12 ounces *fusilli*, cooked in boiling salted
    water until al dente, drained
½ cup grated Asiago or Parmesan cheese

In a pot, cook the spinach in a large amount of boiling salted water until just tender. Do not overcook. Remove with a large fork and drain well. When cool enough to handle, squeeze out as much liquid as possible with your hands. Purée in a food processor or blender and reserve.

In a saucepan, over medium heat, melt the butter, stir in the Gorgonzola, stirring until it has melted and is smoothly blended with the butter. Add the spinach, broth, Marsala, cream, garlic, and a liberal milling of black pepper. Blend well. Lower heat and simmer 10 minutes, stirring frequently. Taste for seasoning before adding salt.

In a hot bowl, toss the hot pasta with half of the sauce, a few tablespoonfuls at a time, tossing well after each addition. Spoon the pasta into hot bowls and top with spoonfuls of the remaining sauce. Sprinkle with grated cheese. Serves 4 to 6.

CANNELLONE SPETTACOLOSO RIPIENO

An Unusual Stuffed Cannellone

3 pounds fresh spinach, trimmed,
    stemmed, and washed (or three 10-
    ounce packages of chopped frozen
    spinach cooked according to package
    directions)

2 tablespoons butter

1 garlic clove, minced

2 cups ricotta, set in a sieve over a bowl
    to drain

1 cup grated Asiago or Parmesan cheese

1 whole egg

2 egg yolks

Salt and freshly ground black pepper to taste

¼ teaspoon nutmeg

⅛ teaspoon cinnamon

⅛ teaspoon cayenne

1 teaspoon sugar

½ recipe Pasta Fresca all'Uovo (page 57)

⅔ recipe (about 1⅔ cups) Béchamel
    Sauce (page 85) to which ⅓ cup
    grated Asiago or Parmesan cheese has
    been added

In a large pot, cook the fresh spinach in a large amount of boiling water until just tender, about 10 minutes. Drain well and when cool enough to handle, squeeze liquid out with your hands. Chop. If using frozen spinach, cook and squeeze liquid out. In a frypan over medium heat, melt the butter and cook the garlic for 1 minute, or until soft. Do not brown. Add the spinach and cook for 2 minutes, stirring. In a bowl combine and blend well the spinach, ricotta, grated cheese, the egg and egg yolks, salt, pepper, nutmeg, cinnamon, cayenne, and sugar. Set aside.

Make the pasta and roll it into a ¹⁄₁₆-inch-thick rectangle, 12 inches wide (length not important). The rest of the procedure can be handled in two ways:

1. Cook the pasta before stuffing it: Brush the sheet of pasta lightly

with olive oil and cook it in a pasta cooker (a large deep pot with a removable colander). When the salted water in the pot is boiling, carefully lower the sheet of pasta into the colander without allowing the pasta to fold over onto itself. Cook for 45 seconds. Remove the colander with the pasta sheet and plunge into a bowl of cold water. Drain thoroughly and lay on a damp cloth. Pat top dry. With a knife, trim the pasta to have a clean rectangle, 12 inches wide. Spread the spinach filling to within ½ inch of the right and left sides, and to within 1 inch of the side farthest from you. (This is much like filling a jelly or chocolate roll.) Roll, using the towel to move the pasta along as you would use wax paper in making a dessert roll. The finished product will be a large 12-inch-long roll. Place in a 13-by-8-inch buttered shallow baking dish. Spoon on the sauce and bake in a preheated 350° F. oven for 30 minutes, or until golden brown. Allow to rest for a few minutes, then cut into ¾-inch slices.

2. Fill the pasta before cooking it: Trim the pasta sheet and spread the spinach filling on it as directed above. Roll the filled pasta onto a large double thickness of cheesecloth. Tie both ends, encasing the roll in the cheesecloth, so that you have what looks like a large sausage. Bring the salted water to a boil in a fish poacher or a roasting pan with a rack. Lower the roll into the water and simmer for 25 minutes. Carefully lift the roll from the water. (This will be easy with a fish poacher, as the rack usually has handles.) If you are using another vessel, use two large perforated spatulas to remove the roll. Cool slightly and cut into ¾-inch slices. Arrange the slices snugly side by side, in a single layer, in a shallow buttered baking dish. Spoon over the sauce and bake in a preheated 350° F. oven for 25 minutes, or until golden brown. Serves 4 to 6.

RAVIOLI CON SPINACI E RICOTTA

Ravioli with Spinach and Ricotta

1 recipe Pasta Fresca for Ravioli (page 59)
½ pound spinach
½ pound ricotta cheese, drained
1 egg
2 cups grated Parmesan cheese
1 teaspoon salt, or to taste
Milled black pepper
¼ teaspoon grated nutmeg
¼ pound butter, melted

Prepare the fresh pasta dough. Wash spinach thoroughly and cook in a covered pan without water until tender; drain spinach and press out all liquid. Put drained spinach and ricotta through a food chopper and place in a bowl. Blend in the egg and 1 cup of the Parmesan, and season with salt, pepper, and nutmeg; mix well. Roll out dough into thin sheets; place a teaspoon of filling on bottom sheet every 2 inches; cover with the second sheet of dough and cut into squares with a pastry cutter. Dry for 45 minutes. Cook a half dozen at a time in simmering salted water. Remove *ravioli* with a slotted spoon as they are done; drain on paper towels. Serve immediately drenched with hot melted butter. Pass remaining Parmesan at table. Serves 4 to 6.

The following are four similar, yet subtly different, simple tomato sauces for four different pastas, each with its special texture.

FETTUCCE AL POMODORO ALLA MARIA

Maria's Fettucce with Tomatoes

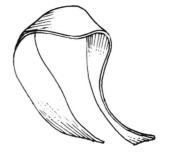

10 plum tomatoes, peeled, seeded, and
    diced
5 tablespoons butter
2 tablespoons olive oil
1 teaspoon dried oregano
1 tablespoon chopped parsley
1 teaspoon salt, or to taste
1 pound *fettucce* (wide *fettuccine*)
½ cup grated Parmesan

Chop the tomatoes and simmer them in a saucepan, uncovered, with the butter, oil, oregano, parsley, and salt for 20 minutes. Cook *fettucce* al dente; drain. Place in individual dishes and spoon the tomato sauce directly from the pan over the pasta. Pass the Parmesan at table. Serves 4 to 6.

NAPLES—Campania

FEDELINI CON POMODORI FRESCHI PICCANTI

Fedelini with Fresh Piquant Tomatoes

With each trip to Italy we discover new pastas; the country's repertoire seems endless. This one, with baked fresh tomatoes, we found in Parma.

8 large dead-ripe but firm tomatoes,
    peeled; with your hands squeeze out
    seeds and liquid, then cut into ¾-inch
    slices
2-ounce can of flat anchovy fillets,
    drained; cut each fillet into 3 pieces
2 teaspoons capers, rinsed and drained
3 tablespoons chopped fresh basil
1 garlic clove, minced
¼ teaspoon (or to taste) crushed red pep-
    per
½ cup olive oil
1 pound *fedelini*, cooked in boiling salted
    water until al dente, drained
Salt to taste
3 tablespoons chopped Italian parsley

In a casserole arrange a layer of half of the tomatoes, overlapping, if necessary. Dot with half of the anchovies, capers, and basil, and all of the garlic. Sprinkle with half of the red pepper and olive oil. Arrange another layer using the remaining halves of the ingredients.

Bake the tomatoes in a preheated 400° F. oven, uncovered, for 30 minutes.

Remove the casserole from the oven. Fork the hot *fedelini* on top and with wooden forks gently toss with the tomatoes, blending well. Taste before adding salt, as the anchovies may have supplied enough. Serve in hot bowls, sprinkled with parsley. Serves 6.

BAVETTE ALLA CIOCIARA

Bavette Peasant Style

1 garlic clove, minced
2 tablespoons olive oil
6 very ripe tomatoes, peeled and diced
¼ teaspoon crushed cherry pepper
½ teaspoon salt
1 pound *bavette* (narrow *linguine*)

In a deep saucepan, over medium heat, sauté garlic in oil until soft; add diced tomatoes and simmer for 15 minutes. Stir in cherry pepper and salt and simmer for another 15 minutes. Cook *bavette* al dente; drain. Place in pan with the tomato-garlic sauce and toss right in the cooking pan. Serves 4 to 6.

CONCHIGLIE ALL'INFERNO

"Shells" with Hot Sauce

2 garlic cloves, minced
2 tablespoons olive oil
8 cups (two 2-pound cans) plum tomatoes
1 teaspoon salt, or to taste
3 tablespoons chopped fresh basil
1 teaspoon crushed red pepper
1 pound *conchiglie*
1 tablespoon butter
½ cup grated Asiago cheese

In a saucepan, over medium heat, sauté minced garlic in the oil until soft. Put tomatoes through food mill and add them to the garlic-oil with the salt, basil, and red pepper, stirring well. Simmer, uncovered, stirring often, until water has evaporated and sauce thickened. Cook the *conchiglie* in rapidly boiling salted water until al dente. Remove the shells with a skimmer or slotted spoon, draining them. Place in warm bowl with the butter and cheese; toss. Add half of the sauce and mix well with the pasta. Serve in warm bowls, each portion topped with a dollop of the remaining sauce. have plenty of wine close at hand to keep the flame down. Serves 4 to 6.

TRIPOLINI ALLA ANTONIO

Tripoli "Bows" Antonio

2 garlic cloves, minced
1 tablespoon chopped parsley
2 tablespoons olive oil
6 ripe tomatoes, peeled, seeded, and
    diced
1 teaspoon salt, or to taste
1 pound *tripolini*
½ cup grated Asiago cheese

In a saucepan, over medium heat, sauté garlic and parsley in the oil until soft; add diced tomatoes and salt. Cook, uncovered, for 35 minutes over low fire. Meanwhile, cook *tripolini* al dente; drain. Pour sauce over pasta and toss with the cheese. Serves 4 to 6.

FUSILLI BUCATI AI POMODORI VERDI

Thin Macaroni "Twists" and Green Tomatoes

6 medium-size green tomatoes, slightly
  yellowish, just beginning to ripen
1 cup flour
1 tablespoon salt
Liberal amount of milled black pepper
6 tablespoons olive oil
1 pound *fusilli bucati*
2 tablespoons butter, melted

Slice tomatoes into ½-inch slices; flour each slice on both sides and season with salt and pepper. In a saucepan, over medium heat, cook in hot olive oil until each side is evenly browned. Cook *fusilli bucati* al dente; drain. Toss with the melted butter, mill in black pepper, and toss again, gently. Place in hot soup bowls, with 3 slices of crisp green tomato atop each serving. In eating, the diner breaks the tomato up with his fork and stirs it into the pasta, releasing its liquid and flavor. Serves 4 to 6.

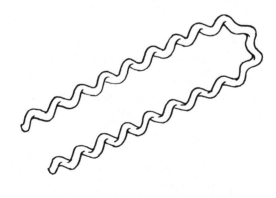

MARUZZELLE VEGETALI

Small "Shells" with Vegetables

8 tablespoons (1 stick) butter

2 tablespoons olive oil

3 medium-size onions, thinly sliced

1 garlic clove, minced

4 medium-size tomatoes, peeled, seeded,
    and coarsely chopped

1 cup rich Beef Broth (page 96), or use a
    Knorr beef bouillon cube dissolved in
    1 cup water

¼ teaspoon dried orégano

2 medium-size heads of fennel (white
    bulb only), trimmed, thinly sliced,
    and cooked in boiling salted water un-
    til crisp-tender

3 medium-size (about 4 inches by 2
    inches) zucchini, cut into halves
    lengthwise, then into ¼-inch slices

½ cup chopped Italian parsley

Salt and freshly ground black pepper to
    taste

1 pound of *maruzzelle*, cooked in boiling
    salted water until slightly firmer than
    al dente, drained

¾ cup grated Asiago or Parmesan cheese

3 tablespoons fresh fine bread crumbs

In a large heavy pot, over medium heat, heat 2 tablespoons of the butter
and the olive oil. Add the onions and garlic and cook for 5 minutes, or
until soft. Do not brown. Add the tomatoes, broth, and orégano. Simmer,
uncovered, for 10 minutes. Add the fennel, zucchini, parsley, salt, and
pepper, and cook until the zucchini is just crisp-tender (do not overcook).
Taste for seasoning.

Toss the hot pasta with 4 tablespoons of butter (in small pieces) and a
generous amount of black pepper until the butter has melted. Arrange a
layer of half the pasta in a buttered shallow baking dish. Spoon on half of

the vegetable mixture. Sprinkle on half of the cheese. Arrange the remaining pasta over the cheese. Spoon on the remaining vegetable sauce. Sprinkle with the remaining cheese and the bread crumbs, and dot with the remaining butter. Place in a preheated 375° F. oven for 25 minutes, or until the top is golden. Serves 6.

LINGUINE E ZUCCHINI ALLA MARIA LUISA
Maria Luisa's Linguine and Zucchini

    2 medium-size zucchini
    4 tablespoons butter
    4 tablespoons olive oil
    1 tablespoon salt, or to taste
    Much freshly milled black pepper
    1 pound *linguine*

Cut zucchini into thin slices about the size and thickness of a fifty-cent piece. In a saucepan, over medium heat, sauté in 2 tablespoons of the butter and the oil until they are deep gold in color. Drain zucchini on paper towels; sprinkle lightly with salt and mill pepper over the slices. Cook *linguine* al dente, drain, and toss with remaining 2 tablespoons butter. Mill black pepper over the pasta and toss again. Serve in individual hot soup bowls, with slices of hot zucchini atop. Serves 4 to 6.

FEDELINI CON ZUCCHINI FRITTI
Thin Pasta with Fried Zucchini

We had this the last time we were in Rome in early summer. The Romans probably have never see a full-grown zucchino. They harvest them when they're not much larger than a thumb, and use them in many ways. Here's one way they dress up a dish of pasta.

2 tablespoons butter

1 tablespoon olive oil

2 garlic cloves, minced

1 large ripe tomato, peeled, seeded, and
    finely chopped

1 small pimiento, cut into slender strips

Salt and freshly ground black pepper to
    taste

1 cup heavy cream

12 ounces *fedelini*, cooked al dente in boil-
    ing salted water, drained

4 very small zucchini, unpeeled, cut into
    matchstick-size strips, lightly dredged
    with flour, then deep-fried in oil,
    drained (French-fried-potato style),
    and kept crisp and warm

In a saucepan, over medium heat, heat the butter and the oil and cook the garlic for 1 minute, or until soft. Do not brown. Stir in the tomato and pimiento and season with salt and pepper. Cook, stirring, for 10 minutes. Stir in the cream and cook, stirring, for 5 minutes, or until the sauce thickens.

   Place the hot pasta in a warm serving bowl and toss with the tomato-cream sauce. Add the crisp warm zucchini and carefully toss with wooden forks, blending with the pasta. Serve immediately in hot soup bowls. Serves 4 for first course.

VENICE—Venezia Euganea

DITALINI E FAGIOLI
"Little Thimbles" and Beans

2 large onions, chopped
1 garlic clove, minced
3 tablespoons olive oil
6 cups Basic Tomato Sauce (page 76)
2 cans (1 pound, 4 ounces each) *cannellini*
    beans
1 cup water
2 teaspoons salt
Milled black pepper
Pinch of red pepper
½ teaspoon dried oregano
¼ pound *ditalini*
¼ cup grated Parmesan cheese

In a deep saucepan, over medium heat, cook onions and garlic in the oil until onions are soft. Add tomato sauce, undrained beans, water, and seasonings. Cover and simmer until mixture thickens, about 30 minutes. Cook *ditalini* firmer than al dente, on the chewy side. Drain; stir slowly into the bean and tomato sauce. Sprinkle with Parmesan and serve in hot soup bowls. Serves 4 to 6.

CONCHIGLIETTE CON FAGIOLI ALLA SORRENTO
"Tiny Shells" with Beans alla Sorrento

2 cups dried Great Northern beans
2 teaspoons salt
2 small celery ribs, chopped
2 small white onions, chopped
3 tablespoons olive oil
6 ripe tomatoes, peeled, seeded, and
    diced

1 tablespoon chopped Italian parsley

4 fresh basil leaves, chopped, or 1 teaspoon dried sweet basil

½ pound *conchigliette*

Soak the beans in water for 6 hours; drain. Place the beans in 4 quarts of water, add 1 teaspoon of salt, and cook over medium heat until beans are al dente—firm but nearly done, about 1 hour; drain.

In a saucepan, over medium heat, sauté the celery and onions in the oil until soft. Sprinkle in remaining salt, then add the tomatoes, parsley, and basil. Simmer for 15 minutes, uncovered, breaking up the tomatoes with a wooden spoon as they cook. Add beans to the pan with the to-matoes and vegetables; stir in well. Cook the *conchigliette* al dente, drain, and add to the bean mixture. Serve in hot soup bowls. Serves 4 to 6.

LUMACHINE CON PATATE

"Small Snails" with Potatoes

This is a farmer's lunch that we had one cold day outside Foggia—an unusual teaming of potatoes and pasta.

2 medium-size white onions, chopped

2 tablespoons olive oil

2 tablespoons butter

1 pound potatoes, peeled and cubed

2 pounds very ripe tomatoes, peeled, seeded, and diced

1½ teaspoons salt, or to taste

Liberal amount of milled black pepper

1 tablespoon minced Italian parsley

1 pound *lumachine*

6 tablespoons grated Romano cheese

In a deep saucepan, over medium heat, sauté onions in the oil and butter until soft; stir in potatoes and simmer, covered, for 15 minutes. Blend in tomatoes and season with salt, pepper, and parsley. Simmer, covered, for

25 minutes; then uncovered for 10 minutes, stirring often. Cook the *lumachine* al dente; drain. Blend pasta into the tomatoes and potatoes, mixing well, add 4 tablespoons Romano and blend. Serve immediately in hot rimmed soup bowls with remaining cheese sprinkled atop. Serves 6.

BAVETTE CON LEGUMI MISTI

Bavette with Mixed Vegetables

    2 tablespoons olive oil
    4 tablespoons butter, in all
    2 small white onions, chopped
    2 small carrots, scraped and chopped
    4 cups (one 2-pound can) plum tomatoes
        with basil leaf
    1 teaspoon salt, or to taste
    Milled black pepper
    1 small eggplant, unpeeled
    3 tablespoons *pignoli* (pine nuts)
    1 pound *bavette* (narrow *linguine*)

In a saucepan, over medium heat, heat the oil and 2 tablespoons of the butter; sauté the onions and carrots until onions are soft. Stir in the tomatoes, breaking them up with a wooden spoon as they cook. Add salt and pepper and cook, uncovered, over a medium flame for 25 minutes, stirring constantly, until sauce is smooth and velvety and thickened. Cut unpeeled eggplant into bite-size pieces and in a saucepan sauté the pieces in remaining 2 tablespoons butter. Stir in the pine nuts and cook until the eggplant is tender. Stir eggplant mixture into the tomato sauce. Simmer for 5 minutes, uncovered. Cook *bavette* al dente; drain. Serve in hot individual rimmed soup bowls, with the tomato-eggplant sauce spooned over. Serves 4 to 6.

VONGOLETTE ALLA GIARDINIERE
"Little Clam Shells" Garden Style

3 celery ribs, scraped
2 medium zucchini
1 small eggplant
2 green medium-size peppers
3 white medium-size onions, chopped
6 large ripe tomatoes, diced
2 tablespoons olive oil
1½ teaspoons salt, or to taste
Milled black pepper
1 pound *vongolette*
½ cup grated Asiago cheese

TAORMINA, the cathedral square—Sicily

Cut celery, zucchini, eggplant, and peppers into 1-inch pieces. In a sauce-pan, over medium heat, stir all the vegetables into the olive oil, add salt and pepper, and cook, covered, for 30 minutes. Cook *vongolette* al dente; drain. Toss with cheese, then with the hot vegetable sauce. Serves 4 to 6.

RIGATONI "TUTTO GIARDINO"

Rigatoni with the Whole Garden

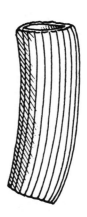

½ cup Italian parsley leaves
1 garlic clove
2 white onions
6 slices of prosciutto
3 small red radishes
3 small carrots
2 small leeks
⅓ cup fresh basil leaves
3 tablespoons butter
3 tablespoons olive oil
1 cup finely chopped cabbage
1 large zucchini, diced
4 medium-size ripe tomatoes, peeled,
    seeded, and diced
1 cup Chicken Broth (page 96)
1½ teaspoons salt, or to taste
Liberal amount of milled black pepper
1 pound *rigatoni* (grooved pasta tubes)
⅓ cup grated Romano cheese
⅓ cup grated Parmesan cheese
6 tablespoons soft butter

Mince finely the parsley, garlic, onions, prosciutto, radishes, carrots, leeks, and basil, and mix all together into what Italians call a *soffritto*. Heat butter and oil in a large pot, stir vegetable mixture into it and simmer until on-ions and carrots are soft; blend in the cabbage, zucchini, tomatoes, and chicken broth; season with salt and pepper. Simmer, covered, for 20 minutes, stirring often, until vegetables are tender. Cook *rigatoni* al dente, drain, and place in a large hot bowl. Sprinkle the mixed cheeses over the pasta and stir in the soft butter; toss well. Add the vegetable sauce and toss again. Serve immediately in hot soup bowls. Serves 8.

SPAGHETTINI ESTIVI

Summer Spaghettini

2 pounds ripe tomatoes
1 pound spaghettini
1 tablespoon chopped Italian parsley
5 fresh basil leaves, chopped
Juice of 1 lemon
1 tablespoon olive oil
1 garlic clove, quartered
½ teaspoon salt, or to taste
Milled black pepper

Dip tomatoes into hot water and peel; slice very thin. Cook spaghettini al dente, drain, and place in a large hot bowl. Add the slices of raw tomato, the parsley, basil, lemon juice, oil, garlic, salt, and plenty of pepper. Using wooden forks, toss well. Serve immediately in hot rimmed soup bowls. Serves 4 to 6.

Note: We introduced Craig Claiborne to this dish. Successful meeting.

CANNELLE CON SALSA FREDDA

"Small Reeds" with Cold Sauce

4 very ripe plum tomatoes, peeled,
    seeded, and chopped

1 sweet green pepper, seeded and
    chopped

1 sweet red pepper, seeded and chopped

4 ribs of white celery with leaves (scrape
    ribs), chopped

1 tablespoon salt, or to taste

Liberal amount of milled black pepper

1 tablespoon capers

1 teaspoon dried oregano

2 tablespoons chopped fresh basil leaves

2 tablespoons wine vinegar

2 tablespoons olive oil

1 pound *cannelle*

Place tomatoes, peppers, and celery in a bowl; add salt and black pepper, capers, oregano, and basil; stir in vinegar. Pour the olive oil over to make a layer on top, cover bowl, and place in refrigerator overnight.

Next day cook *cannelle* al dente, drain, and serve in very hot soup bowls. Stir the cold sauce well and spoon some of it over each serving at table. This is a dish for hot weather and is surprisingly piquant and good. Proving once again that pasta can reach out and grab flavors, hold them, and pass them on. Serves 4 to 6.

LINGUINE PRIMAVERILE
Springtime Linguine

Here's another version of springtime pasta with an uncooked vegetable and seasonings, surprisingly good. We introduced this to the United States in 1968. Today, several versions of this same dish are popular, with several cooks claiming credit.

6 large very ripe tomatoes, peeled,
   seeded, and diced
1 garlic clove, finely minced
8 large fresh basil leaves, minced
2 tablespoons minced Italian parsley
1½ teaspoons salt, or to taste
Liberal amount of milled black pepper
4 tablespoons fine olive oil
1 pound *linguine*
Grated Romano cheese

In a large bowl blend well the tomatoes, garlic, basil, parsley, salt, a lot of pepper, and the oil. Cook *linguine* a dente; drain. Serve immediately in hot bowls with the springtime sauce lavishly spooned atop. Pass cheese at table. Serves 6.

X
Particular Pastas

*H*ere, first, are some of the simplest and therefore among the best of pastas, the ones sauced with olive oil and garlic, butter and cheese, and with added variations on these themes—cream, eggs, anchovies, herbs, nuts, etc. They are followed by a variety of particularly original recipes—those in which cheeses are of major importance; tomatoes stuffed with pasta; a number of unusual baked dishes, including *timballi* (pasta "pies"); and two special sections, one on pasta with truffles and one on the aristocrat of all pastas, *fettuccine*. These recipes do not fit into any general category, but each has a particular quality to recommend it.

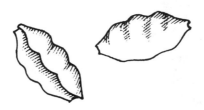

ROME, ancient road into the countryside—Latium

VERMICELLI CON AGLIO ED OLIO

Vermicelli with Garlic and Oil

Here is a dish you can prepare in 15 minutes, at the outside, and be almost completely assured that no guest has had it before. It is a favorite in many parts of Italy as a snack after the theater, much as scrambled eggs are for us.

    2 garlic cloves
    4 tablespoons olive oil
    1 pound *vermicelli*
    Milled black pepper and salt to taste

Mash garlic with the heel of your hand. In a saucepan sauté in the oil, pressing it down with a wooden spoon and swishing it about the oil until it is well browned; discard garlic. Place oil in a warm bowl. Cook *vermicelli* al dente; watch carefully, for this slender pasta cooks quickly; drain well. Immediately fork into the bowl with the hot oil; mill in pepper, add salt, and toss with wooden forks. Serve in hot rimmed soup bowls. Serves 4 to 6.

LINGUINE FINE CON OLIO ED AGLIO

Fine Linguine with Oil and Garlic

Here's another version of a favorite of ours, with a clever way of mixing in the oil.

    12 ounces *linguine fine*
    12 garlic cloves, peeled
    7 tablespoons olive oil
    Milled black pepper
    Salt to taste
    1 tablespoon minced parsley

Cook *linguine fine* al dente, drain, and keep warm. Put 2 garlic cloves in each of 6 ramekins; cover with 2 ounces of cooked *linguine*. Pour a brimming tablespoon of olive oil over each dish of pasta, and sprinkle with pepper, and a pinch of parsley. Cover each ramekin with another very hot ramekin; let oil and garlic blend with pasta for 5 minutes. Turn each ramekin upside down, so the *linguine fine* is served in the hot dish, and the oil will now be distributed evenly; discard garlic. Serves 6.

FETTUCCELLE CON AGLIO E PIGNOLI

Fettuccelle with Garlic and Pine Nuts

3 tablespoons coarsely chopped Italian
parsley

2 garlic cloves

⅓ cup *pignoli*

½ cup grated Asiago or Parmesan cheese

¼ cup olive oil

1 tablespoon fresh lemon juice

½ teaspoon salt

¼ tablespoon freshly ground black pepper

12 ounces *fettuccelle*, cooked in boiling
salted water until al dente, drained

4 tablespoons butter

In a food processor bowl, combine the parsley, garlic, and *pignoli* and process to a paste. Add the cheese, olive oil, lemon juice, salt, and pepper and process until well blended.

Toss the hot pasta with the butter (in small pieces) until the butter has melted. Lightly toss in the garlic-*pignoli*-cheese mixture. Taste for seasoning. Serves 4 to 6 for a first course.

LINGUE DI PASSERI CON LE ACCIUGHE ALLA MARIA LIMONCELLI

Maria Limoncelli's "Sparrows' Tongues" with Anchovies

3 tablespoons olive oil
3 tablespoons butter
3 garlic cloves
2 cans (2 ounces each) anchovy fillets, drained
1 pound *lingue di passeri*

Heat oil and butter in a saucepan. Add garlic and cook over medium heat, until soft; discard garlic. Add anchovies and cook to sauce consistency. Cook *lingue di passeri* al dente, drain, and place in a hot bowl. Pour anchovy sauce over and toss gently with wooden forks. Serves 4 to 6.

SPAGHETTI CON LE ACCIUGHE

Spaghetti with Anchovies

3 tablespoons butter
3 tablespoons olive oil
3 garlic cloves, minced
3 cans (2 ounces each) anchovy fillets
⅛ teaspoon crushed red pepper
1 pound spaghetti
4 tablespoons chopped Italian parsley

In a saucepan, over medium heat, heat butter and oil, stir in garlic. Add undrained anchovies, saving 6 for garnish. Sauté until anchovies have become a paste; stir in the red pepper. Cook spaghetti al dente, drain, and place in a hot bowl. Slowly pour anchovy sauce over pasta; the sauce should be warm but not hot or it will make the pasta gummy. Toss gently with wooden forks until well blended. Add the parsley and toss again. Serve in hot soup bowls with 1 whole anchovy fillet atop each serving. Serves 6.

PENNE ALLA CARABINIERE

"Quills" That Require Fresh Basil

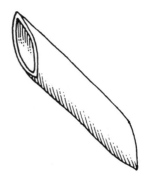

4 tablespoons olive oil

4 medium-size white onions, chopped

8 fresh basil stems and 4 fresh parsley
stems, crushed and tied together

6 large ripe fresh tomatoes, peeled,
seeded, and chopped

1 teaspoon salt

⅛ teaspoon (or to taste) crushed red pepper

4 tablespoons butter

12 ounces *penne*, cooked in boiling salted
water until al dente, drained

1 cup grated Asiago or Parmesan cheese

8 fresh basil leaves, chopped just before
using

In a saucepan, over medium heat, heat the oil and cook the onions for 5
minutes, or until soft and slightly golden. Do not brown. Add the herb
stems, tomatoes, salt, and red pepper. Bring to a boil, lower heat, and
simmer for 15 minutes, or until most of the watery content evaporates and
the sauce thickens, stirring occasionally.

Add the butter and cook, stirring, for 5 minutes. Remove from heat
and taste for seasoning. Remove and discard stems.

Toss the hot pasta with half of the sauce and serve in hot bowls. Top
each serving with the remaining sauce, a sprinkle of cheese, and a sprinkle of the freshly chopped basil. Pass the remaining cheese at the table.
Serves 4 to 6 for a first course.

PIZZOCHERI

Whole Wheat Spaghetti with Potato, Red Onion, and Cream

4 tablespoons butter

1 medium-size potato, cooked in its skin
    until just done, peeled and diced

1 medium-size red Italian onion, coarsely
    chopped

4 tablespoons heavy cream

Salt and freshly ground black pepper to
    taste

12 ounces whole wheat spaghetti, cooked
    in boiling salted water until al dente,
    drained

½ cup grated Asiago cheese

In a deep saucepan, over medium heat, melt 2 tablespoons of the butter
and cook the potato and onion for 5 minutes, or until golden, stirring. Blend
in the cream, salt, and pepper and simmer for 3 minutes. Add the hot
pasta, remaining butter (in small pieces), and with wooden forks toss well.
Serve immediately in hot soup bowls. Pass the cheese at the table. Serves
4 to 6 for a first course.

TAGLIOLINI CON PEPE

Noodles with Black Pepper

*This is a simple dish whipped up in a hunting camp when we were bird shooting
in the Po Valley. Despite its limited ingredients, it has surprisingly good flavor,
a testament to the natural goodness of pasta.*

¼ pound sweet butter

1 pound *tagliolini*

Salt to taste

1 tablespoon cracked black peppercorns

Soften butter in a pan until it is warm and half melted; place in a warm bowl. Cook *tagliolini* al dente; drain. Place in the bowl with the butter and toss gently, using wooden forks. Add salt and pepper (open pepper mill for coarse grating, or crack the peppercorns by pounding). Toss again. Serve in hot bowls. Serves 4 to 6.

TAGLIATELLE AL DOPPIO BURRO
Noodles with Double Butter

1 recipe Pasta Fresca all'Uovo (page 57)
5 tablespoons butter
3 tablespoons heavy cream
½ cup grated Asiago cheese
Salt to taste

Prepare the fresh pasta dough, cut it into *tagliatelle* (page 58), and dry. During the last 10 minutes of the drying, melt the butter in a saucepan and stir in cream and cheese. Add salt. Set aside. Cook the fresh *tagliatelle* carefully; it cooks faster than the dry commercial type. When al dente, drain and place in a hot bowl. Reheat butter, cream, and cheese and pour over the pasta, one fourth at a time, gently tossing it with wooden forks. Serves 4 to 6.

TRENETTE CON PESTO ALLA GENOVESE
Narrow Noodles with Pesto

This is surely one of the great regional dishes of Italy. Pesto—made with pine nuts, butter, and fresh basil, among other things—is served also on other pastas, such as fettuccine, and is used in soups. The recipe is given in the chapter on basic and special sauces. See page 92.

SPOLETO, the Church of San Pietro—Umbria

THE INCREDIBLE, EDIBLE ITALIAN FLAG

1 pound *fusilli* (or other short thick
   pasta), cooked in boiling salted water
   until al dente, drained
6 tablespoons butter
1½ cups *Filetto di Pomodoro* (page 80)
1½ cups *Pesto Alla Genovese* (page 92)
¾ cup grated Asiago or Parmesan cheese

In a bowl toss the hot pasta with the butter (in small pieces) until the butter has melted and blended with the pasta.

Arrange the pasta on individual hot serving dishes in as much of a rectangular shape as possible. On the right-hand third of the pasta, spoon 3 tablespoons of the *filetto* sauce. Sprinkle cheese on the *filetto* sauce and on the center third of the pasta. Spoon 3 tablespoons of the *pesto* sauce on the left-hand third of the pasta.

Serve the remaining sauces and cheese at the table. Serves 6.

MEZZANI TAGLIATI CON MANDORLE

Macaroni with Almonds

1 pound cut *mezzani* (short medium-size
   macaroni)
½ cup butter, melted
1 cup heavy cream, whipped
½ pound almonds, finely minced
5 tablespoons grated Parmesan cheese
5 tablespoons grated Romano cheese

Cook *mezzani* al dente; drain. Place in a large hot bowl; add the butter, cream, almonds, and half of the cheeses, which have been mixed; toss well. Serve immediately in hot rimmed soup bowls. Pass additional cheese at table. Serves 6.

DITALINI ALLA PANNA
"Little Thimbles" in a Cream-Ham Sauce

We had this in Rome, with white truffles. But here that's like sprinkling pasta with gold dust, so we've substituted dried mushrooms. No comparison, but it's still a good recipe.

3 tablespoons butter

6 medium-size dried mushrooms, soaked in warm water
½ hour, drained, and each cut into 6 wedges

1 pound *ditalini,* cooked in boiling salted
water until al dente, drained

½ cup chopped *prosciutto*

1 cup heavy cream

2 egg yolks

¾ cup grated extra-sharp provolone cheese

Salt and freshly ground black pepper to taste

Freshly grated nutmeg

In a saucepan, over medium heat, melt the butter, add the mushrooms, and cook for 4 minutes, stirring occasionally. Lower heat. Stir in the hot pasta, prosciutto, the cream and egg yolks first blended together, and the grated cheese. Simmer for 3 minutes, stirring constantly and carefully. Add pepper. Taste for seasoning before adding salt, as the cheese and ham may have supplied enough. Lightly grate nutmeg over the top and toss well. Serve in hot bowls. Serves 6.

GEMELLI CON SALSA DI PROSCIUTTO
"Twins" with Ham Sauce

Here is a pasta that will make the uninitiated who think all spaghetti is the same sit up and take notice. Called "twins" because it is made of entwined twists of pastas, gemelli *starts off as a conversation piece. The sauce places it further in the unusual category.*

1 recipe Ham Sauce (page 85)

1 pound *gemelli*

2 tablespoons butter

4 tablespoons grated Asiago cheese

Prepare ham sauce. Cook the *gemelli* al dente; drain well. Place the butter in a warm bowl, pour in the hot pasta, and add cheese. Toss well with wooden forks. Pour half of the ham sauce over pasta and toss again. Serve in warm bowls with the remaining sauce spooned over individual portions. Serves 4 to 6.

SPAGHETTINI VERDI

Green Spaghettini

Here is one of the simplest and yet most impressive pastas to present, and, in our opinion, one of the tastiest. The recipe is from a friend in Rome.

6 tablespoons butter

2 tablespoons olive oil

3 garlic cloves, mashed

8 tablespoons minced Italian parsley

1 pound spaghettini

Liberal amount of milled black pepper
    and salt to taste

¼ cup grated Parmesan cheese

Heat butter and oil in a saucepan; sauté garlic until brown, then discard garlic. Stir in the parsley; simmer for 4 minutes. Cook spaghettini al dente; drain. Place in a large hot bowl; mill in much black pepper, the salt, add the cheese, and toss well. Add hot butter and parsley sauce; toss again. Serve immediately in hot rimmed soup bowls. Serves 6.

LINGUINE CON ACCIUGHE ED UOVA
Linguine with Eggs and Anchovies

    4 tablespoons butter
    2 tablespoons olive oil
    1 garlic clove, minced
    1 can (2 ounces) anchovy fillets, drained
    4 tablespoons minced parsley
    1 teaspoon capers
    4 hard-cooked egg yolks, mashed
    2 tablespoons wine vinegar
    Liberal amount of milled black pepper
    1 pound *linguine*

Heat butter and oil in a saucepan. Stir in the garlic and anchovies; simmer for 8 minutes until of sauce consistency. Add the parsley, capers, and mashed egg yolks. Stir in the vinegar and mill in black pepper. Blend everything well and simmer for 5 minutes. Cook *linguine* al dente, drain, and place in a hot bowl. Pour the sauce over, toss well, and serve immediately in hot soup bowls. Serves 4 to 6.

TAGLIATELLE AL LATTE
Noodles with Milk

    1½ quarts milk
    1 teaspoon salt
    1 pound *tagliatelle*
    8 tablespoons butter
    1 pound ricotta cheese
    Milled black pepper
    ½ cup grated Parmesan cheese
    ¼ cup flour
    1 bouillon cube
    ½ pound prosciuttini, diced
    1 cup heavy cream

Pour milk into a pot, add the salt, and bring to boil. Cook *tagliatelle* in the milk, one third at a time, removing them with a slotted spoon and draining them; cook less than al dente; they should be firm and chewy. Save the milk. Toss the drained noodles in a warm bowl with 2 tablespoons of the butter. In another bowl season the ricotta with pepper and stir in enough of the milk the pasta cooked in to make the mixture smooth and creamy. Butter a baking dish. Cover the bottom with a layer of noodles and cover noodles with some of ricotta mixture. Sprinkle Parmesan over that and dot with butter. Continue the layers until noodles and ricotta have been used. In another pot melt 3 tablespoons of butter and stir in the flour, making a golden paste. Then slowly stir in 2 cups of the milk in which the pasta cooked. Add the bouillon cube and 1 tablespoon Parmesan, mill in black pepper, and stir until mixture is a rich smooth sauce. Pour this over the noodles and cheese. Sprinkle with remaining Parmesan and dot with remaining butter. Bake in a preheated 400° F. oven for 20 minutes. Remove from oven and arrange the diced prosciuttini in a crown on the noodles. Warm the cream and serve at table where each diner can pour a small amount over his dish of hot pasta and cheese. Serves 6.

PENNINE ALLA PAPRICA
Small "Quills" with Paprika Sauce

We haven't been able to determine where this sauce originated, but it's certainly a unique one. We discovered it in Sardinia.

4 tablespoons olive oil

4 garlic cloves, peeled (crush 3, reserve 1 whole)

2 tablespoons sweet paprika (preferably Hungarian)

½ cup dry red wine

4 medium-size ripe tomatoes, peeled, seeded, and finely chopped

1 teaspoon salt

12 ounces *pennine,* cooked in boiling salted water al dente, drained

3 tablespoons butter

1 cup grated Asiago or Parmesan cheese

In a saucepan, over medium heat, heat the olive oil and cook the crushed garlic cloves for 5 minutes, or until slightly golden. Discard garlic. Add the paprika and cook, stirring, for 2 minutes. Add the wine and cook over high heat, stirring, until the wine is reduced by half. Reduce heat, stir in the tomatoes and salt, and simmer, stirring occasionally, for 10 minutes, or until much of the liquid has been evaporated. Using a garlic press, add the reserved garlic clove to the sauce and cook until the sauce has thickened. Taste for seasoning.

In a hot bowl, toss the hot pasta with the butter (in small pieces). Spoon the sauce onto the pasta and toss. Sprinkle on half of the cheese and toss. Serve remaining cheese at the table. Serves 4 to 6 as a first course.

VERMICELLI CON PROVOLONE
Vermicelli with Provolone Cheese

This simple but most tasty recipe we learned from an artist friend in Genoa. Out walking one day, we stopped in the market, admired the yard-long tubes of yellow cheese, thigh-thick, hanging from cords outside a cheese store. The sunlight was on them and they gleamed like giant nuggets of Inca gold. He bought two pounds and had the grocer slice off pieces which we munched while we finished our walk. Provolone is a nutty cheese with a marvelous flavor, not often used with pasta, but my friend used nothing else. He is a man who does nothing the ordinary way.

¼ pound sweet butter
1 pound *vermicelli*
1½ cups grated very sharp provolone
    cheese
Liberal amount of milled black pepper

Half melt the butter and place in a warm bowl. Cook *vermicelli* al dente; watch carefully, for the "little worms" cook quickly; test every few seconds. Drain and place in the bowl with the butter; toss, using wooden forks. Add half of the cheese, mill in pepper, and toss gently again. Add remaining cheese, more pepper, and toss again. Serve in hot bowls. Serves 4 to 6.

OSTUNI—Apulia

SPAGHETTINI CON DUE FORMAGGI

Spaghettini with Two Cheeses

1 pound spaghettini
½ cup melted butter
1 cup grated Parmesan cheese
½ cup grated Romano cheese
Much milled black pepper

For this dish the pasta must be perfectly cooked, precisely al dente, and well drained. Pour the butter over it in a hot bowl. Using wooden forks, toss the spaghettini gently. Mix the two cheeses, mill in black pepper, and mix again. Sprinkle half into the bowl with the pasta and toss; serve the rest of the cheese at table. Serves 4 to 6.

MEZZANI CON PANNA ROSA AL FORNO
Baked Mezzani with Cream and Tomato

5 tablespoons butter

1 medium-size onion, finely chopped

2 tablespoons flour

1 cup heavy cream

½ cup dry white wine

¼ cup tomato purée

⅛ teaspoon (or to taste) cayenne pepper

1½ cups grated Fontina or Gruyère
  cheese

Salt to taste

½ pound *mezzani* (or elbow macaroni),
  cooked in boiling salted water until
  slightly firmer than al dente, drained

Fine bread crumbs

In a saucepan, over medium heat, melt 3 tablespoons of butter. Add the onion and cook for 2 minutes, or until soft. Do not brown. Stir in the flour and blend well. In small amounts, add the cream, wine, and tomato purée and cook, stirring constantly, to a smooth thickened sauce. Add the cayenne and cheese, stirring until the cheese has melted. Taste before adding salt, as the cheese may supply enough.

Mix half of the sauce with the pasta. Spoon into a buttered baking dish. Spoon remaining sauce over the top. Sprinkle lightly with bread crumbs and dot with the remaining butter. Bake in a preheated 350° F. oven for 20 minutes, or until the sauce is bubbling and the top is golden. Serves 4.

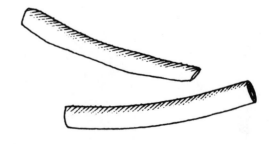

LASAGNE BIANCHE
Lasagne with a White Sauce

10 tablespoons butter

1 tablespoon olive oil

¾ pound small fresh mushrooms, thinly
    sliced

1 garlic clove, minced

1 tablespoon fresh lemon juice

Salt and freshly ground black pepper to
    taste

1 pound *lasagne ricce*, cooked in boiling
    salted water slightly firmer than al
    dente, drained

1½ cups ricotta, set in a sieve over a
    bowl to drain

1 cup grated Fontina or Gruyère cheese

1 tablespoon flour

1½ cups heavy cream

¼ teaspoon nutmeg

½ cup grated Asiago cheese

In a frypan, over medium heat, heat 3 tablespoons of the butter and the oil. Add the mushrooms, garlic, and lemon juice; cook for 5 minutes, or until the mushrooms are crisp-tender. Season with salt and pepper. Raise heat and cook off any excess liquid in pan.

In a buttered square or rectangular baking dish, arrange a layer of one third of the pasta. Cover with half of the mushrooms, half of the ricotta, and half of the Fontina. Dot with 2 tablespoons of butter. Repeat, arranging half of the remaining pasta in a layer, covering with all the remaining mushrooms, ricotta, and Fontina, and dot with 2 tablespoons of butter. Cover with remaining pasta.

In a saucepan, over medium heat, melt 3 tablespoons of butter, add the flour, and cook, stirring to a smooth paste. Gradually add the cream and cook, stirring to thicken slightly. Stir in the nutmeg, salt, and pepper. Pour the cream sauce over the pasta and sprinkle with Asiago. Cover with foil and bake in a preheated 350° F. oven for 30 minutes. Remove the foil and bake until the top is golden. Serves 6.

ZITI AL FORNO ALLA MERETRICE

Baked "Bridegrooms" with Harlot's Sauce

4 cups Harlot's Sauce (page 87)
3 tablespoons butter
¼ pound sharp provolone cheese, grated
1 pound *ziti*, broken into 2-inch pieces

Prepare the harlot's sauce. Place 2 tablespoons of the butter and half of the grated cheese in a hot bowl. Cook *ziti* until half done, or very chewy, and drain. Toss with the butter and cheese. Place one third of the hot sauce in a buttered casserole; add the *ziti*. Spoon the remaining sauce over the *ziti*, sprinkle with the rest of the cheese, and dot with remaining butter. Bake in a preheated 400° F. oven for 15 minutes, until cheese is melted and golden and *ziti* are properly al dente. Serves 4 to 6.

TUFOLI IMBOTTITI

Baked Stuffed Tufoli

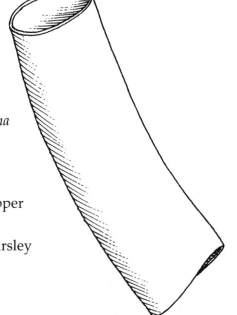

3 cups Bolognese Sauce (page 82)
½ cup freshly grated *Ricotta Siciliana*
    cheese or Parmesan cheese
1 pound ricotta cheese, drained
1 cup diced mozzarella cheese
Liberal amount of milled black pepper
2 eggs, beaten
1½ tablespoons chopped Italian parsley
½ pound *tufoli* (very large tubes)
1 tablespoon olive oil, in all

Prepare Bolognese sauce and keep hot. Place all of the cheeses in a bowl and add pepper, eggs, and parsley; blend well. Cook *tufoli* in lightly salted water with ½ tablespoon of the olive oil to keep pasta from sticking; cook for 8 minutes, or just less than al dente. Remove with a skimmer and drain.

When cool enough to handle, fill with the cheese mixture; place *tufoli* side by side in a casserole rubbed with remaining olive oil. Place a liberal spoonful of Bolognese sauce over each *tufolo*. Bake in a preheated 400° F. oven for 15 minutes. Pass boat of extra sauce at table. Serves 4 to 6.

MANICOTTI CON QUATTRO FORMAGGI
Baked Manicotti with Four Cheeses

½ cup freshly grated Asiago or Parmesan
    cheese
½ cup freshly grated *Pecorino di Tavola*
    cheese
¼ pound mozzarella cheese, diced
1 pound ricotta cheese
4 walnuts, chopped
2 tablespoons chopped Italian parsley
3 eggs, beaten
⅛ teaspoon grated nutmeg
½ tablespoon salt, or to taste
Liberal amount of milled black pepper
4 cups Mushroom and Cheese Sauce (page 86)
2 *manicotti* per person
1½ tablespoons olive oil

Mix all the cheeses in a bowl; add the walnuts, parsley, eggs, nutmeg, salt, and plenty of pepper; blend everything well. Heat the mushroom and cheese sauce. Cook *manicotti*, five at a time, in boiling salted water to which 1 tablespoon olive oil has been added to prevent the big pasta from sticking to itself or to the pot. Cook for 5 minutes, remove with slotted spoon or skimmer immediately, drain well, and fill with cheese mixture. Repeat until the number of *manicotti* desired are cooked and filled. Place in a baking dish greased with remaining ½ tablespoon oil. Spoon liberal portions of the heated mushroom and cheese sauce over all the *manicotti*. Bake in a preheated 400° F. oven for 15 minutes. Pass boat of extra sauce at table. Serve 2 *manicotti* per person; the recipe makes enough to fill 10 *manicotti*.

PENNE AL MASCARPONE

Short Pasta Tubes with Gorgonzola and Italian Cream Cheese

¼ pound butter

¼ pound *Mascarpone* (cheese prepared
    with layers of Gorgonzola and Italian
    cream cheese)

½ cup heavy cream

1½ ounces brandy

2 tablespoons mild tomato sauce

12 walnuts, coarsely chopped

12 ounces *penne*, cooked in boiling salted
    water until al dente, drained

1 cup grated Asiago or Parmesan cheese

Freshly ground black pepper

Salt to taste

3 tablespoons chopped Italian parsley

In a saucepan, over medium heat, melt the butter, then the *Mascarpone*.
Stir in the cream, brandy, tomato sauce, and walnuts. Remove from heat.

Once the pasta is cooked, set the cheese sauce on low heat, add the
pasta, tossing it well with the sauce. Sprinkle with half the grated cheese,
mill in a generous amount of black pepper, and toss again. Taste for seasoning before adding salt. Serve in hot bowls, garnished with chopped
parsley. Serve the remaining grated cheese at the table. Serves 4 as a first
course.

PERCIATELLI CON MOLTI FORMAGGI
"Pierced" Pasta with Many Cheeses

This is a northern Italian classic. The recipe, from a writer friend there, departs from tradition, requiring that you break the pasta before cooking.

4 tablespoons butter
1 teaspoon olive oil
1½ teaspoons flour
1½ cups cream
3 ounces Gouda cheese
3 ounces Gruyère cheese
3 ounces aged provolone cheese
3 ounces Fontina or *Taleggio* cheese
½ cup grated aged Asiago or Parmesan
    cheese
1½ pounds *perciatelli,* broken in half
Freshly milled black pepper

Melt half the butter in a saucepan, stir in olive oil, add flour, and blend well. Stir in cream slowly, about a teaspoon at a time. Cook for 7 minutes, stirring all of the time; do not boil. Remove from heat but keep warm. Cut all the cheeses (except Asiago or Parmesan) into slivers, and stir them into butter-cream mixture. Cook *perciatelli* al dente, drain, and place in a hot bowl with remaining 2 tablespoons butter. Toss well, but gently, with wooden forks. Put cheese-cream mixture back on fire, and stir well until cheeses are all just about melted. Pour this over the pasta in the bowl, toss well with wooden forks. Mill in pepper, toss again. Pass the grated Asiago or Parmesan at the table. Serves 6.

STUFFING FOR RAVIOLI OR TORTELLINI

Should fill enough ravioli to serve 6:

½ pound ricotta set in a sieve over a
   bowl to drain
4 ounces Gorgonzola, at room temperature
4 ounces *Mascarpone* cheese prepared
   with layers of Gorgonzola and Italian
   cream cheese, at room temperature (if
   unavailable, use 3-ounce package of
   cream cheese and additional Gorgonzola)
3 egg yolks
¼ cup grated Asiago or Parmesan cheese
½ teaspoon ground mace
Freshly ground black pepper to taste

In a bowl mash together the ricotta, Gorgonzola, and *Mascarpone*. Add the
egg yolks, grated cheese, mace, and pepper and blend well. Fill the *ravioli*
or *tortellini* as directed on page 59, cooking as suggested.

RAVIOLI CON CINQUE FORMAGGI
Ravioli with Five Cheeses

1 recipe Pasta Fresca for Ravioli (page 59)
12 ounces Parmesan cheese, grated
½ pound ricotta cheese, drained
6 ounces Romano cheese, grated
6 ounces Emmentaler cheese, grated
6 ounces Gruyère cheese, grated
1 egg, beaten
1 cup heavy cream

¼ teaspoon grated nutmeg

2 tablespoons minced parsley

Liberal amount of milled black pepper

¼ pound butter, melted

Make fresh pasta dough and roll into sheets. Set aside half of the Parmesan to use later and blend all the rest of the cheeses in a bowl. Stir in the egg, cream, nutmeg, and parsley; mill in much black pepper; mix well. Spread out the bottom sheet of dough; place a spoon of cheese filling every 2 inches. Cover with the second sheet of dough, press firmly around fillings, and cut into squares with a pastry cutter. Cook a few *ravioli* at a time in simmering salted water, removing with a slotted spoon when cooked; drain. Serve in hot soup bowls, drenched with the melted butter. Sprinkle Parmesan atop. Serves 6.

ZITI ALLA SICILIANA
A Sicilian Ziti

2 cups ricotta, at room temperature

½ cup grated *Ragusano* or Asiago cheese

½ teaspoon sugar

½ teaspoon cinnamon

1 pound *ziti* (or other short tubular
 pasta), cooked in boiling salted water
 until al dente, drained

3 tablespoons chopped Italian parsley

In a large bowl, combine and blend well the ricotta, grated cheese, sugar, and cinnamon. Add 2 or 3 tablespoons of the hot water in which the pasta cooked.

After the pasta has been drained, return it to the pot in which it cooked. Set on medium-low heat. Add the ricotta mixture and mix well but carefully for 1 minute, until heated through. Sprinkle parsley on each serving. Serves 6.

Note: Ragusano is a spicy, rich, and nutty Sicilian cheese.

ZITI TAGLIATI AL FORNO

Baked "Short Bridegrooms"

Do they serve the perennial American favorite, macaroni and cheese, in Italy? Yes, not usually with elbow macaroni as we do, but with larger varieties, such as ziti. Here's a version we had in Naples.

1 pound cut *ziti*
¼ pound butter
4 tablespoons flour
3 cups milk
1 teaspoon salt, or to taste
Liberal amount of milled black pepper
2 cups grated Parmesan cheese
4 cups (one 2-pound can) plum tomatoes, put through food mill

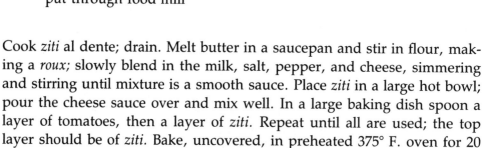

Cook *ziti* al dente; drain. Melt butter in a saucepan and stir in flour, making a *roux;* slowly blend in the milk, salt, pepper, and cheese, simmering and stirring until mixture is a smooth sauce. Place *ziti* in a large hot bowl; pour the cheese sauce over and mix well. In a large baking dish spoon a layer of tomatoes, then a layer of *ziti*. Repeat until all are used; the top layer should be of *ziti*. Bake, uncovered, in preheated 375° F. oven for 20 minutes, or until top is brown and sauce bubbling. Serves 6.

POMODORI RIPIENI DI ORZO

Baked Tomatoes Stuffed with Pasta "Barley"

6 large firm ripe tomatoes
Pinch of sugar
1 teaspoon salt, or to taste
Milled black pepper
½ teaspoon dried oregano

½ cup cubed mozzarella cheese

4 tablespoons butter

1 onion, minced

½ pound *orzo*

4 cups Chicken Broth (page 96), approximately

4 tablespoons grated Parmesan cheese

Remove center pulp and seeds from the tomatoes, hollowing them out well. Lightly sprinkle into each a little sugar, salt, pepper, and oregano; place 4 cubes of mozzarella in each tomato. Melt butter in saucepan and sauté onion in it until soft; stir in *orzo*, stirring well so each grain of pasta is coated. Pour in 2 cups of the broth, stir well, and simmer until broth is absorbed, adding more broth gradually until *orzo* is about three-quarters cooked, firmer than al dente. Blend in the Parmesan, stirring it in well. Spoon *orzo* into the hollowed tomatoes, filling them. Place in a casserole or baking dish with ½ cup of hot broth in the bottom. Bake, covered, in a preheated 400° F. oven for 25 minutes; remove the cover for the last 10 minutes of cooking. Serves 6.

SPAGHETTINI ALL'ABRUZZI
Spaghettini with White Onions and Bacon

This is a simple but classic sauce much served in Rome but created in Abruzzi, that province responsible for so many excellent chefs throughout Italy (including Maria Luisa's parents). It's a deceptive recipe, much tastier than the eye would lead you to believe.

8 slices of lean bacon

2 large white onions, minced

2 garlic cloves, crushed

1 pound spaghettini

3 tablespoons freshly grated Asiago or Romano cheese

Cut bacon into very thin slivers, sauté in saucepan with onions (use no other fat) and garlic. When onions are soft and yellow, discard garlic, remove saucepan from fire but keep warm. Cook spaghettini al dente; drain and place in a hot bowl. Return onion-and-bacon to fire, and when mixture is very hot, pour right from saucepan onto pasta in the hot bowl. Toss well with wooden forks, sprinkle on cheese, toss well again. Serve immediately in hot soup bowls. Serves 4.

PASTA "RISOTTO" MILANESE

No one makes a risotto *like the Italians, who invented the dish. Here's one made with pasta that we feel compares well with the rice version. We serve it with a* scaloppine.

    4 tablespoons butter
    8 scallions, white part only, chopped
    1 garlic clove, minced
    2 cups *acini di pepe*
    2½ cups boiling Beef Broth (page 96)
    1 cup grated sharp provolone
    Salt and freshly ground black pepper to
        taste

In a deep saucepan, over medium heat, melt the butter and cook the scallions and garlic, stirring, for 5 minutes, or until soft. Do not brown. Stir in the *acini di pepe,* add the beef broth, stir, and cook for 3 minutes. Cover pan, remove from heat, and let stand until beef broth is absorbed. Add the cheese, stirring until blended and melted. Taste for seasoning before adding salt and pepper, as the broth may have supplied enough. Serves 6 to 8.

L'AQUILA—Abruzzi

POMODORI RIPIENI ALLA SICILIANA
Baked Stuffed Tomatoes Sicilian Style

1 cup small pieces of spaghetti

6 good-sized tomatoes

2 small white onions, chopped

2 tablespoons olive oil

8 canned sardines, chopped

1 tablespoon chopped parsley

1 tablespoon chopped green olives

1 teaspoon capers, chopped

2 tablespoons dry white wine

Milled black pepper

Salt

6 teaspoons bread crumbs

Butter or oil

Cook spaghetti al dente, drain, and put aside. Slice off tops of tomatoes and scoop out centers, being careful not to break the skins. Mince pulp and drain. In a saucepan, over medium heat, sauté onions in oil until soft; stir in the minced tomato pulp, sardines, parsley, olives, and capers. Blend in wine, mill in black pepper, add salt to taste, and stir in the drained spaghetti. Fill tomatoes with this mixture, lightly sprinkle with bread crumbs, and dot with butter or add a few drops of oil. Bake in a preheated 400° F. oven for 15 minutes, or until tomatoes are cooked through. Serves 6.

GNOCCHI DI SEMOLINO ALLA PERUGINA
Semolina Dumplings Perugia Style

½ cup water

2 cups milk

1 teaspoon salt

4 ounces Italian semolina or fine yellow cornmeal

   4 tablespoons sweet butter

   1 egg, beaten

   1½ cups freshly grated Asiago cheese

Place water and milk in pot and bring to a boil. Take pot from heat, stir in salt, then slowly stir in semolina, a spoonful at a time, mixing well. Replace on low heat and, stirring often, cook for 20 minutes until mixture is smooth and thick. (If too thick, add a small amount of boiling water, stirring well.) Remove from fire, add 1 tablespoon of the butter, then the egg, quickly, blending well. Moisten a large platter or bread board with cold water and spread the *gnocchi* mixture on it in an even smooth layer ½ inch thick. Cool. Cut into 1½-inch circles with cookie cutter. Butter individual ramekins and place 6 or 8 circles in each, slightly overlapping. Dot with remaining butter and sprinkle with Asiago. Place under broiler until golden, watching carefully so *gnocchi* do not burn. Serve immediately as a first course. Serves 6.

SOUFFLÉ DI CAPELLI D'ANGELO

"Angel's Hair" Soufflé

   1 recipe Béchamel Sauce (page 85)

   ½ pound *capelli d'angelo*

   3 eggs, separated

   ¼ cup grated Parmesan cheese

Prepare Béchamel sauce. Cook *capelli d'angelo* in boiling salted water for exactly 60 seconds; remove and drain. In a bowl beat the egg yolks; stir in Parmesan. In another bowl whip egg whites until stiff, then stir into the yolks and cheese, and mix in the drained *capelli*. Butter a soufflé dish and pour in the mixture. Bake in a preheated 450° F. oven for 15 minutes until soufflé rises and is browned. Serves 4 to 6.

SFORMATO DI FETTUCCINE VERDI CON ROGNONI E FUNGHI

Green Fettuccine Mold with Kidneys and Mushrooms

1 recipe Mornay Sauce (page 86)

1 pound green *fettuccine*

4 tablespoons butter

½ cup grated Parmesan cheese

4 tablespoons bread crumbs

½ pound veal kidneys, trimmed and diced

1 tablespoon flour

1 teaspoon salt, or to taste

Milled black pepper

1 teaspoon sherry

1 cup Chicken Broth (page 96)

½ pound mushrooms, sliced

Prepare Mornay sauce. Cook the *fettuccine* firmer than al dente; drain well. Toss with 2 tablespoons of the butter and Parmesan; stir in the Mornay sauce and mix well. Pour the noodles and sauce into a 9-inch cooking mold with a 3-inch center well, which has been buttered and then dusted with the bread crumbs. Place in a preheated 400° F. oven for 15 minutes. Meanwhile, in a saucepan, over medium heat, sauté the kidneys in 2 tablespoons of butter for 5 minutes; do not overcook, as it toughens them. Sprinkle lightly with flour, season with salt and pepper, and stir in sherry, broth, and mushrooms. Cook just until gravy thickens, stirring it to a smooth sauce. Kidneys should be pinkish and mushrooms crunchy. Turn the pasta mold upside down on a warm platter; fill the center well with the kidneys and mushrooms in their gravy. Serve immediately from platter at the table. Serves 6.

Note: This mold makes an attractive and versatile luncheon dish, the ring of noodles centered on a platter, the center well filled with anything from creamed chicken, lobster or game, to chicken livers or creamed vegetables.

TIMBALLO DI TUBETTINI E SALMONE
"Tiny Tubes" and Salmon Pie

The Italians make a pasta pie, or pasta in a pastry shell, called a timballo. *It apparently gets its name from a round musical instrument of that name. This dish we had in a home in the south of Italy and it was actually made with a can of red salmon, perhaps in deference to us, for many Italians sincerely believe that Americans prefer their food from cans. We offer it as we saw it prepared. First, make* half *of the following pastry recipe. (Or make the full recipe and refrigerate half; it keeps well.)*

Pastry for a Two-Crust Pie:
Full Recipe

2 cups flour
1½ teaspoons salt
¾ cup shortening
5 tablespoons water

Half Recipe

1 cup flour
¾ teaspoon salt
6 tablespoons shortening
2 to 3 tablespoons water

Sift flour and salt into a bowl, add about two thirds of the shortening, and blend with hands or pastry blender until well mixed. Then add the rest of the shortening and blend all very well. Add the water all at once, mix well with a fork, and work with hands into a smooth ball. Roll out fairly thin between 2 sheets of wax paper until the circle of dough is about 2 inches larger than a 9-inch pie pan. Place the pastry in a pie pan, trim off excess pastry, and flute edge.

Salmon Filling

2 tablespoons butter

1 small white onion, minced

1 can (1 pound) red salmon, with its
    liquid

½ teaspoon salt

Milled black pepper

1 tablespoon chopped fresh dill

3 eggs

½ cup heavy cream, heated

1 cup light cream, heated

3 tablespoons *tubettini*

In a saucepan, over medium heat, melt the butter and sauté the onion in it until soft. Stir in the salmon, bones and skin removed, with the liquid; add salt, pepper, and dill. Mash the fish with a fork until mixture is smooth. Beat the eggs in a bowl, adding warm heavy and light cream as you beat, or use a blender. Slowly add the smooth salmon mixture from its saucepan to the eggs and cream, beating until smooth. Cook the *tubettini* al dente, drain well, and stir into the salmon and cream. Blend well.

Pour the mixture into the pastry-lined pie pan. Bake in a preheated 400° F. oven for 45 minutes, or until the crust is brown and filling has set. Serves 6.

TIMBALLO DI MACCHERONCELLI E POLLO

Macaroni and Chicken Pie

4 tablespoons olive oil

4 tablespoons butter

4 slices of prosciutto, minced

1 carrot, minced

2 shallots, minced

1 celery rib, minced

1 chicken (3 pounds)

1 teaspoon salt

Milled black pepper

2 cups Chicken Broth (page 96)

1 recipe Pastry for a Two-Crust Pie
    (page 363)

½ recipe Béchamel Sauce (page 85)

3 chicken livers, chopped

6 mushrooms, quartered

½ pound *maccheroncelli* (small macaroni)

¼ cup grated Asiago cheese

Heat 3 tablespoons of the oil and 3 of the butter in a large pot. Sauté the prosciutto, carrot, shallots, and celery until soft. Add the chicken, season with salt and pepper, and brown evenly. Add the chicken broth and braise the chicken, covered, in a preheated 350° F. oven for 2 hours, basting often, until tender. Remove bird; cool.

Prepare pastry; use half to line a 10-inch pie pan. Prepare Béchamel sauce. In a deep saucepan, over medium heat, sauté chicken livers and mushrooms in remaining butter and oil for 5 minutes. Skin and bone the chicken and cube the meat. Add it to mushrooms and livers. Strain ½ the broth from the chicken pot into the mixture of chicken, mushrooms, and livers. Cook *maccheroncelli* al dente, drain, and place in a large bowl. Stir in the Béchamel sauce and cheese, and the chicken, mushrooms, and livers in sauce; blend. Pour into the pastry-lined pie pan; cover with the second sheet of dough, cut off overhanging dough with a pastry cutter, and flute edges. Bake in a preheated 400° F. oven for 20 minutes, or until crust is brown. Serves 4 to 6.

TIMBALLO DI DITALINI
"Little Thimbles" Pie

Here is another of the famous timballi, *which we had at a friend's in Taranto. In this city of fresh fish and marvelous seafood, the citizens are ostentatiously proud to serve meat, feeling seafood is ordinary. We feel otherwise. This pie came as the luncheon entrée served with a salad and a bottle of Barolo, a dependable red wine.*

    1 recipe Pastry for a Two-Crust Pie
        (page 363)
    2 cups Basic Tomato Sauce (page 76)
    1 tablespoon olive oil
    ¼ pound veal, ground
    ½ teaspoon salt, or to taste
    Milled black pepper
    ½ pound *ditalini*
    ⅓ cup grated Asiago cheese
    2 eggs, beaten
    ¼ cup heavy cream

Make pie pastry, roll it out, and arrange half of it in a 10-inch pie plate. Roll the remainder into a circle large enough to fit the top of the pan and set aside. Make the tomato sauce.

In a saucepan, over medium heat, heat the oil and sauté veal until brown, sprinkling with salt and pepper. Cook *ditalini* firmer than al dente, drain well, and place in a bowl. Stir in the veal in its oil, the cheese, and the tomato sauce, blending well. Pour the mixture into the pastry-lined pie pan. With a whisk beat the eggs and cream well; pour this over the rest of the ingredients in the pie pan. Place the second sheet of pastry atop, seal, cut off any overhanging dough, and flute the edge. Bake in a preheated 350° F. oven for 35 minutes, until crust is lightly browned. Serves 4 to 6.

Near VIESTE, on the Adriatic—Apulia

TRUFFLES

A truffle, in Italian *tartufo*, for those who haven't had the pleasure, is an edible fungus that grows under the ground and is greatly prized by gourmets in Italy and France and, in fact, the world over. Truffles are scented by specially trained dogs and pigs and sold either canned or fresh. Everybody else who assembles a cookbook quotes Brillat-Savarin, so we might as well conform: That fastidious old French epicure called them "the diamonds of the kitchen." And he just about had it. Today truffles exported from Italy and France, the only two countries we know where they are found, are exorbitant. For example, a 2-ounce can of either black or white truffles costs $20 ($160 a pound), in the United States. Some think they are worth the price; some think the whole idea preposterous. We think they are worth the price. The French believe the black are the best; most Italians swear by the white. We don't think there is any contest; the white are by far the tastier.

Of course, we are somewhat prejudiced, having first had white truffles in Italy's Piedmont region, in Alba, where the finest are found. What these brownish-gray bits of fungi, usually no larger than a walnut, do is to bring a sweet perfume to any dish they decorate, a flavor that is difficult to describe—piquant, different. As for Scotch whisky, you must acquire a taste for them. But once you've had them—thinly sliced over *fettuccine* or riding atop a butter-sautéed boned turkey breast that has had Fontina cheese sliced and melted over it in the oven—or had a dish of hot pasta with just butter and white truffles, the way it is served in Alba—then you become a member of the club, and $20 for a tiny two ounces of the chief of the tribe *Tuber magnatum* doesn't seem in the least expensive. Try it once and see.

On page 380 is our friend Harris Ravetto's dish of *fettuccine* with truffles. This is the best we ever ate. There follow here three other recipes with truffles, beginning with the one from Alba.

VERMICELLI ALL'ALBA
Vermicelli with White Truffles and Butter

   1 white truffle
   ¼ pound butter
   1 pound *vermicelli*
   ½ cup grated Parmesan cheese

Slice the truffle as thin as a razor-sharp knife can. Melt the butter in a pan, stirring in half of the truffle. Cook the *vermicelli* al dente, drain, and place in a warm bowl. Pour in half of the melted butter and truffle and all of the cheese; toss well but gently. Serve in hot soup bowls, with the remaining butter-truffle mixture poured over, and the rest of the sliced truffle atop. Serves 4 to 6.

Note: If the truffle is canned, add the liquid to the butter in the first stage of cooking.

SPAGHETTI CON TARTUFI
Spaghetti with Truffles

    1 garlic clove
    4 tablespoons olive oil
    3 anchovy fillets
    Milled black pepper
    1 pound spaghetti
    1 white truffle, minced

In a saucepan, over medium heat, sauté halved and mashed garlic clove in oil until brown; discard garlic. Cut the anchovy fillets into small pieces and add to the oil; mill in pepper. Simmer slowly, stirring until oil and anchovies make a paste. Cook spaghetti al dente; drain well. Place in a hot bowl and pour the oil-anchovy sauce over. Use wooden forks and toss well but gently. Serve in hot soup bowls with minced truffle atop each portion. Serves 4 to 6.

SPAGHETTI ALLA CHITARRA CON TARTUFI ED ACCIUGHE

"Guitar Strings" with Truffles and Anchovies

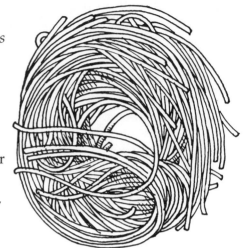

- 2 tablespoons olive oil
- 2 tablespoons butter
- 2 garlic cloves, mashed
- 5 anchovy fillets, soaked in cold water and drained
- 2 large ripe tomatoes, peeled, seeded, and diced
- Light pinch of salt
- Liberal amount of milled black pepper
- 1 pound spaghetti *alla chitarra*
- 2 black truffles, grated
- 1 tablespoon minced parsley

Heat oil and butter in a saucepan; add mashed garlic and sauté until brown; remove and discard garlic. Stir in the anchovies; when they have cooked to a sauce, add the tomatoes, salt, and pepper. Stir well and simmer, uncovered, for 20 minutes. Cook spaghetti al dente, drain, and place in a hot bowl. Sprinkle with grated truffles and toss well with wooden forks. Pour half of the anchovy-tomato sauce over the pasta and toss again. Serve in hot soup bowls with some of the remaining sauce spooned over each portion and parsley sprinkled atop. Serves 4 to 6.

PENNE RIGATE ALLA VODKA

Short Grooved "Quills" with Tomato, Cream, and Vodka

Note: This dish must be begun 10 days before you cook it.

- A fifth of vodka (this is more than needed, but keep it refrigerated; you'll use it again and again)
- 4 teaspoons crushed red pepper

Add the red pepper to the vodka, cap it, shake well, and refrigerate for 10 days. Remove vodka from refrigerator 3 hours before using. When you're ready to prepare the dish, proceed with:

2 tablespoons olive oil

3 medium-size fresh ripe tomatoes,
    peeled, seeded, and coarsely chopped

1 teaspoon salt

1 tablespoon chopped fresh Italian
    parsley

12 ounces *penne rigate,* cooked in boiling
    salted water until al dente, drained

4 tablespoons butter

3 tablespoons heavy cream

3 tablespoons grated Asiago or Parmesan
    cheese

In a saucepan, over medium heat, heat the oil and stir in the tomatoes, salt, and parsley. Cook, stirring occasionally, for 10 minutes, or until the tomatoes are soft and satiny and most of the liquid has evaporated. Remove from heat. Taste for seasoning.

Place the hot pasta in a deep saucepan. Set over medium heat for i minute, allowing any moisture to evaporate, stirring carefully so the pasta doesn't break up. Shake the vodka bottle well, measure out 4 ounces, and pour over the pasta. Stir well. Strike a kitchen match and, standing back a bit, ignite the vodka-doused pasta. When it flames, stir well again. When the flame subsides, stir in the butter (in small pieces) and the cream, blending well. Add the tomato sauce, sprinkle on the cheese, and toss. Serves 4 to 6 for a first course.

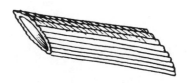

FETTUCCINE

The glamour noodle of the pasta tribe is without question *fettuccine,* thus it deserves special treatment here as a "Particular Pasta." The Romans ate something very close to this pasta about the year 1200. Quite a few years ago a man named Alfredo caught the headlines when Douglas Fairbanks and Mary Pickford presented him in his Roman restaurant, Alfredo alla Scrofa, with a gold fork and spoon, thus honoring him for his dish of *fettuccine,* which was tossed at the diner's table with those utensils. Currently there are three Alfredos in Rome and several in the United States, none related to the original in Rome.

Perhaps back in the days of Fairbanks and Pickford, the Alfredo *fettuccine* was indeed superb—we are sure that it was. But we have tried the three Alfredos and each time found them wanting, the noodles overcooked, served just barely warm, the service sloppy, the restaurants noisy and full of tourists. And perhaps that is the reason for the decline of their *fettuccine.* One manager told us that they had to cook the pasta soft or the tourists wouldn't eat it. But this sounds like pure alibi to us, like saying that the Chinese have to serve their chicken deep-fried Southern style to please their customers. There is no reason why pasta of any type should be overcooked in Rome, of all places. And mostly it isn't. Excellent *fettuccine* is available in many restaurants and *trattorie* there—and prepared in many ways.

The best *fettuccine* we have eaten was not prepared in Rome, not even in Italy, but in Yorktown Heights, New York, in Ravetto's Restaurant. The method of serving and the recipe for *Fettuccine Ravetto* can be found on page 380. We have seldom seen it equaled, never surpassed.

The classic *fettuccine* is *Fettuccine con Parmigiano e Burro,* simply served with butter and cheese, and black pepper, mixed at the table before the diner's eyes, one of the pleasures of the dish. Also, they should be cooked al dente or firmer, well drained, and brought to your sideboard in the dining room where the art of mixing the sauce and serving is displayed. They should be tossed in a chafing dish with plenty of butter, and served in hot bowls to your guests as they watch you perform. Following is the classic *fettuccine* dish.

CAMOGLI—Liguria

FETTUCCINE CON PARMIGIANO E BURRO
Fettuccine with Parmesan and Butter

1 pound *fettuccine*
¼ pound butter
½ cup grated Parmesan cheese
Much milled black pepper

Cook the *fettuccine* firmer than al dente, for the noodles will cook slightly more when you toss them in the chafing dish with butter and cheese. If the pasta is fresh, be especially careful, for it will cook more quickly. Drain well and carry into the dining room where you have the butter melting in the chafing dish. Add the noodles; using wooden forks, toss gently, mixing in the butter. Add the cheese, grated directly from a cylinder-type hand grater; toss. Add more cheese, tossing until the cheese is used up; mill pepper in just before each tossing. Serve immediately in hot soup bowls as first course. Serves 4 to 6.

Note: To make this dish taste exactly right, use nothing but nutty aged Parmesan and for the pepper, preferably Tellicherry.

FETTUCCINE ALLA BOLOGNESE

2 cups Bolognese Sauce (page 82)
1 pound *fettuccine*
4 tablespoons butter
⅓ cup grated Parmesan cheese

This is a happy mating, one of the great sauces with the prince of noodles. As the sauce is so rich, less cheese and butter are needed, but the procedure is the same. Cook the *fettuccine* al dente, drain, and bring to the chafing dish at the dining-room sideboard. Toss in the melting butter and grate cheese directly onto it. Serve in hot soup bowls, with piping hot Bolognese sauce lavishly topping each serving. Serves 4 to 6.

Near CORTONA—Tuscany

FETTUCCINE ALLA PIETRO

¼ pound butter
½ pound lean pork, finely chopped
1 teaspoon salt, or to taste
Milled black pepper
½ cup dry white wine
2 cups Basic Tomato Sauce (page 76)
4 tablespoons fresh peas
8 small mushrooms, sliced
1 pound *fettuccine*

In a saucepan, over medium heat, melt half of the butter and in it cook pork until brown. Add salt and pepper, the wine, and tomato sauce. Simmer for 20 minutes, uncovered. Boil peas for 5 minutes; drain. Add peas and mushrooms to the remaining butter and cook until soft. Blend with pork-tomato sauce. Cook *fettuccine* al dente, drain; serve in hot bowls with sauce spooned over each serving. Serves 4 to 6.

FETTUCCINE CON PANNA ED UOVA
Fettuccine with Cream and Eggs

1 pound *fettuccine*
¼ pound butter
½ cup grated Parmesan or Asiago cheese
Much milled black pepper
2 egg yolks
½ cup heavy cream, warmed

Cook *fettuccine* al dente, drain, and add to the chafing dish in which the butter is melting. Have everything else ready at dining-room sideboard—yolks in eggshells, cream, and cheese. Toss the noodles gently with two forks, coating the strands of pasta; from time to time grate in cheese and mill in pepper. When cheese is well mixed, add egg yolks, breaking them

SIENA, the Piazza del Campo—Tuscany

into the pasta with the wooden stirring fork. Toss the noodles again, then add the cream, and toss again. Serve in hot soup bowls immediately. Serves 4 to 6.

FETTUCCINE CON PISELLI E FUNGHI

Fettuccine with Peas and Mushrooms

   2 tablespoons fresh peas
   ⅓ cup mushrooms, sliced
   ¼ pound butter
   1 pound *fettuccine*
   ½ cup grated Parmesan cheese
   Milled black pepper
   ½ cup heavy cream, warmed

Cook peas lightly in salted water until slightly less than tender; drain. Sauté sliced mushrooms for 3 minutes in the butter in a chafing dish at dining-room sideboard. Cook *fettuccine* al dente; drain. Add to the butter and mushrooms and toss; grate in cheese, mill in pepper, and toss well. Just before serving add the peas and cream and toss again. Serves 4 to 6.

FETTUCCINE CON PROSCIUTTO

   1 pound *fettuccine*
   8 thin slices of prosciutto, cut into
      julienne strips
   ¼ pound plus 1 tablespoon butter, in all
   ½ cup grated Parmesan cheese
   Milled black pepper

Cook *fettuccine* firmer than al dente. In a saucepan, over medium heat, sauté prosciutto in 1 tablespoon of the butter until crisp. Add pasta and ham to chafing dish in which ¼ pound of butter is melting. With two forks, toss together noodles and crisp ham in the melting butter. Grate in cheese and mill in pepper; toss well. Serve in hot soup bowls. Serves 4 to 6.

FETTUCCINE ROSE

Pink Fettuccine

Some restaurants in Italy serve fettuccine *with just a touch of tomato sauce to give the dish personality. We suggest that you prepare marinara sauce, use what is required for this* fettuccine *dish, and save the rest in the refrigerator for another meal; it keeps well.*

1 pound *fettuccine*
4 tablespoons Marinara Sauce (page 81)
¼ pound butter
½ cup grated Asiago cheese
Milled black pepper

Cook *fettuccine* al dente; drain well. Bring to dining room with the piping-hot marinara sauce. Place noodles in chafing dish with the melting butter; toss; grate in ½ cheese, mill in pepper, and toss. Add the sauce and toss well again with two forks until the pasta is pink. Add the rest of the cheese, toss again, and serve in hot soup bowls. Serves 4 to 6.

FETTUCCINE VERDI CON GAMBERETTI

Green Fettuccine with Shrimps

½ pound small shrimp
1 pound green *fettuccine*
¼ pound butter
Milled black pepper
Salt to taste
½ cup heavy cream, warmed

Peel shrimp and in a pot half-cook them (just until pink) in a small amount of salted water. Remove shrimp and cut them into halves. Cook the fresh *fettuccine* firmer than al dente; drain. Place shrimp in chafing dish with the melting butter, mill in black pepper and salt to taste, and sauté shrimp for 3 minutes. Add the *fettuccine* and toss with shrimp and butter. Add the cream and toss it into the pasta and shrimp just before serving in hot soup bowls. To follow the classic Italian pattern, do not use cheese with this seafood dish. Serves 4 to 6.

FETTUCCINE RAVETTO

Fettuccine with Cheese, Cream, Egg, and Truffle

We have never seen fettuccine *served more skillfully, or had it taste better than at the restaurant of our friend Harris Ravetto, in Yorktown Heights, New York. Harris, a tall, slim, handsome fellow who has never made a clumsy movement in his life, performs as gracefully before a table of guests as Toscanini did for an audience at Carnegie Hall. First a waiter wheels in a table with chafing dish aflame, a bowl of* fettuccine *freshly cooked al dente beside it, next to an eggshell with a yolk gleaming in it. The rest of the ingredients are a little glass pitcher of heavy cream, a hand cheese grater and a large piece of Parmesan, a pepper mill and, in a small silver bowl, one white truffle.*

As you watch, Harris calls the waiter for a half cup of soft butter, puts this in the chafing dish, then the noodles, tossing them gently until they are well mixed with the butter. Now the cream goes in and much black pepper is milled over the fettuccine. *Harris then hand-grates at least a half cup of cheese into the pasta, tosses it again to mix it, adds the egg yolk, tosses lightly again. While the* fettuccine *stays warm in the chafing dish, the flame now lowered under it, Harris deftly slices the white truffle on a small wooden block, shaving it wafer-thin. He adds a few wafers to the pasta, tosses again, then the waiter serves it into hot bowls and pauses before Maestro Ravetto while more white truffle goes atop each serving. We have never had it so good, even in Rome. That is the method. Instead of using the chafing dish in the dining room (which is most impressive and eye-pleasing, half the pleasure of any meal), you can use a pot on the stove and do the serving in the kitchen. Ingredients follow.*

1 pound *fettuccine*

¼ pound fresh unsalted butter

½ cup heavy cream

Much freshly milled black pepper

5 ounces Parmesan cheese (about ½ cup
   grated)

1 egg yolk

1 white truffle, thinly sliced

Save the liquid from the truffle if it was canned and add to the *fettuccine* just before serving, tossing it to set the flavor. Serves 4 to 6.

Note: Unfortunately, the *fettuccine* performance at Ravetto's is now history. Harris Ravetto has retired, the restaurant is in other hands. Harris still makes his *fettuccine* magic, but at home in Florida.

VITERBO, the Piazza del Gesù—Latium

XI

Recipes from Friends, Romans & Countrymen

*T*his may be the most rewarding chapter in the book, resulting as it does from the generosity of others—of friends, chefs, people we have met in passing as we traveled the world, taxi drivers, barbers, hotel clerks, restaurant and hotel owners, hosts and hostesses, even pilots of planes on which we have flown. All the recipes have been carefully tested. Some are credited with the name of the person who contributed it, some with initials, others with just a "friend" or a "chef," depending upon the desires of the donors.

There are too many to thank individually on an acknowledgments page, so we thank them collectively here instead. We are grateful for the time and effort all of these kind people took to help us put pasta in its proper place—high on the list of the world's superb foods.

MINA TRIO

We begin with three recipes from Palmina Thompson, the youngest of Maria Limoncelli's three talented daughters, but as adept as her sisters.

Although there are recipes for making fresh pasta dough in Chapter III, two of Mina's are given here, for her way is somewhat different.

1. BAKED MANICOTTI THOMPSON

Dough

6 eggs
3 cups flour
2 cups milk
½ teaspoon milk

Filling

1½ pounds ricotta cheese, drained
2 eggs
½ cup freshly grated Parmesan cheese

Sauce

2 cups Basic Tomato Sauce (page 76)

In a bowl, beat the 6 eggs, add flour, milk, and salt, and blend well. Drop 1 tablespoon of this batter onto a heated griddle and cook lightly on both sides until golden and set, like a small pancake or crêpe. Continue until batter is used up.

In a bowl blend the ingredients for the filling well. Place 1 teaspoon of filling on each *manicotti* pancake and roll up. Place in a baking dish and spoon warm tomato sauce over each little roll. Bake in a preheated 350° F. oven for 30 minutes. Serves 4 to 6.

2. CAVATELLI CON CAVOLFIORE
Curled Noodle Strips with Cauliflower

3 cups flour
1 egg
½ teaspoon salt
2 tablespoons vegetable shortening,
    melted
1 cup water

1 small head of cauliflower
4 tablespoons butter, melted
Liberal amount of milled black pepper

Sift flour on a pasta board and make a well in center. Into this put the egg, salt, and shortening, and half of the water. Slowly whip up, bringing flour from around edges and mixing together; add more water or flour if needed to form a firm ball. Cover ball with a bowl and let rest for 10 minutes. Clean pasta board and again knead dough until it is elastic and smooth. Cover dough ball again and let stand for another 10 minutes. Now roll out to ⅛-inch thickness. Cut into strips ½ inch by 1 inch. Shape *cavatelli* by taking each small strip and pressing your index and middle fingers down on it and then pulling them toward you; this will make the little strip curl up. Dry for 45 minutes, then cook al dente in 7 quarts of boiling water to which has been added 1 tablespoon of salt.

Boil the cauliflower in lightly salted water until tender; separate into flowerets. Put the melted butter in a warm bowl and add the cauliflower and the *cavatelli*, well drained. Mill black pepper generously over this, toss gently, and serve in hot bowls. Serves 4 to 6.

3. CAPPELLETTI CON POLLO
"Little Hats" with Chicken

2 whole chicken breasts
1 onion
1 carrot
1 celery rib with leaves
Salt and pepper
½ cup freshly grated Asiago cheese
1 tablespoon chopped parsley
1 egg, beaten
1 teaspoon salt
1 recipe Pasta Fresca for Ravioli (page 59)
Melted butter

In a pot boil chicken breasts, as you would for soup, in water with the onion, carrot, celery rib, and a little salt and pepper. When chicken is tender, remove from broth; strain the cooking liquid and reserve it. Discard skin and bones, and grind or mince the meat. Place minced chicken in a bowl, add half of the cheese, the parsley, egg, and salt. Blend well.

Make the dough for *ravioli*, roll into sheets, and cut into 2½-inch rounds. Put 1 teaspoon of the filling on each pasta round, then crimp the edges up around the filling closely to make the "little hats," or *cappelletti* that look rather like old-fashioned mob caps. Seal them well; let them dry for 1 hour after sealing. Drop the hats, one by one, into the simmering broth in which the chicken breasts cooked. Cook al dente and be careful; fresh pasta cooks quickly. Remove with a slotted spoon to paper towels for draining. Serve in hot bowls with the remaining cheese sprinkled over and with about ¼ teaspoon of hot melted butter over each hat. Serves 4 to 6.

—from Palmina Thompson, Elmira, New York

AMORINI MADDALENA

Maddalena's Beef Soup with "Little Cupids"

    3-pound "arm" chuck beef roast
    2 potatoes, peeled and diced
    3 carrots, peeled and diced
    2 celery ribs with leaves, diced
    3 small white onions, diced
    1 pound *amorini*
    ½ teaspoon freshly milled black pepper
    4 to 6 teaspoons chopped parsley

Cook beef and vegetables in 8 quarts water with 1 tablespoon salt in a covered pot over slow fire for 4 hours, or until the beef is tender but still firm enough to cut without shredding or being stringy. When meat is done, remove to a warm platter for second course. Cook broth over high fire, stirring often, until it has reduced by half. Put broth and vegetables through a food mill or strainer into another pot. Cook *amorini* al dente, drain, and add to the strained broth. Sprinkle in the black pepper and simmer pasta

CALABRIAN HILLS

in broth for 5 minutes. Serve in soup bowls with a teaspoon of chopped parsley afloat each serving. Serves 4 to 6.

Note: This can be attractively varied by using narrow or very fine noodles, and can make a one-dish luncheon by adding half of the beef, diced.

—*from Maria Luisa's oldest sister, Maddalena Altman, Elmira, New York*

ZUPPA DI VERMICELLI ALLA ROMANO
A Roman Soup

1 medium onion
¼ pound ham fat
1 garlic clove
1 tablespoon olive oil
4 tomatoes, peeled, seeded, and cut into
    strips
1 quart water
1½ teaspoons salt
Liberal amount of milled black pepper
¼ pound *vermicelli*, broken into 1½-inch
    pieces
¼ pound Romano cheese, grated

Mince onion, ham fat, and garlic and sauté in the oil in a large pot. When ham fat is brown, stir in tomatoes, add the water, salt, and pepper. Simmer for 15 minutes, then add the *vermicelli* directly to the pot. When it is al dente, serve the soup in hot bowls with Romano sprinkled atop. Serves 4 to 6.

—*from Carlo, Roman chef*

OCCHI DI PASSERI E MINESTRONE DI VERZA

"Sparrows' Eyes" and Savoy Cabbage Soup

½ pound dried peas
1 large Savoy cabbage
4 potatoes, diced
1 small turnip, diced
10 cups Chicken Broth (page 96)
½ pound pork, lean and fat, chopped
1 small white onion, minced
1 carrot, scraped and minced
1 celery rib, scraped and minced
1 tablespoon minced parsley
3 tablespoons butter
2 teaspoons salt, or to taste
Liberal amount of milled black pepper
½ pound *occhi di passeri*
¼ pound Parmesan cheese, grated

Soak peas in water for 5 hours; drain. Remove stalks and tough portions of cabbage and cut leaves into strips ½ inch by 2 inches. Parboil in salted water for 8 minutes; drain. Place in a 10-quart pot; add the potatoes, turnip, and half of the broth. Cover the pot and simmer for 15 minutes. In a saucepan, over medium heat, sauté the pork, onion, carrot, celery, and parsley in butter until pork is brown; stir into the cabbage. Add salt and much pepper and simmer for 1½ hours.

Boil the peas separately in salted water until almost tender, drain, and stir into soup pot. Add the rest of the broth and simmer for 15 minutes. Cook *occhi di passeri* separately in boiling salted water until al dente, drain, then stir into the soup pot. Serve in hot soup bowls. Pass the Parmesan. Serves 6 to 8.

Note: In Italy much black pepper is used with cabbage.

—*from C. S., Foggia*

UDINE, the clock tower—Friuli-Venezia Giulia

VERMICELLI AND RICOTTA

1 pound *vermicelli*
3 tablespoons melted butter
½ pound ricotta cheese
Freshly milled black pepper
½ tablespoon chopped parsley
½ cup grated Asiago cheese

Cook *vermicelli* al dente; drain. Place in a warm bowl with 2 tablespoons melted butter. Over medium heat, stir ricotta in a pan with 1 tablespoon of butter until smooth and warm; pour over hot *vermicelli*, mill pepper over the pasta, sprinkle with parsley and grated cheese, and toss. Serves 4 to 6.

—from Luisa R., Portofino

FETTUCCE AND BROOK TROUT

6 brook trout
7 quarts water
2 small white onions
2 garlic cloves
2 celery ribs, cut into 2-inch pieces
2 teaspoons salt
3 tablespoons olive oil
6 tablespoons butter, in all
1 pound *fettucce* (wide *fettuccine*)
Liberal amount of milled black pepper

Clean the trout and remove heads and fins. In a pot place heads and fins in the water with onions, garlic, celery, and salt. Cover and simmer for 1½ hours. In a saucepan, over medium heat, sauté fish in the oil and half of the butter until golden-crisp. Remove the center bone or spine from each fish carefully, pulling out most of the rest of the bones with it. Keep fish on a warm platter. Strain the water the heads and fins were cooked in, return to the pot, and bring to a boil. Cook the *fettucce* in this al dente; drain. Place the remaining 3 tablespoons of butter in a hot bowl and toss the hot *fettucce* in it. Mill in black pepper; toss again. Serve in hot soup bowls with one boned trout atop each portion. Serves 4 to 6.

—from J. R., Manchester, Vermont

GIANT SHELLS STUFFED WITH LOBSTER

3 cups Red Lobster Sauce (page 89)
1 live lobster (1½ pounds)
18 giant pasta shells (3 per person)
2 tablespoons olive oil, in all
2 tablespoons butter

You need two lobsters for this dish, as one is used to make the sauce. Prepare the sauce. Boil the 1½-pound lobster for 10 minutes, or just until it turns red (don't overcook). Save the water. Remove the meat from the shells, and cut it into thumbnail-size pieces; put aside. Cook pasta shells in the boiling lobster water with only 1 tablespoon of salt and with 1½ tablespoons of oil added to keep the shells from sticking. When they are firmer than al dente, not yet tender, remove the pasta shells one at a time with a skimmer or slotted spoon; drain on absorbent paper and let cool. Stuff each shell with lobster meat. Use also the lobster that you prepared the sauce with to stuff some of the shells. Grease a casserole with the butter and remaining ½ tablespoon of oil (the oil keeps the butter from burning). Place stuffed shells in the casserole and spoon sauce lavishly over each one. Bake in a preheated 400° F. oven until sauce bubbles and shells are heated through. Serves 6 as a first course.

—from Maria Luisa Scott

LINGUINE CON LUMACHE ALLA PASQUALE

Linguine with Snails Pasquale

2 pounds Italian snails in shells
6 cups Marinara Sauce (page 81)
1 tablespoon chopped Italian parsley
1 pound *linguine*
1 tablespoon butter

Scrub each snail well with a stiff brush. Place in a large pot of cold water with weighted cover so snails can't escape; this will bring snails partly out of shell. Soak overnight, then remove and discard any snails that haven't opened. In a large pot of boiling salted water, cook snails for 15 minutes. Make marinara sauce; when it is completed, add the drained snails, cover the pan, and cook for 15 minutes. Remove cover, stir well with a wooden spoon, add parsley, and stir. Cook the *linguine* al dente, drain, and toss with the butter in a warm bowl. Spoon ½ cup of sauce over *linguine*, toss, and serve. Follow with the snails in their sauce in soup bowls; use toothpicks to lever the sweet meat from the shells. Serve hot buttered Italian bread and a salad of romaine and Boston lettuce with this. Serves 4 to 6.

Note: Live snails may be obtained from many Italian food stores.

—from Maria Luisa's father, Pasquale Limoncelli

SPAGHETTI AND SHRIMP SAMMY

1 pound fresh shrimp, peeled and cleaned
½ garlic clove, minced
1 large white onion, chopped
1 large green pepper, seeded and chopped
1 tablespoon peanut oil
½ teaspoon salt
1 pound spaghetti

In a saucepan, with a small amount of water, cook shrimp just until they turn pink. Peel shrimp. In another saucepan, sauté garlic, onion, and green pepper in peanut oil until soft. Add cooked shrimp and salt and mix well. Cook spaghetti al dente, drain, and toss gently with shrimp and vegetables until well blended. Serve in hot, rimmed soup bowls. Serves 4 to 6.

—from Sammy Ashida (formerly with Young's Hotel), New Milford, Connecticut

CANNERONI CON SALSA DI CARNE
"Large Reeds" with Meat Sauce

2 pounds boned stewing beef

2 onions, peeled and halved

2 garlic cloves, minced

Salt

Freshly milled black pepper

3 tablespoons olive oil

¼ cup flour

4 ripe tomatoes, peeled, seeded, and
    chopped

1 pound *canneroni*

3 tablespoons butter

Place the stewing beef in a deep saucepan and add water to cover it. Add onions, garlic, and salt and pepper to taste; bring to a boil. Simmer, covered, until meat is tender, for about 1½ hours. Shred the meat and reserve it. Measure out 2 cups of the cooking liquid. Heat the oil in a saucepan and add the flour. Stir constantly until flour is golden brown. Stir in the reserved liquid. When the mixture is thickened and smooth, add tomatoes and shredded beef. Simmer for 20 minutes. Cook *canneroni* al dente, drain, and toss with butter. Spoon sauce over individual servings. Serves 4 to 6.

—from P. P., Naples

NAPLES, the Palazzo Reale—Campania

QUADRUCCI GIUSEPPE

"Small Squares" Giuseppe

6 white onions, chopped
2 garlic cloves, minced
2 tablespoons olive oil
¼ pound butter
4 cups (one 2-pound can) plum tomatoes,
     put through food mill
1 bay leaf
¼ teaspoon dried oregano
¼ teaspoon dried marjoram
½ teaspoon salt
Liberal amount of milled black pepper
1 pound beef round, ground
1 pound *quadrucci*
¼ cup grated Romano cheese
¼ cup grated Parmesan cheese

In a deep saucepan, over medium heat, simmer onions and garlic in oil and butter until soft. Add tomatoes and bring to a simmer. Stir in bay leaf, oregano, marjoram, salt, and pepper; cook for 20 minutes. Discard bay leaf. Slowly add meat and simmer, uncovered, for 1 hour. Cook *quadrucci* al dente; drain. Mix the cheeses and toss with the pasta. Spoon meat sauce over each serving of pasta and pass more grated cheese at the table. Serves 6.

—*from Joseph H., Buffalo, New York*

TAGLIOLINI DEL BUONGUSTAIO

Gourmet's Noodles

¾ pound beef sirloin, chopped
2 raw egg yolks
2 shallots, chopped

2 tablespoons fresh caviar (lumpfish caviar will do)
Liberal amount of milled black pepper
1 teaspoon salt, or to taste
1 pound *tagliolini*
2 tablespoons butter, melted

In a bowl mix beef, egg yolks, shallots, caviar, pepper, and salt together well. Cook *tagliolini* al dente, drain, and toss with melted butter in a hot bowl. Place in hot soup bowls with a good spoonful of the meat mixture atop each serving. Each person tosses and mixes for himself. Serves 4 to 6.

—from Paolo Crossi, Rome

ZITI CON RICOTTA MARIO

Baked "Bridegrooms" with Cheese Mario

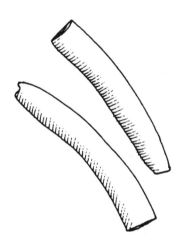

3 cups Bolognese Sauce (page 82)
½ pound fresh ricotta cheese
¼ teaspoon grated nutmeg
1 teaspoon salt
Freshly milled black pepper
1 tablespoon chopped Italian parsley
1 pound *ziti*
1 tablespoon olive oil

Make the Bolognese sauce. Place the ricotta in a strainer and drain; then put in a bowl and mix in the nutmeg, salt, pepper, and parsley, mixing well. Break *ziti* into 3-inch pieces and cook in rapidly boiling salted water until firmer than al dente, on the chewy side; drain well. Toss in a bowl with the ricotta mixture, until each piece of pasta is well coated. Oil a baking dish, put in the *ziti*, and cover with warm Bolognese sauce. Bake, uncovered, in a preheated 400° F. oven for 15 minutes. Serves 4 to 6.

—from Mario, Mario's Restaurant, Arthur Avenue, Bronx, New York

BUCATINI BRUNO

½ pound lean pork, chopped
1 tablespoon olive oil
1 pound beef sirloin, chopped
1 teaspoon dried oregano
1 teaspoon salt, or to taste
Liberal amount of fresh-ground black
    pepper
2-pound can of plum tomatoes
1 pound *bucatini* (small macaroni)
½ cup freshly grated Parmesan cheese
1 white truffle

In a deep saucepan, over medium heat, sauté chopped pork well in the oil for 20 minutes. Add sirloin seasoned with oregano, salt, and black pepper. Cook until beef is less than half done, red and still moist. Put tomatoes through food mill and add to saucepan with the meat. Simmer for 20 minutes, uncovered, stirring well.

Cook the unbroken *bucatini* in rapidly boiling salted water until al dente; drain. Toss in a bowl with the cheese, then place in the pan with the meat and tomato mixture; mix gently and toss again. Serve in individual hot bowls with thinly shaved white truffle on top. Serves 4 to 6.

—*from Bruno Ranieri, Washington, Connecticut*

PORTOFINO—Liguria

BAKED LASAGNE

1 garlic clove, minced

3 small white onions, chopped

3 tablespoons olive oil

8 cups (two 2-pound cans) plum tomatoes, pushed through food mill

1 tablespoon sugar

½ teaspoon salt

1 teaspoon dried sweet basil

1 pound ground meat (mixture of beef
and pork)

½ pound *lasagne*

½ pound ricotta cheese

½ pound mozzarella cheese

½ cup grated Parmesan cheese

In a saucepan, over medium heat, sauté garlic and 2 chopped onions in 1 tablespoon of the oil; add tomatoes, sugar, salt, and basil. Simmer, uncovered, stirring, for 1 hour over a low flame until most of the moisture has evaporated. Meanwhile, in another, deep, saucepan, sauté the third onion in another tablespoon of oil, add the ground meat, and brown all together lightly. Add the tomato sauce.

Cook *lasagne* in boiling salted water with remaining 1 tablespoon oil until al dente; drain. Alternate strips of *lasagne* with layers of sauce in a large baking dish. On each layer of sauce spread ricotta, sliced mozzarella, and grated Parmesan. End with a layer of sauce. Bake in a preheated 400° F. oven for 20 minutes. Serves 4 to 6.

—*from R. D., SAS Pilot, Copenhagen*

ROME, Trajan's Column

BAKED LASAGNE MAMMA LUCIA

2 garlic cloves, peeled and left whole

1 Bermuda onion, chopped

4 tablespoons butter

7 tablespoons olive oil, in all

½-pound piece of beef rump

¼ pound mushrooms, sliced

1 cup red wine

3 cans (2 pounds, 3 ounces each) peeled
    plum tomatoes, strained

Salt and pepper

1 pound mild Italian sausage (½ pound if
    you want a less rich stuffing)

1 pound broad *lasagne*

1 cup grated Parmesan cheese

1 pound mozzarella cheese, sliced thin

Miniature Meatballs (see below)

1½ pounds fresh ricotta cheese

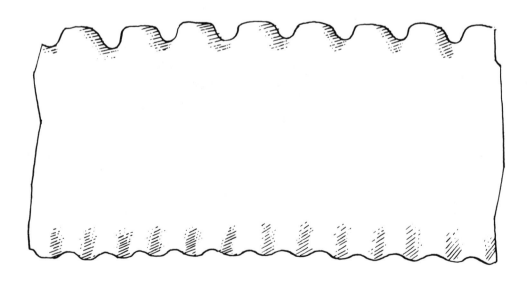

Brown garlic and onion in butter and 6 tablespoons of the oil in a large pot. Place the piece of beef on top and brown evenly. Add mushrooms and brown for 5 minutes, then add wine and cook until it evaporates completely. Remove garlic. Add the tomatoes and season with salt and pepper. Bring to a boil over a high flame, then lower heat. Simmer about 2 hours, covered, until sauce is a rich dark red and thickened. Remove beef (it will be good for hero sandwiches).

Sauté sausage in a frypan for 15 minutes, or until evenly browned, then cut it into small pieces. Make the meatballs. Cook *lasagne* in boiling salted water with remaining tablespoon of oil added to keep noodles from sticking to each other; cook over high heat for 15 minutes, until tender but not soft.

Pour a few tablespoons of sauce on the bottom of a square baking pan and place a layer of *lasagne* on it. Sprinkle with grated cheese and spoon a layer of sauce over that. Then arrange slices of mozzarella, pieces of sausage, and the small meatballs. Now blend the ricotta with some of the sauce, and spoon some of this over the layer of meats. Repeat this procedure in layers until you have used all the ingredients (but you should have sauce left over). Use only sauce and a sprinkling of Parmesan for the top layer. Bake in preheated 350° F. oven for 20 minutes, and serve immediately. Serve the remaining sauce and more grated Parmesan separately at the table. Serves 6.

Miniature Meatballs

1 cup dry whole-wheat bread cubes
Milk
½ pound beef chuck, ground
1 garlic clove, squeezed through a press
1 teaspoon minced parsley
1 teaspoon grated Parmesan cheese
1 egg, beaten
Salt and pepper
Butter

Soak the bread cubes in milk to cover for a few minutes, then squeeze the milk from them well until they are almost dry. In a bowl mix together bread, ground beef, garlic, parsley, cheese, and egg until well blended. Season with salt and pepper. Shape mixture into small meatballs the size of shell almonds, and sauté in a little hot butter until browned.

—*Lucia Abbot, Bethlehem, Connecticut*

LASAGNE RICCE IMBOTTITE ALLA MARIA LUISA
Baked Stuffed "Curly" Lasagne Maria Luisa

1½ pounds *lasagne ricce*
4 tablespoons olive oil
2 tablespoons butter
1 onion, minced
1 garlic clove, minced
2 pounds beef round, ground twice
Salt and pepper
3 tablespoons chopped parsley
4 cups Basic Tomato Sauce (page 76)

3 pounds ricotta cheese

3 small mozzarella cheeses, sliced

1 cup grated Parmesan cheese

In a large pot, cook *lasagne ricce* in boiling salted water with 2 tablespoons of the oil until slightly firmer than al dente; drain.

In a saucepan, over medium heat, in remaining 2 tablespoons oil and the butter, sauté onion and garlic until onion is soft; add ground beef and salt and pepper to taste and cook for 10 minutes. Add parsley. Put this mixture in a strainer so all excess fat and liquid drains off.

Into a square or oblong casserole pour a small amount of tomato sauce, enough to cover the bottom. Arrange a layer of the pasta in the casserole, one of each of the 3 cheeses, one of the meat mixture, then more sauce. Repeat until casserole is almost full; ingredients expand a little. End with sauce and Parmesan. Bake in a preheated 350° F. oven until bubbling. Serves 12.

—from Maria Luisa Scott

LASAGNE VERDI ALLA DORIS

Green Lasagne Doris

1 recipe Pasta Verde (page 60)

1 recipe Béchamel Sauce (page 85)

2 tablespoons butter

1 medium-size white onion, chopped

1 carrot, chopped

1 small celery rib, chopped

¼ pound salt pork, minced

½ pound lean pork, ground fine

Salt

¼ cup dry white wine

3 tablespoons Basic Tomato Sauce (page 76)

¼ cup grated Parmesan cheese

Prepare green pasta dough, cut it into 4-inch squares, and dry on cloth for 1 hour. While it is drying make Béchamel sauce. Now in a deep saucepan, over medium heat, sauté in butter the onion, carrot, and celery until onion is soft; stir in the minced salt pork and cook until it is almost crisp; then add the ground lean pork; stir well with a wooden fork. Sprinkle lightly with salt and simmer until meat is brown. Blend in wine and tomato sauce, stir well, and simmer, covered, for 15 minutes. Boil pasta squares, 2 at a time, in boiling salted water; drain. Place a layer of the squares in a buttered dish. Spoon a layer of meat sauce over this, make another layer of pasta squares, and cover with Béchamel sauce. Make another layer of pasta, then meat sauce, and end with Béchamel; top with Parmesan. Bake in a preheated 400° F. oven for 10 minutes until sauce bubbles and top browns. Serves 4 to 6.

—from Doris Limoncelli, Reston, Virginia

BUCATINI CON POLPETTE D'AGNELLO E SALSA DI UOVA

Bucatini with Lamb Meatballs and Egg Sauce

2 pounds lamb, ground
Salt
Freshly milled black pepper
3 eggs, in all
¼ cup grated *Incanestrato* cheese
1 tablespoon chopped parsley
1 tablespoon chopped raisins
1 garlic clove
2 tablespoons olive oil
½ tablespoon flour
½ cup dry white wine
Juice of ½ lemon
1 pound *bucatini* (small macaroni)

Place ground lamb in a bowl and season with salt and pepper to taste. Add 1 egg, beaten, the cheese, parsley, and raisins. Blend well and form into tiny meatballs half the size of a walnut. In a saucepan, over medium heat, sauté garlic in the oil until brown; discard garlic. Add the meatballs to the oil and lightly sprinkle with flour. Brown. Add the wine and cover the pan for 3 minutes. Remove cover and stir the meatballs and liquid with a wooden spoon, scraping the cooked particles from the side into the sauce. In a bowl beat remaining 2 eggs with lemon juice; add to meat pan, stir well, and simmer for 3 minutes. Cook *bucatini* al dente, drain, and place in a bowl. Pour meatballs and egg sauce over pasta and toss well. Serves 4 to 6.

—*from A. De Rossi, Genoa*

FETTUCCINE VERDI E BIANCHE

Green and White Fettuccine

4 tablespoons butter
1 tablespoon olive oil
4 slices of prosciutto, cut into julienne strips
2 garlic cloves
8 small mushrooms, sliced thin
2 cups Basic Tomato Sauce (page 76)
2 tablespoons cooked or canned fava beans
1 pound *fettuccine* noodles, half green, half white
¼ pound Parmesan cheese, grated

In a saucepan, over medium heat, in 2 tablespoons of the butter and the oil sauté the prosciutto. Add the garlic and mushrooms and sauté until garlic is brown; discard garlic. Stir in the tomato sauce and beans; simmer, uncovered, for 10 minutes. Cook *fettuccine* al dente; drain. Place in a bowl with the remaining butter and toss. Serve in soup bowls, with sauce liberally spooned atop. Pass the Parmesan. Serves 4 to 6.

—*from "Nick," chef, Naples*

BAKED STUFFED GIANT SHELLS

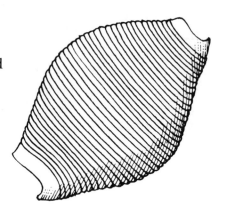

    6 cups Basic Tomato Sauce (page 76)
    18 giant pasta shells
    1 tablespoon olive oil
    1½ pounds fresh ricotta cheese, drained
    4 tablespoons grated Parmesan cheese
    6 slices of prosciutto, finely diced
    2 tablespoons minced parsley
    1 egg yolk
    Pinch of sugar
    Liberal amount of milled black pepper
    ½ teaspoon salt, or to taste

Prepare the tomato sauce; simmer. Cook the shells in salted boiling water with the olive oil; cook firmer than al dente, remove with slotted spoon, drain, and cool. In a large bowl mix ricotta, Parmesan, prosciutto, parsley, egg yolk, sugar, pepper, and salt; blend well. Stuff each shell with some of this mixture. Spoon some tomato sauce into a glass casserole or baking dish; arrange the stuffed shells in the sauce. Spoon more tomato sauce atop each shell. Bake in a preheated 400° F. oven for 20 minutes. Serve 3 shells to each person for a first course. Serves 6.

—from Maria Luisa Scott

LINGUINE ALLA CARBONARA
Linguine with Ham-Egg Sauce

    8 slices of bacon, in thin strips
    1 tablespoon olive oil
    ½ cup diced lean prosciutto

   3 egg yolks
   1 cup grated Parmesan cheese
   1 pound *linguine,* cooked and drained

In a saucepan, over medium heat, brown the bacon in the olive oil; mix in the ham until slightly browned. Drain off half the fat and discard it. In a bowl beat the egg yolks, then stir in ¼ cup of the cheese. Toss hot *linguine* with the bacon mixture, then immediately with the egg-yolk mixture. Serve sprinkled with the remaining cheese. Serves 4 to 6.

—from Fanny Graef, New York City

MAGLIETTE RIGATE ROBERTO

"Grooved Links" Roberto

   1 pound *magliette rigate*
   ¼ pound butter
   ½ pound prosciutto
   3 egg yolks
   ½ cup heavy cream
   ⅓ cup freshly grated Parmesan cheese

In a pot cook the *magliette rigate* in boiling, lightly salted water until al dente; gently remove with slotted spoon or skimmer, but be careful not to break the pasta. In a deep saucepan melt the butter and add the prosciutto cut into thin strips. Sauté for 2 minutes. In a bowl beat the egg yolks with the cream. Now place the pasta in the pan with the butter and prosciutto, add the beaten egg and cream, and stir carefully so as not to break the pasta. Place on a low fire and simmer for 30 seconds, continuing to stir gently. Grate cheese over the dish and serve while the sauce is creamy, before the eggs solidify. Serves 4 to 6.

—Bob Neville, a writer friend in Rome

RIGATONI ALL'ARRABBIATA

Raging Rigatoni

This remains a favorite in Rome; it is guaranteed to bring a stuffy dinner party alive, drive the pompous to their knees, and raise the languid from their seats.

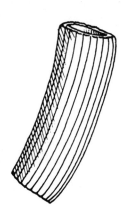

    6 slices of bacon, chopped
    2 tablespoons olive oil
    4 cups (one 2-pound can) plum
        tomatoes
    Black pepper
    ½ teaspoon salt, or to taste
    2 large fresh chili peppers (*peperoncini*)
    1 pound *rigatoni* (grooved pasta tubes)
    2 tablespoons butter
    ½ cup grated Romano cheese

In a saucepan, over medium heat, sauté chopped bacon in the oil until soft; drain off half the fat and discard it. Add tomatoes, breaking them up with a wooden spoon as they simmer. Mill in black pepper and add the salt. Chop hot peppers and blend into the tomato mixture, stirring well. Simmer, uncovered, for 15 minutes longer until sauce is thickened. Cook *rigatoni* al dente; drain. Place in a warm bowl with the butter and cheese; toss gently with wooden forks. Serve in hot soup bowls with *arrabbiata* fire sauce spooned over each serving. At the elbow of each diner place one large glass of cold water and one large glass of wine. Both will be needed. Serves 4 to 6.

—from Mary Neville, Rome

SPAGHETTI ALLA CARBONARA OLGA

    2 small white onions, chopped
    4 tablespoons butter
    ¼ cup dry white wine

5 slices of bacon, chopped

3 eggs, beaten

2 tablespoons chopped parsley

½ cup grated Parmesan cheese

Liberal amount of milled black pepper

1 pound spaghetti

In a saucepan, over medium heat, sauté onions in butter until soft. Stir in wine and add bacon; cook until wine evaporates. In a large bowl, put beaten eggs, parsley, cheese, and black pepper; beat. Cook spaghetti al dente; drain. Fork spaghetti from pot into bowl, toss, and garnish with hot onions and bacon. Serves 4 to 6.

—from Olga Ravetto, Yorktown Heights, New York

SPAGHETTI ALL'AMATRICIANA GRAEF

Spaghetti with Bacon Sauce

½ pound bacon, chopped

2 white onions, chopped

½ cup dry white wine

1½ pounds tomatoes, peeled, seeded,
    and diced

½ teaspoon freshly ground black pepper
    and salt to taste

1 pound spaghetti, cooked and drained

½ cup grated Pecorino cheese

½ cup grated Parmesan cheese

In a saucepan, over medium heat, cook the bacon and onions until browned but not crisp. Add the wine, tomatoes, and pepper; cook over medium heat until wine has evaporated and sauce has thickened. Spoon over individual dishes of hot spaghetti. Pass mixed cheeses at table. Serves 4 to 6.

—from Fanny Graef, New York City

SPAGHETTINI PRIMAVERILE

Springtime Spaghettini

12 small very ripe plum tomatoes
2 tablespoons olive oil
1 garlic clove, halved
8 slices of bacon, diced
½ cup fresh basil leaves, shredded
3 grindings of fresh black pepper, or to taste
1 pound spaghettini

Peel tomatoes by plunging into hot water, then stripping off the skins. Squeeze out seeds by holding a tomato in the hand and closing the fist; most seeds will pop out. Do this over the sink. Then dice the tomatoes.

Place the oil and garlic in a frypan and sauté until garlic is golden and soft; then add bacon pieces. Sauté until soft but not crisp. Add diced tomatoes, basil leaves, and black pepper. Cook over medium fire, using a wooden spoon to stir and break up tomatoes as they cook. Cook for 25 minutes, uncovered, until water has evaporated from sauce.

Boil spaghettini al dente in boiling, lightly salted water; drain. Place directly in serving bowls and spoon tomato sauce on top. This dish has a taste right from the garden. Serves 4 to 6.

—from Fortunato E., Perugia

LINGUINE ALLA LUIGI

3 tablespoons olive oil
2 white onions, chopped
6 mushrooms, sliced thin
6 artichoke hearts, diced
6 chicken livers, diced
3 cups Ham Sauce (page 85)
Pinch of grated nutmeg
1 pound *linguine*

In a saucepan, over medium heat, sauté in the oil the onions, mushrooms, and artichoke hearts until soft, about 10 minutes. Stir in the livers; cook for 5 minutes, stirring often with a wooden spoon. Add the ham sauce and the nutmeg, stir well, and simmer for 10 minutes. Cook *linguine* al dente, drain, and toss with half of the sauce. Spoon the remainder generously atop individual servings in hot soup bowls. Serves 4 to 6.

—from Luigi, chef, Parma

Note: The ham sauce in this recipe of course was made from the local ham in Parma, the world's best prosciutto.

MAGLIETTE SPACCATE ALLA TOMMASO

"Split Links" Tommaso

1 garlic clove, minced
2 four-inch-long sweet Italian sausages,
    sliced thin
3 tablespoons butter
3 tablespoons olive oil
8 small firm mushrooms, sliced thin
2 tablespoons peas, cooked
2 tablespoons lima beans, cooked
½ teaspoon salt, or to taste
Liberal amount of milled black pepper
1 pound *magliette spaccate*
½ cup grated Parmesan cheese

In a saucepan, over medium heat, sauté the garlic and sausages in butter and oil until sausages brown; add mushrooms and simmer for 5 minutes. Stir in peas and beans and sprinkle in salt and pepper; simmer 5 minutes. Cook *magliette spaccate* al dente; drain. Place in a large warm bowl, add half of the cheese, and toss well. Add half of the sauce and toss again. Serve in hot bowls with the rest of the sauce spooned atop and the remaining cheese sprinkled over all. Serves 4 to 6.

—from Tommaso Bona, chef, Rome

TAGLIATELLE VERDI CON FUNGHI

Green Noodles with Mushrooms

  1 recipe Pasta Verde (page 60)
  Two 4-inch sweet Italian sausages
  2 medium-size veal sweetbreads
  3 tablespoons butter
  4 slices of prosciutto, diced
  12 mushrooms, sliced thin
  2 large very ripe tomatoes, peeled,
     seeded, and diced
  1½ teaspoons salt, or to taste
  Liberal amount of milled black pepper
  2 cups Chicken Broth (page 96)

Prepare the pasta and cut it into ¾-inch strips for *tagliatelle* (page 58). While it is drying, remove sausage casings and break meat into pieces. Parboil the sweetbreads, remove skin and membranes, and dice sweetbreads. In a deep saucepan, over medium heat, sauté in butter the sausage pieces, prosciutto, and sweetbreads until brown. Stir in the mushrooms and simmer for 5 minutes. Add the tomatoes, salt, and pepper and simmer for 10 minutes. Stir in the chicken broth and simmer for 25 minutes, stirring often with a wooden spoon, until sauce becomes smooth and thickened. Cook *tagliatelle* al dente; watch carefully, as fresh pasta cooks more quickly than dry; drain. Place in a warm bowl, spoon in 4 tablespoons of sauce, and toss gently. Serve in hot soup bowls with remaining sauce spooned generously atop. Serves 4 to 6.

—*from Giorgio, chef, Amalfi*

CHICKEN AND LINGUINE LUCIA

  1 frying chicken (3 pounds), cut into pieces
  Flour
  4 tablespoons butter

2 tablespoons olive oil

1 garlic clove, crushed

Salt and pepper

2 large fresh tomatoes, cut into small slices, or 20 cherry tomatoes,
   peeled

1 small can (10 ounces) pitted black ripe olives, halved

¼ pound fresh mushrooms, sliced

1 small onion, sliced thin, or 4 scallions, minced

1 tablespoon minced parsley

1 cup dry white wine

1½ cups (one 14-ounce can) peeled
   tomatoes

1 pound *linguine*

Roll pieces of chicken in flour and in a saucepan, over medium heat, brown them evenly in half of the butter and oil with the garlic. Sprinkle with salt and pepper. Pour 1 tablespoon of the oil into a shallow oblong ovenproof casserole and arrange the chicken pieces in it. On top and sides of chicken pieces arrange all the sliced ingredients evenly—sliced tomatoes, olives, mushrooms, and onion or scallions. Sprinkle with parsley. Pour the wine over the vegetables and dot with remaining butter. Bake in a preheated 375° F. oven for 45 minutes, turning chicken from time to time. When chicken is tender and has a nice golden color, remove casserole from oven, take out the chicken, and keep it warm.

Pour all the juicy sauce from the casserole into a saucepan and add to it the canned tomatoes. Let the sauce cook briskly for about 10 minutes; crush tomatoes with a spoon while cooking. Cook *linguine* al dente; drain. Place *linguine* in a warm serving bowl, cover with the sauce, and serve. Serve chicken as a second course, with fresh string beans flavored at the last minute with garlic and olive oil and a sprinkle of lemon juice. Serves 4.

—from Lucia Abbot, Bethlehem, Connecticut

FETTUCCE ALLA BIANCA
Fresh Noodles Bianca

    1 recipe Pasta Fresca all'Uovo (page 57)
    2 small white onions, minced
    3 tablespoons olive oil
    3 tablespoons butter
    1 teaspoon salt, or to taste
    ½ chicken breast (one side), diced
    4 slices of prosciutto, slivered
    4 very ripe tomatoes, peeled, seeded,
        and diced
    1½ teaspoons flour
    1½ cups white wine
    2 large chicken livers, chopped

Prepare the fresh pasta and cut it into ½-inch widths to make *fettucce*. While it is drying, in a saucepan, over medium heat, sauté the onions until soft in the oil and butter. Add the salt and diced chicken breast. Simmer until brown. Add prosciutto and tomatoes, sprinkle in the flour, and stir well. Add wine and cook, stirring with a wooden spoon, until moisture evaporates and sauce is smooth, about 20 minutes. Stir in the chicken livers; simmer for 10 minutes, stirring often. Cook the fresh *fettucce* noodles al dente; watch carefully, as they cook more quickly than the dry. Drain; serve in hot bowls with sauce liberally spooned over each portion. Serves 4 to 6.

—*from Mrs. B. R., Cremona, Lombardy*

FETTUCCE RICCE GIORGIO
"Curly Ribbons" Giorgio

    1 whole chicken breast, boned
    2 tablespoons olive oil
    3 tablespoons butter

1 teaspoon salt, or to taste

Freshly milled black pepper

¼ pound thinly sliced prosciutto

½ cup freshly grated Parmesan cheese

2 tablespoons heavy cream

1 pound *fettucce ricce*

Flatten boned chicken breast under wax paper with a wooden mallet or cleaver. In a saucepan, over medium heat, put chicken in the oil and butter; season with salt and pepper and turn often; sauté until brown and cooked through, but still moist. Remove and cut into thin strips 1 inch long. Cut the ham into similar strips. Add them both to the saucepan in which the chicken cooked, warming them over a low flame and mixing them together. Add half of the cheese and all of the cream. Stir all together well. Cook *fettucce ricce* until al dente; drain. Toss in a warm bowl with the mixture of ham, chicken, and cream. Serve in individual warm bowls with remainder of cheese on the side. Serves 4 to 6.

—from Giorgio L., Milan

SPAGHETTI CON FEGATINI DI POLLO

Spaghetti with Chicken Livers

This came from the Trulli area, from a little restaurant on a hill outside Alberobello, that astonishing place of the Moorish, whitewashed, conical-roofed houses. The livers used were kid, or young goat, but for obvious reasons we have substituted chicken livers.

1 small sweet red pepper, seeded and
   diced

4 teaspoons butter

1 teaspoon salt, or to taste

⅛ teaspoon crushed red pepper

1 pound chicken livers, diced

1 pound spaghetti

In a saucepan, over medium heat, sauté the sweet pepper in butter for 15 minutes; sprinkle in the salt and stir in the crushed red pepper and the chicken livers. Simmer for exactly 5 minutes. Livers, properly cooked, should be pink. Stir well. Cook the spaghetti al dente, drain, and toss with half of the liver sauce. Serve in hot bowls; spoon remaining sauce atop individual portions. Serves 4 to 6.

—*from Giovanni, Alberobello*

TAGLIOLETTE CON CONIGLIO
Baked Rabbit with Noodles

⅓ pound *tagliolette*
8 mushrooms, quartered
2 tablespoons butter
1 tablespoon pine nuts
1 whole young rabbit
1 garlic clove, mashed
4 tablespoons olive oil
1½ teaspoons salt
Liberal amount of milled black pepper
2 white onions, quartered
1 cup white wine

Cook *tagliolette* until they are half done, very chewy. Drain and place in a bowl. In a saucepan, over medium heat, sauté mushrooms in the butter with the pine nuts; add to the *tagliolette*; toss. Wash and dry the young rabbit; fill with the noodles; sew skin across the cavity so it is completely closed. Rub the rabbit with the mashed garlic and 2 tablespoons of oil; sprinkle with salt and mill pepper over it liberally. In a roasting pan place the remaining oil and the onions; brown the onions, with the rabbit, on top of the stove over a high flame for 10 minutes. Add the wine, cover the pan, and bake in a preheated 400° F. oven for 45 minutes, or until rabbit

ALBEROBELLO—Apulia

RAVENNA, the Basilica of San Vitale—Emilia-Romagna

is tender, basting often; add more liquid (hot water) if necessary. Rabbit should be browned and tender but moist. Serve it whole on a warm platter; carve at table and spoon out noodle stuffing to go with each serving of rabbit. Serves 4.

—from Aldo Moro, Taormina

CHITARRA WITH MUSHROOMS AND PURÉED PEAS

6 medium-size mushrooms, quartered
3 tablespoons butter
1 pound fresh peas, shelled
1 pound *chitarra* ("guitar strings")
Liberal amount of milled black pepper
⅓ cup freshly grated Romano cheese

In a saucepan, over medium heat, sauté mushrooms in the butter until half done, on the firm side. Cook peas in salted water until tender, then purée in a food mill. Place purée in a warm bowl. Cook *chitarra* al dente in boiling salted water; drain. Combine mushrooms with puréed peas, grind in black pepper, and blend. Add pasta and cheese to the bowl with the peas and mushrooms; toss well. Serve in warm bowls. Serves 4 to 6.

—from Maria Luisa Scott

MEZZANI TAGLIATI AL FORNO

Baked Macaroni

2 white onions, minced
2 tablespoons butter
2 tablespoons olive oil
8 small mushrooms, sliced thin
2 tablespoons flour
2 cups milk
8 black olives, sliced
1 teaspoon salt, or to taste
1 cup grated Romano cheese
1 pound cut *mezzani* (short medium-size
    macaroni)
¼ cup buttered bread crumbs

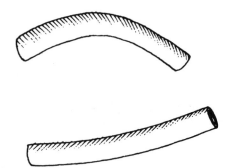

In a saucepan, over medium heat, sauté onions in butter and oil until soft. Stir in mushrooms and simmer for 10 minutes. Add the flour, stirring in well, and blend in milk, olives, and salt, stirring well with a wooden spoon until the sauce becomes smooth as it simmers. Add half of the cheese and blend in well. Cook cut *mezzani* al dente; drain. Stir into the onion-mushroom sauce. Pour into an ovenproof casserole; sprinkle the rest of the cheese atop, then the bread crumbs. Bake in a preheated 400° F. oven for 20 minutes, or until the sauce bubbles and the top browns. Serves 4 to 6.

—from S. G. L., Ravenna

FETTUCCE FRESCHE ALLA MARIA LUISA

1 pound Pasta Fresca all'Uovo (page 57)
3 tablespoons butter
½ cup freshly grated Asiago cheese
2 cups sliced fresh small mushrooms
Freshly milled black pepper
4 tablespoons heavy cream

Prepare fresh pasta dough and cut it into ½-inch strips to make *fettucce*. When dried for 1 hour, cook in boiling salted water. Watch carefully, for fresh pasta cooks more quickly than dry. When al dente, remove with a fork, shake off water, and place in a warm bowl with 1 tablespoon of the butter. Toss, add grated cheese, and toss gently again. In a saucepan, over medium heat, sauté mushrooms slightly in remaining 2 tablespoons butter until not quite soft but still firm; do not overcook. Add mushrooms to the pasta. Now mill in pepper, add the cream, and toss again. Serve in hot bowls. Serves 4 to 6.

—from Maria Luisa Scott

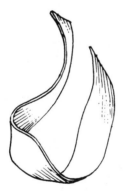

BAKED STUFFED RIGATONI

1 large white onion, chopped fine

3 tablespoons olive oil

8 cups (two 2-pound cans) plum toma-
     toes, put through food mill

1 tablespoon sugar

2 teaspoons salt

1 bay leaf

½ teaspoon dried oregano

1 pound ricotta cheese

2 eggs, beaten

2 tablespoons chopped parsley

¾ cup grated Parmesan cheese

⅛ teaspoon black pepper

1 pound *rigatoni* (grooved pasta tubes)

In a saucepan, over medium heat, sauté onion in oil until soft. Add tomatoes, sugar, 1 teaspoon of the salt, the bay leaf, and oregano; cover.
Simmer for 40 minutes, covered, then for 15 minutes uncovered, stirring
often. Remove bay leaf. In a bowl combine ricotta, eggs, parsley, ¼ cup
Parmesan, remaining 1 teaspoon salt, and the pepper. Cook *rigatoni* al dente;
drain. Stuff *rigatoni* with cheese mixture. Alternate layers of stuffed *rigatoni* and sauce in a square casserole. Sprinkle with remaining Parmesan.
Bake, uncovered, in a preheated 400° F. oven for 20 minutes. Serves 6.

—from R. L., barber, Rome

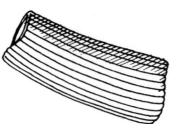

ZITI TAGLIATI AL FORNO

Baked "Short Bridegrooms"

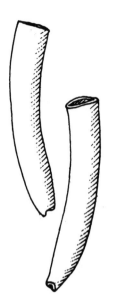

4 shallots (or scallions fresh from the
    garden), minced
8 tablespoons butter
8 very ripe tomatoes, peeled and diced
1 teaspoon salt, or to taste
Liberal amount of milled black pepper
1 cup white Chianti
1 pound *ziti tagliati*
½ cup grated Romano cheese
½ cup grated Parmesan cheese

In a saucepan, over medium heat, sauté the minced shallots in 4 tablespoons of the butter until soft. Stir in the tomatoes, salt, and pepper; simmer for 10 minutes. Add the wine and simmer, stirring often, for 25
minutes. Put all through food mill. In a saucepan, stir 2 tablespoons of
butter into the purée and simmer into a smooth velvety sauce. Cook *ziti
tagliati* al dente; drain. Place in a large bowl and toss with half of the sauce.
Butter a baking dish and pour in half of the pasta. Sprinkle over this half
of the Romano and Parmesan, which have been well mixed. Add the remaining pasta, spoon the sauce over, and add the rest of the cheese. Fleck
the top with the remaining butter. Bake in a preheated 400° F. oven, uncovered, for 10 minutes, or until sauce is bubbling and top is brown.
Serves 6.

—from T. A., Siena

FLORENCE, detail of the Church of Santa Croce—Tuscany

Index of Illustrations

SIENA, doorway adjoining the Duomo—Tuscany

General Index